SOCRATES' WAY

OTHER BOOKS BY RONALD GROSS

Peak Learning

The Lifelong Learner

Individualism: Man in Modern Society

The New Professionals

The Independent Scholar's Handbook

Independent Scholarship: Promise, Problems, and Prospects

The Great School Debate

Radical School Reform

The New Old

The Children's Rights Movement

Pop Poems

SOCRATES' WAY

Seven Master Keys to
Using Your Mind to the Utmost

RONALD GROSS

Foreword by Michael J. Gelb

JEREMY P. TARCHER/PUTNAM
a member of Penguin Putnam Inc.   *New York*

Most Tarcher/Putnam books are available at special quantity discounts for bulk purchase for sales promotions, premiums, fund-raising, and educational needs. Special books or book excerpts also can be created to fit specific needs. For details, write Putnam Special Markets, 375 Hudson Street, New York, NY 10014.

Jeremy P. Tarcher/Putnam
a member of
Penguin Putnam Inc.
375 Hudson Street
New York, NY 10014
www.penguinputnam.com

Library of Congress Cataloging-in-Publication Data

Gross, Ronald.
Socrates' way : seven master keys to using your mind to the
utmost / Ronald Gross ; foreword by Michael Gelb ;
illustrations by Kana Philip.
p.   cm.
Includes bibliographical references and index.
ISBN 1-58542-192-8
1. Socrates.   I. Title.
B317.G76   2002   2002070583
183'.2—dc21

Printed in the United States of America
3   5   7   9   10   8   6   4   2

This book is printed on acid-free paper. ∞

Book design by Mauna Eichner
Original illustrations of Socrates and the Owl by Kana Philip

For Bea,

my Aspasia

CONTENTS

6

SPEAK THE TRUTH

"It has been my fixed principle to speak the truth."

7

STRENGTHEN YOUR SOUL

"Oh, my friend, why so little care for your soul?"

SOCRATES' WAY FOR WOMEN

*"To judge a person's capability by gender is like judging
a man's intelligence by the amount of hair on his head."*

APPENDIX A
READING THE SOCRATIC DIALOGUES

APPENDIX B
BEST BOOKS ON SOCRATES AND OUR CLASSICAL HERITAGE

FOREWORD

by Michael J. Gelb

author of *How to Think Like Leonardo da Vinci*

and *Discover Your Genius*

"The unexamined life is not worth living," declared Socrates. He might have added that the unlived life may not be worth examining. In this book Ronald Gross shows you how to both examine and live your life more fully.

Over the last decade, numerous books featuring lessons from historical figures have appeared on the shelves of bookstores around the world. Many of these titles provide a smattering of quotes and a superficial introduction to the historical figure in question.

Ron Gross offers something different: an authentic immersion in the life and work of one of the greatest teachers of all time. Socrates stands with Leonardo da Vinci, Nicholas Copernicus, Charles Darwin, and Albert Einstein as a beacon of inspiration for independent thinkers. But Socrates came first.

Based on the master's famed "method," Plato, his greatest disciple, founded the "academy" to cultivate people's ability to think productively and to live wisely. Today, the word *academic* is often associated with impractical theory. In the business world it is frequently used as a synonym for *irrelevant*. In this book, however, Ron Gross restores the original spirit of the academy and guides you to deepen your own relationship with truth, beauty, and goodness.

I first met Ron in the early 1980s, and he immediately impressed me with his rare combination of enthusiastic openness and critical intelligence. Ron is not just a champion of lifelong learning; he is a role model for it. This book flows naturally from his decades of inquiry into how we can deepen and accelerate our self-education.

Ron is renowned for appearing at educational and corporate conferences in the garb and character of Socrates. But this works only because, even when he's not wearing a chiton, he exemplifies the Socratic principles expressed in this book.

Socrates refused to be recognized as a teacher, Plato tells us. Instead, he asked to be seen as a "midwife of ideas." *Socrates' Way* works in that "midwife" tradition. In each chapter you will meet one of the master's principles, then as you do some of the exhilarating exercises you will learn even more about yourself.

This book is about Socrates, but it's really about you and how you can bring more truth, beauty, and goodness into your life every day. Cicero said of Socrates that "he called philosophy down from the skies and into the lives of men." In *Socrates' Way*, Ron Gross calls Socrates up from the past to invigorate and enrich our lives today.

PREFACE
SOCRATES, MY MENTOR

My first encounter with Socrates was at the age of twelve, when I noticed an odd practice of my father's. Each day, before leaving the house for work, he would walk over to the bookcase in the living room, take down the same thick book from the top shelf, open it, and carefully tear out exactly six pages. Folding them neatly and tucking them into his jacket pocket, he'd go out the front door. Each night, as put his wallet, keys, and change on the hall table, he would carefully unfold those pages and place them back in the book.

One day, after he left, I took down the book and read its spine: *Dialogues of Plato.*

That evening I asked him about this. He did not patronize me, but explained the practice in adult terms: "My work doesn't bring me into contact with stimulating ideas," he said. "But for forty-five minutes every day, on the way to and from work, I can spend my time with some of the smartest people who have ever lived. They talk about the most important issues. They really listen to each other, rather than just shouting their own positions. And, together, they gradually grow wiser."

So each day on the subway he would read a few pages of one of Plato's dialogues, then reread them on the way home.

Socrates became part of him, and changed his life. Throughout my adolescence I would notice how often he'd pose just the right question to start a conversation going or to propel it to a higher level.

When I began asking about who Socrates was, my father took me to see my first Broadway show. I was thirteen. It was *Barefoot in Athens,* a play about Socrates by Maxwell Anderson. I actually saw my father's hero tramping around Athens, questioning the high and low, enjoying his devoted friends, challenging authority, and having the time of his life.

I refused to wear shoes for an entire week. I was hooked. The Socratic ideal dominated my view of learning throughout my school and college years.

My first book, *The Lifelong Learner,* invited readers to use Socrates' methods to facilitate their self-development, just as my father had. Since then, as a professional speaker, I regularly don the chiton (the Greek version of the toga) to question groups of professionals and businesspeople, ranging from the Group Health Association of America and the YMCAs of North America to senior executives of McDonnell Douglas and U.S. Steel.

Socrates will be with me right up to my final moments: I never leave home without having in my wallet a little card from The Hemlock Society—named, of course, for his final act of integrity. This card declares my wishes in the event of a life-and-death situation. It is based on Socrates' powerful conviction, expressed to his oldest friend, Crito, on the evening before his death, that the *quality* of life is more important than the mere continuance of biological existence.

I cite Socrates' impact on me to show how he can function as a mentor to an ordinary person. But his influence is far more impressive than that. For more than 2,500 years, Socrates' methods have been the subject of a vast "longitudinal study" extending over generations. Century after century, the brightest people have made Socrates their model.

He has been "the mentor of the mentors" not just for intellectuals, but for men and women who have taken bold action on behalf of their beliefs. Henry David Thoreau, Mahatma Gandhi, and Martin Luther King, Jr., evoked him in their jail cells.

·　·　·

Socrates' principles relate to our world today. He calls on us to think for ourselves, to challenge authority, to do the right thing, to speak the truth, and to keep our souls alive through friendship and love.

Socrates' principles, which you will master in this book, reveal the glaring flaws in our lives and point to the steps we need to take to get back on the right path, personally and politically. If he walked among us today, Socrates would point out that:

- We have become frenzied consumers, working ourselves mercilessly in order to purchase things we don't really need, and despoiling our environment. We should look less to our possessions and more to our inner development; hence, we must reaffirm the importance of STRENGTHENING OUR SOULS.

- We have plunged the world's greatest economic system into crisis by our corporations' widespread lies and deceptions. We must learn to SPEAK THE TRUTH.

- We have surrendered our minds to the mass media, which distract us as we virtually amuse ourselves to death. We must THINK FOR OURSELVES.

- We have failed to nurture our bonds of friendship and community. We must revive the art of joyous and substantive conversation, and learn to GROW WITH OTHERS.

I have found Socrates' principles applicable to personal relationships, family life, community affairs, and the workplace. In fact, they are often so relevant that I have the sense *they* are using *me:* they are *demanding* that I apply them to get the job done right.

One example I'll never forget included most of Socrates' principles—asking questions, involving people in dialogue on basic values, learning from each other, thinking creatively, and working together—and even ended up with my being "given the hemlock."

I was serving on the board of one of the national voluntary health organizations whose mission was to prevent birth defects. It supported scientific research and information programs to help pregnant women who were at-risk for delivering impaired babies because of poverty, drug usage, or other problems. I and my fellow board members prided ourselves on making progress in reducing birth defects.

Then one morning, the *Washington Post* reported that the Nixon administration was pulling the rug out from under an array of federal programs that also ministered to these women. Hundreds of "well-baby" clinics in poor neighborhoods would be shut down, despite having proved to be immensely successful in achieving the goal we shared: reducing birth defects. So devastating were the impending cuts that they would clearly negate any impact our modest grants might be having.

At a board meeting the next week, I raised the kinds of questions that I imagined Socrates might pose. Were we not compelled to help lead the fight against these cuts? My fellow board members disagreed. They recoiled from "taking on" the government.

But I felt a Socratic imperative to continue asking the obvious questions: How many birth defects do our grants prevent? How many will occur because of these cuts? What will be the human, medical, and social costs of those bad outcomes? Who is responsible for contesting this change in policy?

I had no choice but to became a kind of "gadfly," as Socrates did, raising the issue at every board meeting. I reminded my colleagues about the underlying mission and values of the organization and why I felt that we were obligated to take action. Together with a few colleagues, I launched between-meeting "dialogues," like Socrates', where we tried to think creatively about how the organization might deal with the new challenge.

Inspired by Socrates' deep respect for expertise (he admired people who were really superb at their craft, trade, or profession, whether it was sandal making or statecraft), we conducted a "benchmarking" survey of how other comparable organizations had succeeded in their fields. Using those findings, we came up with some innovative strategies that we felt would work.

Our efforts did not escape the notice of the majority of the board, who opposed our course of action, just as Socrates' constant questions finally impelled his fellow Athenians to prosecute him. Within six months my cup of bureaucratic "hemlock" arrived: a letter informing me that at a meeting I had not been told about I had been ousted from my position on the board. My only satisfaction was that within seven months of my departure, the organization changed its policies and confronted the challenge. "Your raising the issue and insisting that we deal with it started the ball rolling," the president confided to me.

In this instance, I had used Socrates' principles, but they had also "used" me. Specifically, I felt obliged to follow in his footsteps to the best of my ability. To do that I had to do my best to:

- Persistently raise significant questions.

- Involve people in dialogue about their basic values.

- Learn from those with authentic expertise.

- Think productively with friends and colleagues.

- Work together toward the truth.

- Do the right thing.

There's hardly a day when the spirit of Socrates doesn't stir me to think something through a little better, or when his robust laugh doesn't help me see the humor in some frustrating turn of events. For example, I'll be engaged in an aimless conversation that is sapping my energy, and suddenly Socrates will nudge me with the thought: *What question could I ask that could elevate this conversation above the mundane?* Or I'll be facing a day full of routine and obligations, and I'll find myself wondering, *How would Socrates find some benefit or advantage from these necessary activities?* Or someone at work will say something bigoted, prejudiced, or hurtful, "just as a joke." And over his or her shoulder, an ectoplasmic Socrates will glare at me, demanding to know whether I'm going to let it pass or say: "I think we really need to discuss what you just said. . . ."

Occasionally he's gotten me into hot water, as you have seen. I've been fired, ousted, and blacklisted when I found myself, as he did finally, caught in a situation where I had to draw the line about what I could in good conscience do.

But Socrates also inspires me to achieve things I might not otherwise even try. I'll be starting to plan a new major project—like this book, for instance—and I will quietly ask Socrates to add to my strength with his patience, wit, integrity, and joy in life.

I hope you find those qualities helpful to you as you invite him into your life.

INTRODUCTION

SOCRATES'
LIFE AND TIMES—
AND OURS

Why should Socrates, who lived 2,500 years ago, be so relevant today? Here are four reasons:

- Socrates and his fellow Athenians were the first to express *our* most treasured values and principles.

- Those Socratic values and principles have shaped much of our subsequent history.

- Most of the earth's people now aspire to those values and principles.

- Most important, Socratic values and principles can inspire and guide people to live fuller lives and to create a better society.

Among those Athenian values and principles are:

- Self-understanding is the basis for authentic living.

- We must question "conventional wisdom" to verify the truth for ourselves, rather than rely on tradition.

- The individual has moral and spiritual authority over his or her own "soul."

- Free speech, open dissent, and questioning of authority are essential to a healthy society.

- To be most productive, thinking should be disciplined by logic and personal experience.

- Our human dignity mandates that we rule ourselves through participation in constitutional government.

- A sound economy should have due respect for private property, markets that work, and individual enterprise.

- The state's military powers should be under civilian control.

- We should value and appreciate the body, physical fitness, and the enjoyment of our sexuality.

Of course, we often fall short of achieving these ideals—as did the Athenians themselves. But they were the first to declare their *commitment* to them as well as their willingness to examine where they fell short of achieving them.

THE FIRST "GOLDEN AGE"

Athens in the fifth century B.C. experienced the first of those "golden ages" that have occurred periodically in Western history. Think of the Roman Empire under the enlightened rule of Augustus, or Renaissance Italy, which produced Leonardo and Michelangelo, or Elizabethan England, or colonial America in the generation of the Founding Fathers.

Athens was not a vast or populous place, merely one of hundreds of city-states. In Socrates' time you could walk across it in two hours. The total population was about 350,000, and of those, the number with full citizenship and the right to vote—adult Athenian-born males—was only about 40,000.

Athens' shining era started in 480 B.C., when it miraculously beat back an invasion by the colossal Persian Empire in a crucial naval engagement in the strait around Salamis. Capitalizing on this military triumph, Athens assumed leadership of the Greek city-states, forming the so-called League of Delos for mutual protection. Eventually some two hundred cities along the seacoast of Greece and among the islands of the Aegean became members.

In return for paying taxes to Athens, league members received protection and the encouragement of their commerce. The league's armed forces kept the seas clear of pirates and the roads free of bandits, so that merchants could travel freely. The result was an era of some forty years during which Athens grew mightier and richer each year. It was at peace with distant powers like Persia, and rival city-states like Sparta were not yet strong enough to challenge its preeminence.

But even more astonishing than this military and political achievement was its commercial, cultural, and intellectual corollary. Athens hummed with vitality and energy. Magnificent marble temples shimmered in the brilliant sunlight. The Parthenon, a temple honoring the city's patroness, the goddess Athena, was constructed on a hill overlooking the city called the Acropolis. Ships thronged Athens' port, Piraeus. Merchants of many lands did business in the Athenian marketplace.

Most important for us, Athens was also a great marketplace of *ideas*. In 461 the Athenians selected a great leader, Pericles, and committed itself to excellence in all things. Socrates' generation lit a torch of freedom, excellence, and beauty that has been kept burning down the ages.

The leading thinkers, artists, and writers were drawn to Athens. The city was a mecca for innovators in science and philosophy, like Anaxagoras, who challenged the idea that the sun was a god, and Protagoras, who famously proclaimed that "man is the measure of all things."

At the Theater of Dionysus, Athenians applauded the plays of the founders of Western drama: Aeschylus, Sophocles, Euripides, and Aristophanes. For nearly half a century, Athens was the center of the Western world.

The *locus classicus* of Athenian ideals is the funeral oration that Pericles delivered over the fallen soldiers of the war against Sparta. It is the Gettysburg Address of antiquity. Its declaration of principles for an open society has been a touchstone throughout world history:

> *Our city is thrown open to the world, and we never expel a*
> *foreigner or prevent him from seeing or learning anything of*

which the secret if revealed to an enemy might profit him. We rely not upon management or trickery, but upon our own hearts and hands.

We are called a democracy; for the administration is in the hands of the many and not the few. No man is barred from public service because of poverty or low birth. Personal merit is the standard for which a citizen is distinguished.

Not only in our public life are we liberal, but also as regards our freedom from suspicion of one another in the pursuits of everyday life; for we do not feel resentment at our neighbor if he does as he likes, nor yet do we put on sour looks which, though harmless, are painful to behold.

We are lovers of the beautiful, yet simple in our tastes, and we cultivate the mind without loss of manliness. Wealth we employ rather as an opportunity for action than as a subject for boasting. With us it is no disgrace to be poor; the true disgrace is in doing nothing to avoid poverty.

We alone regard a man who takes no interest in public affairs, not as one who minds his own business, but as one who is good for nothing. We Athenians decide public questions for ourselves in open debate.

We alone do good to our neighbors not upon a calculation of interest, but in the confidence of freedom and in a frank and fearless spirit.

Athens is the school of Greece. Each Athenian, in his own person, seems to have the power of adapting himself to the most varied forms of action with the utmost versatility and grace. For in the hour of trial Athens alone among her contemporaries is superior. *

---

*Like all the English versions of Greek texts in this book, including those leading off each chapter, this one is my free adaptation based on several standard translations. I have endeavored to render the sense of each passage in terms that best fit its function in the book.

The Legacy

What the Athenians achieved in those miraculous forty years has resonated down the ages. Our modern world was launched by the recovery of the Greek classics, including Plato's *Dialogues*, as Sir Kenneth Clark notes in this remarkable passage from his survey of Western history, *Civilization*:

Much as one would like to say something new about the Renaissance, the old belief that it was largely based on the study of antique literature remains true. In Florence the first thirty years of the fifteenth century were the heroic age of scholarship when new texts were discovered and old texts edited. . . . It was to house these precious texts, any one of which might contain some new revelation that might alter the course of human thought, that Cosimo de' Medici built the library of San Marco. It looks to us peaceful and remote—but the first studies that took place there were not remote from life at all. It was the humanist equivalent of the Cavendish Laboratory. The manuscripts unpacked and studied under these harmonious values could alter the course of history with an explosion, not of matter, but of mind.

Even closer to our time and place, the Athenian vision influenced the formation of our own government and culture. Visitors to Washington today find themselves walking amid Greek "revival" buildings, observing institutions pioneered in fifth-century Athens, like Congress and the courts, viewing sculpture and city planning based on Hellenic models, and recalling the ideals adapted from the classics by Thomas Jefferson and other founders of our republic.

The influence of classical Greek culture, however, is more than a mere relic. Rather, it has been a constant goad to radical thinking for the present and future. "All through the history of the West the Greeks have continued to spur innovation," concluded Professor Bernard Knox after a lifetime of studying our history. "Their role has always been innovative, sometimes indeed subversive, even revolutionary."

The ideals and practices of Periclean Athens have never exerted more power in the world than they do today. Having inspired the West's rise to world leadership, these ideals and practices are now the ones to which many of the world's people and nations aspire.

"The traditions of the Greeks explain why Western culture is so uniquely dynamic," declare Professors Victor Hanson and John Heath, "and why its tenets . . . are now sweeping the globe." That's the thesis of their stirring book on the "recovery of Greek wisdom," *Who Killed Homer?* The authors point out:

> What most [people] on this earth desire . . . started with the Greeks and with the Greeks alone. . . . Billions of this world seem to want more . . . of the personal freedom, political liberty, and material comfort that began with the Greek approach.

SOCRATES: THEN AND NOW

One person more than any other exemplifies the spirit of classical Athens that is the driving force of modernism. As the great historian Arnold Toynbee says: "The finest flower of Athens during this half century was not a statue, building, or play, but a soul: Socrates." Indeed, the whole history of Athens in this period can best be seen through Socrates, according to Professor J. W. Roberts of Oxford University. He writes in his *City of Sokrates:*

> Sokrates is central to our understanding of Classical Athens. He had at some time conversed with most, if not all, of the leading men of Athens . . . he examined most of the religious, moral, social and political norms of the city; he was aware of the intellectual and artistic innovations taking place. In his lifetime, Athens rose to the zenith of her power.

Fortunately, Socrates is a figure from whom we can learn much, because he was very much an "everyman." Socrates did not wield immense political power like Pericles; he was not a man of great artistic talent like the sculptor Phidias or the playwright Sophocles; he was not an Olympic champion or a great business success or even good-looking. Socrates always insisted that any of us could do what he did if we were willing to give full expression to our innate capacity to ask questions, learn from everyone, challenge our own beliefs, and stand up for what is right.

Socrates did not contend that following him was "the way"—just *a* way to find *your* way. I can't promise you that it will be easy. Like all really true friends, Socrates will be tough with you when he needs to be. "He is the only person who makes me ashamed of the way I waste my life," confesses the high-living Alcibiades, in Plato's dialogue the "Symposium." But Alcibiades goes on to explain why he submits himself to such a troubling experience: "If you stick with him—if you really listen and join him in his questioning, and see how he lives his life—then you will find that there is nothing but sound sense there. You will begin to see how everything he says, and everything he has done, has important applications in your life, too."

In every generation, men and women have followed Alcibiades in finding Socrates to be not only a fascinating character, but also a soul-shaping mentor. During his seventy years (469–399 B.C.) he was con-

Socrates' Life and Times

Note: Some of the dates in this time line cannot be verified precisely. In such cases, I have made reasonable estimates based on the research of leading scholars.

Each entry after the first two begins with the age of Socrates at the time of the event.

479 B.C. The Athenians defeat the Persians and establish their domination of Greece.

476 B.C. Athens organizes the League of Delos for mutual defense of Greek city-states.

469 B.C. Birth: Socrates is born to Sophroniscus, a stonecutter, and Phaenarete, a midwife.

461 B.C. Age 8: Pericles, Athens' greatest leader, assumes control of the state and launches a forty-year period of growth, prosperity, and achievement.

457 B.C. Age 12: Athens negotiates a truce with Sparta, a rival city-state, securing peace and prosperity for several years.

457–450 B.C. Ages 12–19: Socrates spends his youth in Athens as the city enters its most prosperous, creative decades. He is apprenticed to his father as a stonecutter, but he soon realizes that his true vocation lies elsewhere.

cerned with the same issues that concern us today: friendship, love, work, the creation of a better society and lives that matter. In each case he struck a chord that others, in his time and later, have found inspiring and useful.

Everything we know about him is a tribute to his gift for friendship.

We would know nothing about Socrates were it not for the affection and admiration of his friends. He never wrote down his thoughts—there's no work by him in any library. Socrates believed that genuine philosophizing required "live" dialogue. "The trouble with a book," he said, "is that if you ask the book a question, it just keeps repeating the same thing, over and over again." He thrived on the give-and-take of great conversation.

Fortunately, Socrates' friends Plato and Xenophon cared so deeply that they devoted much of their lives to recording his conversations. And, significantly, the titles that Plato gave to these dialogues are quite different from the usual works of philosophy. Rather than having titles like "A Treatise on Logic" or "Prolegomenon to Any Future Metaphysics," the Socratic dialogues are simply named for the friend who figured prominently in each one: Laches, Meno, Protagoras, Phaedrus, Euthyphro, Timaeus, and so on.

As Socrates demonstrated, we only become ourselves most fully through our relationships with others: friends, mentors, and those we love and who love us.

He was respectful of his parents—and therefore could benefit fully from their gifts.

Socrates said often that his work was basically the same as his mother's and father's: "bringing forth that which is within." His mother was a midwife; his father was a stonecutter. Just as his mother helped women bring forth newborns, Socrates helped people bring forth their best ideas. Reading the *Dialogues,* we often hear him saying, in effect: "Push! PUSH! You *can* bring forth a better idea." The process was often painful, but immensely gratifying.

He also followed in his father's path, actually apprenticing as a

448 B.C. Age 21: Socrates studies with Anaxagoras and Archelaus, who are leading natural philosophers and cosmologists, and begins to understand that his own destiny lies in bringing philosophy "down to earth" by dealing with ethical rather than scientific issues.

447 B.C. Age 22: Construction begins on the Parthenon, the greatest work of Greek architecture, on the Acropolis overlooking Athens. The city becomes the center of the Mediterranean world, attracting the best and brightest in every field.

443 B.C. Age 26: Socrates attends Sophocles' *Antigone*, which portrays a woman of integrity standing firm against a tyrant.

442 B.C. Age 27: Socrates learns that the Delphic Oracle has declared that "there is no man wiser than Socrates" (pages 82–83). He searches Athens for a man wiser than himself, realizes that his strength lies in knowing how little he knows, and dedicates himself to a lifelong search for valid knowledge and deep understanding (pages 83–84).

stonemason in his youth. But then he discovered that his real work was to carve and shape not stone, but his own character.

Like Socrates, each of us can profit from taking a closer look at the most important qualities—positive and negative—we have acquired from our parents.

 He lived well on modest means.

As he tramped barefooted around the central marketplace of Athens, the agora, Socrates often remarked: "How many things are here that I do *not* need." His lifestyle of "voluntary simplicity" was so well known that it was satirized by his fellow Athenians, one of whom hails him as:

> Stout fellow! Where can we find you some respectable clothes?
> You're an affront to shoemakers!

The sophist Antiphon derided him by saying that "a slave made to live in this fashion would have run away." But Socrates was slave to no man, as the verse quoted just above concludes: "Yet you never have to stoop to flatter anyone."

Socrates lived modestly but agreeably on a small income. He thrived not on material possessions but on friendship, service, and using his mind. He liked to point out that the gods got along on the mere smoke coming from sacrificial offerings. For him, the unencumbered life was best.

But this was not easy on his family. His wife, Xantippe, must have had her hands full with raising their sons with a husband who produced no income and devoted his days and nights to dialoguing—often in places from which she was excluded. We can imagine her lamenting about this famed conversationalist: "He never *talks* to me."

Legend portrays Xantippe as a shrew. There are countless stories in the collections of Athenian gossip, such as the one about her following him into the agora, haranguing him at the top of her voice, and then unceremoniously emptying a pisspot on his head. When his friends expressed amazement at how philosophically he took this, Socrates said simply, "Haven't we all learned from childhood that after the thunder comes the rain!"

As Socrates demonstrated, we can benefit from reexamining how much "stuff" we really need—and weighing it against the cost, to ourselves and our families.

 ## He found his calling late but ultimately discovered his mission in life.

Socrates was told his destiny by no less an authority than the Oracle at Delphi, but his reaction was to reject the advice and seek his own destiny. His quest resulted in a profound insight into his real mission, as we will explore later.

As Socrates did, we must free ourselves from the expectations of others and discover for ourselves what we are really called to do in the world.

 ## He was a dutiful soldier and a loyal citizen, but he loved Athens too much to not criticize it.

Socrates served with distinction in the Athenian armed forces in engagements right through his forties. His bravery was widely recognized. On one occasion at Potidaea, he stood over his fallen friend Alcibiades and held off the enemy until help arrived.

Moreover, Socrates saw himself as owing Athens his soldierly allegiance in a larger sense. In his "Apology," he pointed out that just as he put his life on the line when commanded to do so in the wars, so he could not desert his position as a gadfly when that was what the state really needed.

Like Socrates, we must define for ourselves what true citizenship means and recognize that dissent may be as patriotic as unthinking obedience.

 ## He gave us the Socratic method.

Socrates was the man who asked questions. He does not offer us *his* insights, conclusions, or tenets. Rather, he interrogates us about *ours*—and provokes us to think things through, consider alternatives, and sometimes make surprising discoveries. Socrates applied this "method" to everything from the nature of courage and wisdom to the causes of the decay of or-

430 B.C. Age 39: Socrates survives the plague that kills one-third of the population of the city.

429 B.C. Age 40: Socrates marries Xantippe, with whom he will have three sons.

425 B.C. Age 44: The Athenians launch a great armada to conquer Sicily that ends in disaster for their fleet.

424 B.C. Age 45: Socrates escapes death in the massacre of Athenian soliders at the battle of Deljum (pages 15–16).

421 B.C. Age 48: Socrates discusses the meaning of courage with two generals, Nicias and Laches (pages 48–51).

Socrates relates his allegory "The Cave" to Glaucon, to illustrate the limits of human knowledge (pages 116–19).

416 B.C. Age 53: Socrates attends the symposium at the home of Agathon (pages 146–47), where he talks about the only subject on which he claimed any expertise, love.

415 B.C. Age 54: Socrates attends the premier of Euripides' passionate anti-war play *The Trojan Women*, in which the playwright protests Athens' growing inhumanity in the Peloponnesian War and which prompts Athenians to associate the two men's views.

ganizations. Plato's "Republic" is the first great management consultant's report, analyzing the emerging problems of Socrates' lifetime "client"— the *polis* of Athens.

With Socrates as our mentor, we can ask the right questions when we examine our lives, our communities, and our organizations.

 ## He was ridiculed, feared, and persecuted as the Gadfly.

Despite his profound gift for friendship, Socrates was no glad-hander. Quite the contrary. His continual questioning of everyone led his fellow Athenians to compare his queries to the incessant bites of the insects that buzzed around the butts of farm animals in the Attic summer. Their stings, like Socrates' questions, could drive a creature crazy. And Socrates spent thirty years doing that to some of the most powerful figures in Athens.

His fellow Athenians bit back. Imagine how Socrates must have felt when he attended the opening performance of Aristophanes' *The Clouds* and discovered that the comic playwright's new work was about *him*. Aristophanes portrayed Socrates as the blow-hard proprietor of a "thinkery." He showed the philosopher suspended in a basket, literally with his "head in the clouds," dispensing nonsense to his rapt disciples.

Athenians loved this kind of free-spirited debate. Legend has it that Socrates himself relished the lampoon and in the middle of the performance stood up so that he'd "make an easier target."

Socrates never let up. He loved his fellow Athenians too much to let them ruin their lives by failing to address the tough questions. But the Athenians grew less tolerant after they lost the war with Sparta, and their city fell on hard times. At the age of seventy, Socrates was brought to trial by three fellow citizens. The charges included failing to worship the accepted gods, introducing new ones (referring to his reliance on his own conscience), and corrupting youth. After a trial (see page 174), he was sentenced to death by hemlock. He died, as he had lived, in the midst of dialogue with his friends.

Like Socrates, each of us must be concerned with how we are living our lives and conducting our public affairs.

415–410 B.C. Ages 54–59: Socrates continues to pursue his "mission" of challenging his fellow Athenians, despite their growing irritation as the war takes its toll on their morale.

406 B.C. Age 63: Socrates, serving as chair of the senate, defies the mob by refusing to permit illegal death sentences for defeated generals.

405 B.C. Age 64: The Spartans triumph in the war, occupy Athens, and establish the authoritarian regime of the "Thirty Tyrants" to take charge and institute a reign of terror.

404 B.C. Age 65: Socrates defies the tyrants by refusing to participate in the illegal arrest of a fellow citizen.

403 B.C. Age 66: The Thirty Tyrants are deposed and a more democratic government takes power. Socrates continues in his gadfly role despite widespread opposition to dissent.

399 B.C. Age 70: Socrates is charged with impiety and corrupting youth, brought quickly to trial, and after a one-day trial is sentenced to death by hemlock (page 174). During a month's incarceration prior to his death, Socrates conducts final dialogues with his friends and respectfully refuses to accept their plan to convey him safely into exile. At the appointed time, he voluntarily takes the hemlock.

He exalted not only reason, but intuition and imagination.

A small inner voice, which Socrates called his daimon, often warned him when he was about to make a bad decision. And he used his imagination to create powerful metaphors and parables such as that of "The Cave" (see pages 116–119), which prophesies our current infatuation with electronic entertainment and virtual reality, and "The Ring of Gyges" (pages 222–223), which poses the ultimate ethical challenge.

Following Socrates, we can become more sensitive to the stirrings of intuition and imagination within ourselves, and in so doing make wiser decisions and enhance our creativity.

 He enjoyed life.

Socrates was invited to dinner practically every evening, because once he arrived the conversation always crackled with energy, relevance, and wit. He thrived on friendship and sociability and could drink most of his friends under the table—but never lost his composure.

One of the few Platonic dialogues *not* named for a friend, the "Symposium," refers not to an academic discussion but to a boisterous party with so many notable attendees that Plato gave up on selecting one of them for its title.

Like Socrates, we can live life fully, enjoying and benefiting from the best that our society has to offer, even while making our mark and doing our part to improve the world.

 He respected and appreciated the humanity of women, slaves, and "barbarians."

At a time when women were not permitted to vote or participate in civic affairs or cultural life, Socrates acknowledged his immense intellectual debt to talented women like Aspasia and Diotima. He insisted that to judge a person's mental capacity by gender was like judging a person's intelligence by how much hair was on his head.

While he did not publicly oppose slavery, which was universally accepted in his world, he declined to accept slaves as a gift and chided friends for depending on their services: "Have you ever reflected," he used to ask, "whether it be your slave or yourself that deserves whipping?"

In the dialogue called "Meno," Socrates coaches an ignorant slave boy to solve one of Euclid's most challenging theorems. He wanted to show that the seeds of truth lie in every person's mind. Socrates' empathy for these "outsiders" may have derived in part from his own widely noted homeliness. In a culture that exalted physical beauty, he was notorious for being ugly by conventional Greek standards. He was short and stout, with a muscular workman's physique. Dubbed "Frog-face" as a child, he had a bulging forehead, protruding eyes, a snub nose, and bulbous lips. When he was awarded a medal for his valor in one military engagement, Athenian wags spread the tale that it wasn't his courage that carried the day but that the opposing Spartans got one look at his face and fled in terror!

As Socrates did, each of us must determine where we stand on issues of equality, fairness, and equity in our society.

 ## He learned constantly and from everyone, everywhere.

Socrates spent his life in the agora—the teeming, rowdy center of fifth-century Athens. He loved to spend hours in the potter's shed, the wine merchant's stall, the workshop of Simon the sandal maker. He wanted to understand what made for excellence in every trade and profession and how it could be a model for wise living or effective action. "His conversation was full of things he learned from the potters, the horse-trainers, the politicians, the prostitutes," said one of his friends. "Most of the philosophers talk just ideas, but Socrates seems to have learned something from everyone, and can use it to make his ideas clear."

Like Socrates, we can and must become lifelong learners, which means enriching our lives with learning every day.

 ## He lived and died at peace with himself.

"Socrates Felix" is the striking title of the concluding chapter of the masterwork on Socrates by the late Professor Gregory Vlastos of Harvard. The phrase is Latin for "Happy Socrates," of course. Vlastos' conclusion after a lifetime of studying Socrates was that the most important thing about him is that he lived and died a happy man.

Everything comes to an end, whether it's a project, a company, an empire, or an individual human life. There comes a time—and it should be earlier than we usually think—when we should focus on what comes next: on succession in the leadership of an institution, on the next generation of our family.

Like Socrates, we should look to our legacy, asking: What will I leave behind in the minds and hearts of my friends and loved ones?

 ## Our world without Socrates

What difference would it have made if Socrates had not been a part of our history? "The entire course of Western philosophical and political thought would have been radically altered," declares Professor Victor Davis Hanson, the distinguished classicist, in the book of historical scenarios *What If?* (volume 2).

Hanson speculates on what would have happened if Socrates had been one of the hundreds of those slain at the battle of Delium, a disastrous military rout of the Athenians in which Socrates participated in 424 B.C. at the age of forty-five. If Socrates had died then, we would know about him only from Aristophanes' portrayal in *The Clouds,* a decade before, as a sophist windbag.

He would never have been known by those who chronicled the mature Socrates. For example, Plato was only five years old in 424. Hence, there would be no book in any library in the world that conveyed the serious thought and character of the man. "Almost everyone who wrote anything about Socrates and his thinking came of age *after* the battle of Delium," Hansen observes. "Socrates' influential students seem to be nearly all acquaintances from his late forties, fifties, and sixties. Had he died in 424, the later Western tradition of philosophy would probably have known almost nothing positive about his life or thought. Moreover, Hanson notes, without the inspiration—and subject matter—of Socrates, Plato's own work "would probably exist [only] as rather abstract utopian and technical theory . . . as little-known to the general reader as [the ideas of] Zeno or Epicurus."

More important, I believe, is that if Socrates had died at Delium:

- It would have robbed us of our most notable model of civil disobedience as an ethical political strategy.

- We would have lost the archetype of the gadfly as a necessary figure in a free society.

- We would have been deprived of the Socratic method as it is exemplified so unforgettably in the *Dialogues*. We would lack this powerful ideal of effective education.

- We would have been denied the most memorable portrayal in world literature of human beings learning, growing, and creating together.

Getting to know Socrates is the best introduction to most of the key values and principles of Western civilization and liberal education.

 He has been a mentor for many.

The figure of Socrates has shone brightly through the centuries, among virtually every generation of educated people. His spirit was kept alive in antiquity by Plato, Aristotle, and Cicero. The early church fathers considered him a pre-Christian saint for advocating "care of the soul." During the Reformation, Erasmus of Rotterdam, a man of reason caught in

Carriers of the Flame

It took more than his good luck at Delium, and the portrayals of him by Plato and Xenophon, to keep Socrates alive for us. It took "carriers of the flame"—men and women of every generation whose minds have been illumined and whose hearts have been warmed by the spark that Socrates provided. Throughout this book I have portrayed and cited some of these carriers of the flame in our time. They have found inspiration and guidance in Socrates, and manifested his values in their own lives. Their experiences can help us use our minds to the utmost.

the crossfire between Catholics and Protestants, invoked "Saint Socrates"! Montaigne, after reading virtually every writer extant at his time, regarded Socrates as "the wisest one that ever was." Benjamin Franklin assigned himself the task: "Imitate Jesus and Socrates."

Thinkers of modern times from Friedrich Nietzsche to Michel Foucault have found their encounter with Socrates to be soul-stirring. A wide range of contemporary writers and artists have been inspired to create their own versions of Socrates. Maxwell Anderson put him onstage in his play *Barefoot in Athens*. Mary Renault portrayed him in her novel *The Last of the Wine*. Iris Murdoch, the renowned British woman of letters, composed two Socratic dialogues that were published under the title *Acostos*. Journalist I. F. Stone rewrote Socrates' "Apology" to strengthen its theme of freedom of expression. Novelist Walter Mosley created the character of Socrates Fortlow, an African-American gadfly who is as fast with his fists as he is with his questions.

The reason for this perennial fascination is suggested by the most recent scholarly study of Socrates' influence: *The Art of Living: Socratic Reflections* by Professor Alexander Nehamas of Princeton University. "Socrates shows by example the way toward establishing an individual mode of life," concludes Professor Nehamas. "His way [does] not force his followers to repeat his life, but compels them to search for their own."

To truly follow Socrates' Way, we must find our own.

CHAPTER

1

KNOW THYSELF

> The unexamined life is not worth living.
>
> SOCRATES, IN PLATO'S "APOLOGY"

S OCRATES DID NOT CONDUCT his inquiries in the tranquil atmosphere of a temple or campus. Rather, he frequented the agora—
the teeming, noisome marketplace for all of Athens. This was the
place where every Athenian came every day to shop, catch up on the
news and gossip, and enjoy life.

The comic poet Eubulus described it vividly:

> You will find everything sold together in the same place in the
> Athenian agora: figs, witnesses to summonses, bunches of
> grapes, givers of evidence, chickpeas, lawsuits, myrtle, laws,
> water clocks, indictments.

Here, in the heat of the Attic sun, Socrates dialogued amid the aro-
mas of freshly baked bread and fish just delivered from the port. He and
his friends had to speak up as the vendors hawked their wares and the
blacksmith hammered at his anvil.

One of Socrates' favorite haunts was the shop of Simon the Cobbler at
the edge of the agora. It has been excavated and identified by the scatter-
ing of hobnails and a fifth-century cup inscribed with the name of Simon.

In this excerpt from a typical conversation, Socrates challenges his
young friend Euthydemus to seek self-knowledge. It is from the *Memoirs
of Socrates,* by Xenophon, who together with Plato gave us the best ac-
counts of Socrates' life and thought.

SOCRATES: Tell me, Euthydemus, have you ever visited the Oracle at
Delphi?

EUTHYDEMUS: Yes, indeed, Socrates. Twice. I always seek the best advice when I have an important decision to make.

SOCRATES: Did you notice the inscription above the entrance, the one
you can't miss as you enter the temple . . . ?

EUTHYDEMUS: Which one is that, Socrates?

SOCRATES: It says KNOW THYSELF [*gnothi seauton*].

EUTHYDEMUS: Oh, yes! But I guess I didn't pay it too much attention.

They hurry you so much to get in and out, I never stopped to think about that.

SOCRATES: But what about later, Euthydemus? Did you think it was worth thinking about, if you were making an important decision?

EUTHYDEMUS: No, I never have, Socrates. By the time I left, I'd gotten the oracle's advice, and I didn't think that further thought was necessary. But I also just assumed that I knew myself, I mean, how could I *not*. I'm really not that complicated, Socrates.

SOCRATES: Well, only you can decide about that, Euthydemus. But let's approach this from another angle. Yesterday I saw you at Aristides', sizing up the horses—were you thinking of buying one?

EUTHYDEMUS: Yes, Socrates, I'm going down there now to close the deal.

SOCRATES: And did you spend much time examining the horse, to determine its strength or weakness, its health and age and temperament?

EUTHYDEMUS: Well, of course, Socrates. I've hung around the paddock and the stable for several hours on different days.

SOCRATES: And did you have in mind how you would want to use the horse and how you would need it to perform?

EUTHYDEMUS: That was uppermost in my mind, Socrates.

SOCRATES: And did you weigh what you learned about examining the horse against the uses you would be putting it to?

EUTHYDEMUS: Exactly, Socrates.

SOCRATES: But, Euthydemus, you didn't go to a soothsayer or priest for advice one way or the other, did you?

EUTHYDEMUS: Why no, Socrates. Why should I? I could examine the horse myself, and it became apparent what is was good for.

SOCRATES: Yet when you have a decision to make that will affect your whole life and those you care about, you accept what the oracle says rather than following the advice to *know thyself* . . .

EUTHYDEMUS: I see your point, Socrates. I could examine myself at least as well as I examine my horse.

SOCRATES: Indeed, Euthydemus. And do you think that people may choose more wisely when they understand their own strengths and weaknesses?

EUTHYDEMUS: That makes sense, Socrates. Wasn't our friend Podocles complaining bitterly yesterday about how he hates his work as a potter and wished he'd gone into something that made better use of his talents?

SOCRATES: Yes, I recall that dialogue. That's why I wanted to have this conversation with you. I thought you might want to consider that those who know themselves know what is appropriate for them and can distinguish what they can and cannot do. By doing what they understand, they both supply their needs and enjoy success. By refraining from doing things that they don't understand, they avoid making mistakes and escape misfortune.

EUTHYDEMUS: I have certainly seen that many times, Socrates, but I never realized how it applied to me. I guess they put KNOW THYSELF above the entrance at Delphi because, if you *don't,* then whatever advice you get from the priestess, you may not understand properly or use well.

Those who do *not* know themselves and are totally deceived about their own abilities are in the same position whether they are dealing with other people or any other aspect of human affairs.

This sharp focus on self-examination is the first of Socrates' major concerns.

The earlier Greek philosophers had focused on the nature of the universe, developing theories about the ultimate form of matter and the place of the Earth in the cosmos. What distinguishes Socrates from the so-called pre-Socratics like Heraclitus and Anaxagoras is that he brings philosophy down to earth. He is the first to apply critical thinking to the challenges of human life and society. "Socrates called down philosophy from the skies," observed the Roman orator Cicero, "and implanted it in the cities and homes of men." By making philosophical inquiry more relevant, Socrates introduces radically new ways to think about ourselves and our lives.

First, he relies on reason rather than revelation, as his questioning of Euthydemus exemplifies. Rather than going to the priests and oracles for guidance, Socrates urges us to use our minds to understand ourselves.

Second, Socrates questions "conventional wisdom." His endeavor in virtually every dialogue is to challenge the easy answers that most of us have for important questions such as: "What is love?" "What is courage?" "What is justice?" "What is friendship?" As we make decisions that affect how we live our lives, Socrates implores us to start by examining our own interests, values, and capabilities. Socrates presses beyond the easy answers, revealing them to be contradictory or mere words without clear meanings. The ideas we find in our heads whenever we start to discuss such issues are, more often than not, confusing rather than helpful in making sound decisions.

Third, Socrates conducts these inquires as dialogues because we need one another to see ourselves clearly. We need to express our ideas, justify them, and hear the reactions of others. Often we do not know what we really think until we hear what we have to say, and only then do we realize that our beliefs and opinions are not as insightful or valid as they might be and could use some revision.

But if we ourselves are the chief instruments for understanding and shaping our lives, then we must begin by understanding better how we use our minds, what our values are, and to what degree we are using our minds to the utmost.

SOCRATES' SPIRIT IN OUR TIME

This book invites you to follow Socrates' Way. But is that really feasible? Isn't it too grand a goal for "ordinary" people like us? Isn't Socrates, after all, one in a million—a uniquely capable individual who cannot be imitated?

Socrates himself answers that question for us, according to Richard Mitchell, the first of my carriers of the flame. Mitchell, a formidable gadfly himself, is widely known as "The Underground Grammarian," after his book of the same title. So naturally he was attracted to Socrates as a model.

Mitchell imagines that an extraterrestrial who knows nothing of lifeforms on our planet arrives to investigate the human race. He selects two typical specimens: Socrates and Mitchell. The visiting scientist begins by noting two things that both specimens have in common and that distinguish them from all other forms of life he finds on earth: self-consciousness and choice.

> We can know ourselves, unlike the foxes and the oaks, and can know that we know ourselves. While we have appetites and urges just like all the other creatures, we have the astonishing power of seeing them not simply as the necessary at-

tributes of what we are, but as separate from us in a strange way . . . we can hold them at arm's length, turning them his way and that, and make judgment of them, and even put them aside, saying yes, that is "me" in a way, but when I choose, it is just a thing, not truly me, but only mine.

Now the extraterrestrial investigator looks for the *differences* between his two specimens, Mitchell and Socrates. He is particularly interested in how each of them compares with respect to these two defining human characteristics.

The conclusions of Mitchell's extraterrestrial scientist are sobering. Comparing himself to Socrates, Mitchell is forced to conclude that "the humanness in me has been somehow 'broken.' . . . Socrates is the normal human, and I, a freak, a distortion of human nature." But, Mitchell notes, he would have one defender—Socrates himself!

Socrates would say, for he said this very often: "No, my young friend is not truly a freak. All that I can do, he can do; he just doesn't do it. And if he doesn't do it, it is because of something else that is natural to human beings, and just as human as the powers that you might find human in me . . . Some of us sleep deeper and longer than others. It may be, that unless we are awakened by some help from other human beings, we sleep our lives away, and never come into these powers. But we can be awakened."

Socrates' very first lesson for us is *we can do what he did,* and, indeed, we *must* do that if we want to master our minds to the utmost. Mitchell goes on to explain exactly how we can go about following Socrates' advice (see Exercise 8 at the end of this chapter).

Socrates always maintained—literally to his dying day—that he was not especially smart or learned or wise. He asserts time after time that he is merely a searcher of truth, slowly and fitfully making his way, just as we do.

To achieve self-mastery and insight requires a lifelong regimen of asking questions, thinking things through, liberating your mind, benefiting from the perspectives of other people, and caring for your soul. The purpose of this book is to awaken you to your full powers as a thinking and ethical human being.

Strengthening Your Socratic Spirit

- Have you critically examined the "conventional wisdom" of your culture, as Socrates urges Euthydemus to do? (Exercise #1)

- Have you identified and fully benefited from the mentors you have already had in your life? (Exercise #2)

- Have you examined the roles that choice and chance have played in your life so far, and have you drawn conclusions for living wisely? (Exercise #3 and #4)

- Do you really think things through when making decisions? (Exercise #5)

- Have you nurtured the Socratic mentor in yourself, to help others whom you care about? (Exercise #6)

- Have you examined your own thinking "style"—which of your several kinds of intelligence (logical, emotional, linguistic, etc.) do you enjoy using the most? (Exercise #7) What time of day is your mind most alert and energized? (Exercise #8)

- Do you capture, refine, and build on your best thoughts about how to live a good life? (Exercise #9)

CHALLENGES, EXPLORATIONS, AND APPLICATIONS

 ## 1. Do better than Euthydemus.

As Socrates revealed, Euthydemus had seen the Delphic Oracle's injunction to KNOW THYSELF but failed to really examine it, appraise it, or use it to enhance his life. This is a constant theme of the *Dialogues:* the need to examine statements that we take for granted but have never examined critically. In different dialogues Socrates challenges his friends to examine concepts they thought they fully understood, like courage, justice, and friendship itself.

Here's your chance to do better than Euthydemus did in his encounter with Socrates. Just as the two looked at the real meaning of "know thyself," you can stir your thinking with slogans and credos of your world.

We are surrounded by such "conventional wisdom"—widely accepted dictums about how we should live our lives. But rarely do we examine them critically, identify their implications and limitations, and decide for ourselves how useful they are. I'd like you to identify three of them and actually reflect on and discuss what they mean, whether or not you agree with them, and how you might apply them in your life. These declarations might be:

- a favorite saying among your family or friends, like "Go with the flow" or "Don't sweat the small stuff" or "Love is all you need"

- the motto or slogan of the organization you work for or a voluntary organization with which you are associated (Boy Scouts, Pledge of Allegiance, Masonic credo)

- an advertising motto that's stuck in your mind, like "Just do it" or "Where's the beef?"

The Owl of Wisdom

For Socrates, the symbol of wisdom was the owl of Athena. Athens was named after her, of course, and she was its presiding deity. A giant gold-and-ivory statue by Phidias stood at the center of the Parthenon. The Athenians also put her on their coins. Our notion of the "wise owl" derives from their belief.

In Homer, Athena supports the Greeks, especially Odysseus during his wanderings, and she often appears in the form of the bird—the stock Homeric epithet for her is *glaucopis,* which can mean either "bright-eyed" or "owl-faced."

Real owls were so pervasive around Athens that the Athenian equivalent of our expression "bringing coals to Newcastle" was "bringing owls to Athens."

"The owl of wisdom only takes flight in the gathering dusk," said the philosopher Hegel, referring to the fact that Socrates reached his prime at the point when Athens had begun its descent from the pinnacle of greatness.

SOCRATIC QUESTIONING VERSUS ORACULAR AUTHORITY

Socrates was on dangerous ground in discussing the Delphic dictum, KNOW THYSELF. Most Greeks treated the oracle with awe and reverence. Going to the Delphic Oracle for advice was an extraordinary experience. Located in lofty hills north and west of Athens, Delphi was the site of the temple of the god Apollo. Approached either by ship from Corinth or by a road winding through the mountain passes from Boeotia, the first view of the gleaming marble, bronze, and gold buildings was stunning.

Men came from all over Greece to put their questions to the oracle. Cities sent envoys to find out how to get rid of a plague or where to found a colony. Important men came to ask whether they would have sons to carry on their name. Each would bring hefty gifts that were stored in "treasury" buildings leading up to the temple.

Questions to the oracle were presented in writing, prior to the supplicant's encounter in the dark, smoky shrine. The answers came from young priestesses through whom Apollo supposedly spoke. They were intoxicated by fumes from a deep fissure over which they sat, which emanated ethylene, which produces euphoria and hallucinations.

In a later chapter, we will discuss what the oracle had to say about Socrates himself—and how he applied his critical intelligence to that pronouncement.

- a phrase on a public building or monument that you see regularly, like "In God We Trust"

- a visual image that has caught your eye, like the eye above the pyramid on the one-dollar bill

Take one of these each day and spend some time reflecting on it. Spark a little dialogue by asking others what they think about it. By the end of the day, decide on whether you agree with it or not, and, if you do, think of one specific way you could apply it to enhance your life.

If you enjoy this challenge, do it with other such sayings. As you identify those that ring true and also hold up under your Socratic scrutiny, post them around your personal spaces—the places in which you like to think, work, create, or reflect. You will be in excellent company in doing this. Michel de Montaigne, the classical French writer often compared to Socrates, posted his selection of the smartest and wisest things he had ever heard. In fact, he had them carved into the wooden pillars of his private study.

2. Revisit a Socratic figure in your life.

You may have already met Socrates in your life but failed to realize it. In every generation and in every life we can find "carriers of the torch." These are the people who fulfill Socrates' role by stimulating us to examine our lives, question our beliefs and values, and think more clearly.

In this exercise you will revisit such a person in your life, either literally or by means of imagination. For you, this Socratic figure may have been one of your parents or even a grandparent, a teacher, a friend, or a professional colleague. Perhaps he or she was an older person, patient and wise, someone who understood you when you were young and searching, who helped you see the world as a more profound place or gave you sound advice to help you make your way through it.

For Mitch Albom, that person was Morrie Schwartz, a carrier of the flame who was his college professor twenty years earlier, as he recounted in his book *Tuesdays with Morrie.* "The last class of my old professor's life took place every week in his home," Albom begins. "The subject was 'The Meaning of Life.' It was taught from experience.

"No grades were given, but there were oral exams each week. You were expected to respond to questions, and you were expected to pose questions of your own."

That's what you will do in this exercise. To maximize its effectiveness, do it at a place where you can be alone and comfortable and at a time when you will be uninterrupted for at least a half-hour.

First, summon up your memories of the favorite Socratic mentor you want to revisit. Picture him or her in one of your favorite places. As you visualize that person savor the physical sensations of the place and time: what you can see, hear, smell, taste, and touch. Then ask yourself the question that Mitch Albom found himself asking himself the first time he was alone with his old professor:

What has happened to me?

That is, reflect on the truly important changes in you that you feel have occurred since you were in touch with your mentor.

Morrie asked some questions that you might ask yourself:

- Do you feel you are doing the right things?

- Are you at peace with yourself?

- Have you become what you feel you were destined to be?

- Are there dimensions of yourself that you regret having neglected?

- Are you giving back to your community?

- Are you trying to be as human as you can be?

- Have you found someone to share your heart with?

Then, *listen* to hear what the mentor you have summoned into your consciousness might have to say.

If you find this exercise rewarding, repeat it several times. You will find that your answers change and grow and that the mentor you have re-visited will have more to tell you each time.

 3. Discover your core values.

Socrates regularly questioned his friends to reveal the core values under-lying their opinions. He was persistent in wanting to know why they be-

"HIS VOICE DESCENDS INTO THE DEPTH OF YOUR SOUL"

So declared the philosopher Friedrich Nietzsche, who had a lifelong love-hate relationship with Socrates. "Socrates teaches you how to listen," Nietzsche continued. "He lets you taste a new yearning . . . he divines the hidden and forgotten treasure, the drop of goodness from whose touch you go away richer, opened, less sure, perhaps, but full of hopes that as yet have no name."

lieved what they said they believed. You can do the same thing by playing The Whys, a game created by cognitive anthropologist Charles Case. He designed this game to carry the flame of Socrates' questioning. It's an exercise in probing into yourself—or an agreeable partner—to discover the basis of your beliefs.

You can start with any belief or conviction, even a trivial one like: "I really like chocolate-covered donuts." The game consists of asking yourself or your partner "why" questions that elicit the reason or motivation for each of your responses. A dialogue about the donuts with yourself or someone else might proceed thus:

Why do you like chocolate-covered donuts?

It's the chocolatey taste and the different textures of the chocolate and the dough.

Why do you like the chocolatey taste, and the different textures of the chocolate and the dough?

Well, for one thing, it reminds me of donuts I used to eat with my father when we went out together on Sunday afternoons.

Why be reminded of donuts you used to eat with your father?

That was the best time of the week for me.

Why was that the best time of week for you?

Because I had him all to myself, and he let me have whatever I wanted, pretty much.

Why have him all to yourself and be allowed to do what you wanted?

Because my mom was very strict, I always felt I had to pretend with her.

As I think you can see, this process can lead to some interesting discoveries about yourself. Granted, it can also get annoying. "At first I found the process maddening," said Judith Hooper, reporting on her experience with The Whys in *Would the Buddha Wear a Walkman?* "It was like conversing with a toddler or an automaton," she says. "But after about thirty or forty whys, I finally hit one I absolutely could not answer. And I discovered that I had arrived at a core belief." That's the ultimate point of The Whys, and each time you play it you get a somewhat different version of one of your core beliefs.

"The question 'Why?' is the most powerful invention of the human mind," contends Case. "When you use it to discover your own beliefs, you can become self-creative and sculpt your own reality. You get 'whyser'!"

 4. "Examine your life" as choice and as chance.

Socrates insisted that we examine our lives. Here is an exhilarating way to begin to do this—by yourself or in dialogue with others.

Each of our lives results from the interplay of choice and chance. On the one hand, we make choices, pursuing our goals and dreams, and thereby nudging our lives in desired directions. But at the same time we are all vulnerable to chance, luck (good and bad), and accident.

In this exercise you will look back on your life in two ways to illuminate the interplay of these two forces in your life. You can do it by yourself, making notes on your thoughts, with another person, or in a small group.

This exercise is adapted from Mary Catherine Bateson, the distinguished anthropologist and author of *Composing a Life* and other books. Bateson is another of my carriers of the flame: She brilliantly "examines her life" and those of other people in ways that Socrates would have admired.

To examine your life in this way, start by briefly describing the high points, beginning with this topic sentence:

HOW SOCRATES TALKED WITH HIMSELF

All the exercises so far have been different kinds of dialogue with yourself and with others. Socrates engaged in such dialogues with himself. At the end of the dialogue "Hippias Major," Socrates bids farewell to Hippias, who has proven to be a dim bulb, and laments that for him, Socrates, this dialogue is not over. He explains that waiting for him at home is an annoying character who is always there and who insists on continuing the day's conversations way into the night.

Socrates meant that, for him, the dialogue continued even when he was alone. The philosopher Hannah Arendt, author of *Eichmann in Jerusalem,* calls this "The Two-in-One." "When Socrates goes home," she notes, "he is not alone, he is *by* himself. Clearly, with this fellow who awaits him, Socrates has to come to some kind of agreement, because they live under the same roof. Better to be at odds with the whole world than be at odds with the only one you are forced to live together with when you have left company behind."

We would call this our self-consciousness or, in ethical matters, our conscience, and Socrates may have been the first to articulate it. But it is one of the key acts of mind that make us human.

"Without the breath of life, the human body is a corpse," Arendt observes. "Without thinking, the human mind is dead." You have already experienced such a dialogue with yourself. Exercises 1–3 have been different kinds of dialogues-with-yourself.

As I look back, I am struck by how much my present situation resulted from choices that I made and goals that I set for myself.

For example . . .

Now create a second version of the major turning points in your life (likely different from those in the first version), beginning with *this* topic sentence:

As I look back, I am struck by how much of my present situation resulted from occurrences (either good or bad) I could not have predicted and over which I had little or no control.

For example . . .

Reflect on or discuss with others the insights you have gained from "examining your life" from these two different perspectives. Are there any implications for how you should be living your life now?

 ### 5. *"Examine your life": Do you think things through?*

Socrates kept his mind keen by working every day to sharpen his thinking. In this exercise, you will judge for yourself how well you are already using the strategies that you will be mastering in this book.

This exercise is based on the plot of the movie *Defending Your Life* with Meryl Streep and Albert Brooks. (You don't need to have seen the movie, but if you haven't, then enjoying it would be an excellent way to energize yourself for this exercise.)

In the movie, Daniel Miller, an advertising man played by Brooks, is driving along a Los Angeles boulevard in his new luxury car listening to Barbra Streisand sing "Something's Coming" when something does come: a bus that hits him head-on. Miller wakes up deceased, but his troubles are just beginning!

In a kind of purgatory presided over by Rip Torn, he's called upon to "defend his life." To do so he must recall instances in his life where he really used his mind to the utmost—and instances where he did *not*. Then he is judged on whether, overall, he really lived fully. (If you're having that feeling of déjà vu, it's because this movie plot recalls Dickens's classic *A Christmas Carol,* in which Scrooge is confronted with examples of his behavior and realizes that he could and must do much better.)

THE CHALLENGE

You will judge your own performance by recalling key incidents in your life and using them to gauge your degree of success thus far.

For each of the categories below, please recollect one occasion in your life when you succeeded maximally and one in which you must admit that you failed. For example, for the first category, recall a time when

SOCRATES' SCORN OF PEOPLE WHO REFUSE TO THINK

Socrates had no patience for people who give up on stretching their minds because our reasoning so often falters and fails. He even coined a word for them: *misologists*—"haters of reasoning."

"It is a sad case," he said, "when a man discovers that some of his cherished beliefs are false and therefore gives up on finding the truth. He should blame himself for failing to validate his belief, but instead he turns against thinking itself. So for the rest of his life he goes on hating reason and speaking ill of it."

Socrates would have recoiled from our common practice of dodging discussion of an important but controversial topic by saying, "You have your opinion, and I have mine. Let's just agree to disagree." To Socrates, this would have been an avoidance of the need to engage in dialogue, to be willing to test our convictions in the give-and-take of discussion. "Let us not let into our souls this idea that perhaps there is no soundness in reasoning," he enjoined his friends. "Let us think instead that we ourselves are not yet sound, and struggle to become better thinkers."

you asked questions that enabled you to act more wisely and a time when your failure to ask questions got you into trouble.

Some people find it easier to remember their successes and more difficult to recall failures. For others, it's just the reverse. Note which is the case for you; you will learn something else about yourself.

Then, for each of the categories, rate yourself from 1 to 10 on your overall performance thus far.

Succeeded . . . Failed

I asked the right question(s) at the right time.

I challenged assumptions and thereby prevented misunderstandings.

I used specific thinking skills to analyze, criticize, and be creative about a situation.

I really thought things through before deciding or acting.

I questioned the basis of my beliefs and either confirmed or changed my initial position.

I made maximum use of friends and colleagues, and experts in the area in which I needed to decide or act.

I stood up for what was right.

I took specific steps to care for my soul.

 6. Evoke the Socratic teacher in you.

In a previous exercise, you revisited a Socratic figure in your life. Now, I'd like you to experience imaginatively and then to consider acting out how you yourself can function as Socrates did.

Imagine you are with a person you care very much about—perhaps a younger person with whom you have a close relationship, one who thinks you are one of the smartest, wisest people that person has ever met. Let yourself imagine how it feels to be with this person. Imagine yourself "Socratizing" with this young person, including:

- engaging in dialogue that helps this person clarify her thinking

- helping this person to discover what she needs to think about

- encouraging her to question her "received ideas"

- stimulating this person to think more deeply than she usually does

- helping this person be more objective and more positive

- strengthening this person in thinking her own best thoughts, made the better by your presence and involvement

You can put this imaginative exercise into action. Choose someone who you think would welcome this kind of Socratic interaction with you. Take the initiative, in an appropriate way to make this happen. It may need to be a long-range plan, in which you take steps to refresh and strengthen your relationship over a period of weeks or months. But those steps, too, should be gratifying for both of you.

7. *What's your thinking style?*

Socrates had a distinctive style as a thinker. So do you. For one thing, Socrates was a slow, careful thinker. He almost always found that the people with whom he engaged in dialogue came up with snappier answers than his. He would ask them to slow down so that he could understand what they were saying. Often, this was ironical. Socrates' insistence on clarity frequently revealed that the people with the instant answers hadn't really thought things through—what they offered sounded good but didn't hold up under scrutiny.

Second, Socrates greatly preferred verbal rather than written communication. In fact, he actively resisted the printed word, as we have noted.

Third, Socrates had an irresistible penchant for challenging "the right answer." He usually wanted to explore alternatives.

In short, Socrates would not have done very well on the kinds of tests used to measure thinking ability for students today. On those tests, students are called upon to make quick selections among multiple-choice items on a written test. Socrates would have taken one look and said, "Let's look more closely at Question #1. I have some problems with the way it's formulated. Could you explain what you mean by the key terms? I wonder whether *any* of the proposed choices are really valid."

In this exercise you will explore the way you like to use your brain. When people think about measuring their capacity to use their brain, they usually think of their IQ. Most of us recall having our IQ measured at some point in our childhood, and most of us know the results. The IQ test was supposed to measure your capacity to think and learn and therefore to predict your success in school. However, contemporary psychologists have debunked this whole idea of a single capacity called *intelligence*. You have not one but at least *seven* intelligences, according to Harvard psychologist Howard Gardner.

- Linguistic intelligence

- Logical-mathematical intelligence

- Spatial intelligence

- Musical intelligence

- Bodily-kinesthetic intelligence

- Intrapersonal intelligence (knowing yourself)

- Interpersonal intelligence (knowing other people)

Here's a simple exercise that will pinpoint some of your strengths. Circle the numbers of those descriptions that you feel apply to you.

1. You easily remember nice turns of phrase or memorable quotes and use them deftly in conversation.

2. You sense quickly when someone you are with is troubled about something.

3. You are fascinated by scientific and philosophical questions like "When did time begin?"

4. You can find your way around a new area or neighborhood very quickly.

5. You are regarded as quite graceful and rarely feel awkward in your movements when learning a new sport or dance.

6. You can sing on key.

7. You regularly read the science pages of your newspaper and look at magazines on science and technology.

8. You note other people's errors in using words or grammar, even if you don't correct them.

9. You often can figure out how something works or how to fix something that's broken without asking for help.

10. You can readily imagine how other people play the roles they do in their work or families and imaginatively see yourself in their roles.

11. You can remember in detail the layout and landmarks of places you've visited on vacations.

12. You enjoy music and have favorite performers.

13. You like to draw.

14. You dance well.

15. You organize things in your kitchen, bathroom, and at your desk according to categories and in patterns.

16. You feel confident in interpreting what other people do in terms of what they are feeling.

17. You like to tell stories and are considered a good storyteller.

18. You sometimes enjoy different sounds in your environment.

19. When you meet new people, you often make connections between their characteristics and those of other acquaintances.

20. You feel you have a keen sense of what you can and can't do.

If *all* three descriptions of any of these trios apply to you, you probably are strong in that intelligence, even if you haven't cultivated it.

Descriptions 1, 8, and 17: linguistic intelligence

Descriptions 6, 12, and 8: musical intelligence

Descriptions 3, 7, and 15: logical-mathematical intelligence

Descriptions 4, 11, and 13: spatial intelligence

Descriptions 5, 9, and 14: bodily-kinesthetic intelligence

Descriptions 10, 16, and 20: intrapersonal intelligence (knowing yourself)

Descriptions 2, 10, and 19: interpersonal intelligence (knowing others)

HOW SOCRATES PERSONALIZED HIS CONVERSATIONS

In Plato's dialogue "Phaedrus," Socrates observes that to engage men's minds, you must know what kinds of minds they have. Each kind demands its own style of discourse. The subjects and strategies that will engage one person will fail to appeal to another.

This was another reason why Socrates declined to codify his thoughts in a book. In writing a book "you can't know whom to address" since the readers are unknown to you as individuals. Socrates therefore insisted on face-to-face dialogue, where he could adjust his message to each individual. In dialogues like "Laches," "Lysis," "Euthyphro," and "Theaetetus," Socrates tailored his conversation to the person he was talking to or the occasion in which he and his friends were involved.

- To military leaders like Laches and his comrades, Socrates chose a topic central to their mission—the nature of courage.

- But when talking to his old school friend Lysis, in the dialogue named for him, Socrates asks, "What is friendship?"

- When he encounters Euthyphro on the steps of the courthouse where he has come to prosecute his own father for an offense against the gods, Socrates asks: "Are actions right because the gods demand them, or do the gods demand them because they are right?"

- Socrates questions young Theaetetus, whose field is mathematics, about the nature of knowledge by asking him, "Is knowing the same thing as seeing and feeling?"

8. When is your mind most alive?

Socrates was not a morning person. When Crito came to visit him in his damp, cold cell during his imprisonment, he arrived early in the morning and had to sit and wait for Socrates to wake up! By contrast, Socrates was notorious for his capacity to outlast his friends as the evening wore on and remain at the top of his form when the other guests had fallen asleep, as demonstrated in Plato's dialogue the "Symposium."

You'll benefit from becoming more aware of your own pattern of mental energy during a typical day. Everyone has a favorite time of day. For some of us it's the early evening, when we are unwinding from work and are eager for the night's activities; we feel more alive and capable, ready to dance until midnight. For others, it's that quiet period at dawn, when few people are up and the day seems fresh and new. A whole new field within psychology, *chronopsychology,* is devoted to researching the patterns of time and energy for each person.

It is now firmly established that each of us is mentally alert and motivated at certain times during the day. "Larks" wake up singing, mentally speaking, while "owls" take hours to warm up and may not reach their peak until late afternoon or evening.

You will obtain three benefits from knowing your peak and valley times for thinking:

- You will enjoy using your mind more when you feel in the mood for it.

- You will think better, because you will not be fighting resistance, fatigue, and discomfort.

- You will make better use of your "low" times by doing things other than trying to think.

The following questions will help you to sharpen your sense of when you think best. You may already be generally aware of your preferences, but these simple questions will help spur you on to act on them. The questions were developed by Professor Rita Dunn of St. John's University, Jamaica, New York.

Answer *true* or *false* to each of these statements.

- I dislike getting up in the morning.

- I dislike going to sleep at night.

- I wish I could sleep all morning.

- I stay awake for a long time after I get into bed.

- I feel wide awake only after 10:00 in the morning.

- If I stay up late at night, I get too sleepy to remember anything.

- I usually feel a *low* after lunch.

- When I have a task requiring concentration, I like to get up early in the morning to do it. I'd rather do those tasks requiring concentration in the afternoon.

- I usually start the tasks that require the most concentration after dinner.

- I could stay up all night.

- I wish I didn't have to go to work before noon.

- I wish I could stay home during the day and go to work at night.

- I like going to work in the morning.

- I can remember things best when I concentrate on them:
  in the morning
  at lunchtime
  before dinner
  in the afternoon
  after dinner
  late at night

Your answers should provide a map of how you prefer to spend your mental energy over the course of the day. To interpret your answers, check whether you answered *true* or *false* for most of the statements that point to a single time of day: morning, noon, afternoon, evening, or night. That will be the period during which you feel that you work either at your best or at your worst.

How can you use these results? There are three simple guidelines for thinking that will give your mind an opportunity to work at its optimum.

First, seize your highs. Know when your mind is most likely to click into high gear and prearrange your schedule whenever possible so that you are free to use it undisturbed during that period. Change appointments and hold phone calls to take advantage of the times when your brain does its best thinking.

Second, shut down before you run out of gas. Know when your mind is *least* likely to be ready for action and plan ahead to do other useful or enjoyable activities at those times, such as socializing, routine work, or relaxing.

Third, give yourself a break and get enough sleep. The majority of Americans are sleep-deprived because of the temptation to stay up late with TV or a movie.

9. Launch your Socratic dialogue on "How to Live (I Think)."

Richard Mitchell, the carrier of the flame you met earlier in this chapter, proposes that each of us should follow Socrates' Way by continually thinking about and discussing the topic of "How to Live (I Think)." Mitchell envisages this as a book that we should each be writing and that we know we will never finish. "The first line is the hardest part," he observes. "But whoever writes even that one line has passed at once into what Socrates called the examined life, the life that *is* worth living."

I would like you to write that first line of your book on "How to Live (I Think)," below. Much of Socrates' Way is a manual for doing what you need to do to continue thinking and discussing this topic.

How to start? Mitchell helpfully notes that many of us can best begin with one of our own favorite quotes or a thought from one of our parents, teachers, or mentors from the Great Tradition. Writing your version of "How to Live" is, to my mind, the ideal syllabus for your own lifelong education. As Mitchell, a professional educator himself, wisely declares:

> The largest and simplest definition of true education that I can imagine is this: It is all that is absent in the lives of those who aren't composing [their own] *How to Live (I Think)*.

Once you've started, I'd like you to develop the habit of jotting down thoughts as they occur to you. Forget about "making a mental note"; write it down. Our memories simply aren't built to move spontaneous thoughts into long-term memory. You'll lose 90 percent of your best ideas if you don't make some note of them the moment they occur.

SOCRATES AND THE PIG

Through the ages thinking people have struggled with this conundrum: Is it better to be a pig, wallowing in the mud, oblivious to its condition but happy from moment to moment or to be Socrates, self-aware and struggling through-out his life with the questions, issues, and dilemmas of being an ethical human being?

The most famous response to this conundrum was that of the philosopher John Stuart Mill. "It is better to be a human dissatisfied than a pig satisfied," Mill declared. "It is better to be Socrates dissatisfied than a fool satisfied. And if the fool or the pig are of a different opinion, it is because they only know their own side of the question. The other party to the comparison knows *both* sides."

From this perspective, ignorance is not bliss. Indeed, "following one's bliss," which was Joseph Campbell's renowned formula for a fulfilling life, specifically involves seeking out "the greatest challenges and the most agoniz-ing struggles," as Campbell put it.

Sometimes, of course, the rigors of self-awareness become irksome. So it's worth hearing from one other thinker who has weighed in on this question: Woody Allen. "The unexamined life may not be worth living," he has said. "But the *examined* life is no picnic either."

Recording your thoughts on paper is essential if you wish to be able to work with them in the future. Newly forming ideas, no matter how vivid they may seem at the moment, are extremely easy to forget. Other activities demand your attention and pull you away from your work for a minute, an hour, a day, or a week. That shimmering idea is like a seed: If it is not tended, it will turn to dust and blow away.

We all have such thoughts continually. However, they have little im-pact, because we don't record them, review them, reflect on them, and re-spond to them. Your journal provides that medium. It is a culture-bed for these seeds of interest that would otherwise be swept away by the breezes of onrushing circumstances.

If you want to start out simply, you can carry a piece of 8½ × 11-inch paper folded into quarters, which provides enough space for the sponta-neous thoughts you're likely to have during one day. A 5½ × 3¼-inch pad is perfect.

Whenever you make a notepad entry, transfer the thought to your journal that same day or shortly thereafter. This gives you a chance to re-examine your initial ideas and "tweak" them as you are transferring them to a permanent record.

Your initial, tentative, preliminary draft of the first sentence of "How to Live (I Think)":

_____

_____

_____

_____

_____

_____

Now, over the next forty-eight hours, reflect on the thought or insight you captured in the box above. See if you can make more of it. You might refine it, express it better, apply it, critique it, generalize it, etc., then transfer it to your journal. Having done this, you will be well launched on your Thinker's Journal—your ongoing personal place in which to think more deeply by capturing your thoughts and then enhancing their meaning.

CHAPTER

2

ASK GREAT
QUESTIONS

My way toward the truth is to ask
the right questions.

SOCRATES, IN PLATO'S "PROTAGORAS"

Picture the outdoor gymnasium of Athens: the training ground for young men. About 150 of them are engaged in exercises in the football-field-size arena. At one end of the field, an armor maker is putting on a show, hoping to attract business.

Watching this exhibition are Socrates and two esteemed Athenian military leaders—Nicias and Laches. These veteran soldiers had earned their city's respect in the Peloponnesian War against the Spartans. Indeed, both would subsequently die in battle: Laches at Mantinea in 418; Nicias in the doomed Sicilian expedition of 413. So this conversation suggests how Socrates might fare today were he to visit West Point and talk to a couple of visiting generals.

Laches and Nicias are discussing whether this sort of training would really be useful or not in actual combat. Nicias thinks it would be, but Laches is not so sure. After "warming them up" for some vigorous thinking, Socrates introduces a more profound subject central to their profession: What is courage?

The following excerpt from Plato's *Dialogues,* titled "Laches," is the longest account of Socrates-in-action that you will be reading. It exemplifies the famed Socratic method.

LACHES: I saw this soldier performing differently, not long ago. He was one of my men, and he was showing off a new spear he had invented, curved like a scythe. He was very proud of what he thought it could do in actual combat.

Well, to make the story short, his scythe-spear got caught in the rigging of an another ship, as we fought in passing. He pulled at it, couldn't get it loose, and had to run along the deck as we passed to keep hold of the handle. Finally he let go of the spear and ran, with the crews of both vessels laughing. We couldn't help it. You should have seen the spear dangling up there in the rigging!

So I rather doubt that this salesman's contraptions are good for much.

NICIAS: I disagree; the equipment looks serviceable to me.

LACHES: What do you think, Socrates? One for and one against. You have the deciding vote.

SOCRATES: Laches, instead of just taking a vote, let's look at the more basic question which you wisely raise. Don't you think that in anything as important as the education of your friends' sons we should find out who is an expert and take his advice?

LACHES: Certainly, Socrates. That makes sense.

SOCRATES: Then what should our expert be an expert in?

NICIAS: Aren't we just considering the question about fighting in armor: whether our young men should learn it or not?

SOCRATES: Yes, Nicias. But don't we have to answer this basic question first? For example, when a man asks about putting a medicine on his eyes, what is he really interested in, medicine or eyes?

NICIAS: Eyes, of course.

SOCRATES: And when he thinks about putting a bridle on a horse or not, surely it is the horse that he is thinking of, not the bridle?

NICIAS: True.

SOCRATES: Then don't you see, Nicias, that learning to fight in armor is just like medicines and bridles, only a means to an end. What we are really thinking of when we talk about different kinds of knowledge is young men. It is the self, the soul, of the young men that this training is going to be applied to.

Now a doctor knows what is good for eyes; a home-trainer, what is good for horses. But which of us knows what is good for the soul, that is the real question!

NICIAS (laughing): I should have seen this coming, Socrates. I've been through this with you before, and it is a strenuous process. But I always leave with a clearer idea than I had at the start. Are you game,

Laches? I'm warning you about what we are about to experience at the hands of this man.

LACHES: I am not one for talk usually unless I know that the man is a doer as well as a talker. But I was with Socrates on the retreat after we lost the battle of Delium. If everyone had behaved the way Socrates did, we would have won. I'll take questions any day from a man like that.

SOCRATES: Thank you, Laches. Let me pose to you the part of this larger question which is of most concern to you in your profession of leading men in combat. What is courage, Laches?

LACHES: That's easy, Socrates. A man who has courage stays at his post and does not run away.

SOCRATES: That is a good definition of courage, as an infantryman sees it, but how about the cavalry, who are always on the move? It is a favorite maneuver among the Scythians, I believe, to run away shooting backward as they go.

LACHES: Good point, Socrates. Those horsemen are as courageous as they come.

SOCRATES: And how about courage in storms at sea, or in sickness, or in poverty, or in political life? And some people are brave in the face of pain but no good when tempted by pleasure. So I ask again . . . What is courage in general, Laches?

LACHES: You're making me think, Socrates. I would say that it seems to me, now that I really think about it, courage is a kind of endurance of the soul.

SOCRATES: Bravo, sir. Now you are giving us a comprehensive concept—perhaps too comprehensive. After all, if real courage is always a virtue, then would mere endurance that was senseless—like doing 1,000 push-ups—still be a virtue?

LACHES: I should have said *wise* endurance.

SOCRATES: But what do we mean by "wise endurance"? How about a man who endures in war and is willing to fight, having calculated wisely that others will help him, that he is fighting against fewer and weaker men than those on his side, and that he holds the stronger position. Would you say that the man who endures with this wisdom and preparation is brave? Braver than a man who has the will to stand firm on the other side?

LACHES: I have no doubt that the soldier who does not need to calculate the risk is braver than the other.

SOCRATES: Then the man who dives into a well, not knowing how to dive, is braver, though more foolish, than the trained diver?

LACHES: I must agree to be consistent with what I said before, Socrates, but I can see that there is something amiss in our reasoning.

What has Socrates accomplished with these two estimable gentlemen? He has revealed as defective a concept central to their generalship—that courage consists of advancing on the battlefield and killing adversaries. (Later in the dialogue, Socrates will show that the idea of courage of these two military men does not take into account the possibility of courage off the battlefield or the connection between courage and knowledge and wisdom.)

Socrates' demonstration of the defect in the officers' concept of courage has some important implications. A commander who believed that ordering a retreat was cowardly would be severely constrained in his options; one who had a broader definition would have more tactical choices.

Socrates points out what a difference that could make by citing those master militarists, the Spartans. "At the battle of Platea," he recalls, "the Spartans came up against the Persians, and their general chose to retreat even though some criticized this as unmanly. The Persians, thinking they were victorious, broke ranks, at which point the Spartans wheeled around fighting like cavalry and won that part of the battle."

The question of what constitutes courage arose dramatically right after the attack on the World Trade Center in New York City on September 11, 2001. Our government denounced the terrorists who caused the devastation as "cowards." But several maverick commentators, while denouncing the act of mass murder, argued that *cowardice* did not seem like the right term for a group of men who, however misguided, martyred themselves on behalf of their beliefs. Susan Sontag argued in *The New*

Yorker that the act took "courage," but added that courage did not have a moral value in a case like this.

Socrates would have relished this dialogue. He would point out that understanding what drove that terrible act of violence would help us prevent further attacks. Our words channel our thoughts. Our concepts drive our thinking. Our ideas shape our actions.

SOCRATES' SPIRIT IN OUR TIME

In our time, too, any serious inquiry must begin by making sure that we know what we are talking about. Just consider how important such clarification is to discussions of such topics as

- "Quality" in a company or nonprofit organization.

- "Poverty" in shaping and implementing welfare policies.

- "AIDS" in diagnosing and treating that illness.

But let's take a much simpler example, one with which there would seem to be little to quibble.

Lillian Rubin, a social scientist at the University of California at Berkeley, undertook a major study of friendship. Surely we've all had

Socrates' Famous "Method"

1. Choose a statement widely accepted as self-evident or unquestionable.

   Courage means standing your ground in battle and not retreating.

2. Now, treat the statement as if it were false. Look for situations in which the statement would not be true.

   When might one be courageous even while retreating?

   When might one stand one's ground, yet not be truly courageous?

3. When you find such exceptions, you know that the definition in inadequate.

   We can see now that it is possible to be courageous even while retreating.

   We can see now that it is possible to stand firm in battle, yet not be truly courageous.

4. Clearly, the original proposition must be modified to accommodate these exceptions.

   Courage in battle may involve both retreat and attack.

5. Continue this process by seeking other situations that clarify the concept. By this process of correcting inadequate concepts, you will approach more and more closely a truly adequate idea of what you are talking about.

Note: This "recipe" just covers the process exemplified by "Laches." Socrates himself used other "methods" to stir thinking, when appropriate, including major metaphors such as "The Charioteer of the Soul" (Chapter 7), allegories like "The Cave" (Chapter 4), and solitary reflection to "invite his soul" (Chapter 6). In this book you will master still other, more recently developed techniques.

enough experience with friendship in our lives to feel that we know what it is. Why don't you jot down your definition below.

Now, let's accompany this modern-day Socrates on a brief quest for a definition of *friendship*.

Just as with Socrates' interlocutors, Rubin's interviewees had no trouble coming up with a quick answer to this "simple" question. And there was notable agreement among their answers:

> Trust, honesty, respect, commitment, safety, support, generosity, loyalty, mutuality, constancy, understanding, acceptance

So far, so good. But when Rubin followed up, using Socrates' method, to test each person's definition of friendship, she made a startling discovery. Let's listen in on one of her little dialogues with a typical respondent, Mike, who has defined *friendship* as "trustworthiness and helpfulness in any situation."

Do you have a best friend?" I asked him, as I had asked everyone else.

Sure do. He's a guy I've known since high school.

How often do you see each other?

Well, in fact, we haven't seen each other since he moved east about ten years ago.

How do you stay in touch, by phone?

Yeah, well, actually, you see, we don't, not really; maybe a couple of times we've talked on the phone since he left.

What makes him a best friend, then?

It's just like I said—trust. That's what it is. I know I can absolutely trust him.

Trust him with what?

With anything I need. I could land on his doorstep in the cold of winter and the dead of night and I know he'd be right there.

Just where is this doorstep on which you'd always be welcome to land?

A moment of silence and then:

I'm not sure. You see, he moved a while back and I don't know exactly where he lives now.

How far back?

I don't remember exactly—a couple of years maybe.

Clearly, Mike's *definition* of friendship just didn't match up with the actual friendship he described, just as Socrates' friends discovered that their initial definition of justice or courage didn't apply to crucial real-life cases. Was this an oddball instance? After all, each of us can tell tales of long-distance friendships in which, after months or years of separation, we were able to "pick up right where we left off."

But Rubin, like Socrates, probed further and used some additional tools. She asked 44 of her interviewees to refer her to *all* those they had named as best friends or even close friends. She ended up with the names of 186 people of whom she contacted 132, with the purpose of discovering if the designation of "close" or "best" friend was *reciprocal*.

In almost two-thirds of the cases, the people contacted made *no* mention of the interviewee on *their* list of friends. Often they responded vaguely, acknowledging that they knew him or her but didn't think of that person as a friend. When prompted, many of them would recall the person, apologize, and explain that this was not an important relationship for them.

Only 14 percent of the people put the interviewee anywhere near the top of their list of friends.

"Such is the elusiveness of the idea of 'friend,'" Rubin concludes, "that not even the people involved can always say which is which . . . without careful questioning. It's practically impossible to know just what people mean when they call someone a friend."

This is what Socrates had discovered about justice, courage, and love. This is why he insisted that the best way to commence an inquiry into any issue or topic is to share our definitions, discuss them, and thereby clarify our awareness and our thinking.

CHALLENGES, EXPLORATIONS, AND APPLICATIONS

 1. Explore the meanings of a key idea of vital interest to you.

You can use the methods of Socrates—and Rubin—to explore a key term, concept, idea, or value that is central to your life or your work. Here are some that many people today find central in thinking about their life:

- Love
- Success
- Excellence
- Peace
- Balance
- Health
- Fulfillment

Explore what these terms really mean to you in these three ways:

- Like Socrates and Rubin, ask people for their definitions and really listen. Probe them with follow-up questions to elicit everything they have to say.

Strengthening Your Socratic Spirit

- Have you explored your understanding of the key ideas and values that shape your life, such as love, success, or health? (Exercise #1)

- Do you ask questions that stimulate thinking? (Exercise #2)

- Do you use both "open" and "closed" questions? (Exercise #3)

- Do you know the most important question you can ask about your primary relationship? (Exercise #4)

- Do you know how to create your own list of the most important questions to ask about your life? (Exercise #5)

- Do you know how to use the question "Why?" to get to the root causes of problems? (Exercise #6)

- Do you encourage questions from the people with whom you work? (Exercise #7)

- Do you know how to use questions to change people's attitudes in a positive way? (Exercise #8)

- Do you know the one question that will reveal what you most need to know about the organization in which you work? (Exercise #9)

- Do you regularly learn how to ask great questions from the expert interviewers on the media? (Exercise #10)

- Do you enhance your learning by questioning what you read, hear, or see? (Execise #11)

- Do you have a checklist of the most powerful questions you can ask as a professional? (Exercise #12)

- Once you have collected at least six *different* definitions or descriptions of each term, initiate dialogues with others—one on one or in a small group—by sharing the collection and thereby stimulating broader and deeper thinking.

- You will now understand this idea or value and what it means in your life much more deeply. Formulate for yourself your refined, thought-through definition of the term. Choose the right people to share it with.

 ## 2. Ask questions that stimulate thinking.

Socrates used great questions as the cornerstone of his "method," a powerful intellectual strategy that has been rediscovered by carriers of the torch in every generation. "Whether the setting be home, place of work, or classroom, questions initiate learning," declares Professor Roland Christensen of the Harvard Business School. "Questions can excite, disturb, discipline, or comfort, but they always stimulate inquiry."

We all began our lives as learners by asking questions. Christensen notes charmingly that even as he wrote the lines quoted above, "in the past several hours, as I sat at my desk overlooking a peaceful New Hampshire lake, two precious grandsons have asked dozens of questions. 'Why does moss grow at the bottom of the tree?' 'Who taught the fish to swim?' 'How does the airplane stay in the sky?' 'If we eat these M&M's now, will Mom be angry?'"

We've all heard such simple and powerful inquiries from the very young. Regrettably, our years in classrooms often stifle rather than nurture this innate curiosity and boldness. Many of us come to feel that our questions are impertinent or aggressive or naïve or annoying or time-wasting or irrelevant or just plain dumb.

On the contrary, asking good questions is the basis of lifelong learning. "Once you have learned how to ask questions—relevant and appropriate and substantial questions—you have learned how to learn and no one can keep you from learning whatever you want or need to know," in the ringing words of Neil Postman and Charles Weingartner in their aptly

SOCRATES MOCKS HIS OWN METHOD

A friend, Critobulus, once challenged Socrates to a contest of wits, as reported by Xenophon. Each of them was to use Socrates' interrogatory method to prove that he was the handsomest. Given Socrates' reputation for homeliness, this was a challenge indeed. Socrates used it to poke fun at his own method.

SOCRATES: Do you hold that beauty is to be found only in man, or is it also in other objects?

CRITOBULUS: Certainly, it is found in horses or oxen or any number of inanimate things, Socrates. A sword or a spear may be beautiful.

SOCRATES: How can it be that all these things are beautiful when they are entirely dissimilar?

CRITOBULUS: Hmm. The reason they are beautiful and fine is that they are well made for the functions for which we use them or naturally well-constituted to serve our needs.

SOCRATES: Let's take eyes. Why do we need eyes?

CRITOBULUS: Obviously, to see with.

SOCRATES: In that case I would contend that my eyes are finer ones than yours.

CRITOBULUS: How so?

SOCRATES: Because, while your eyes see only straight, mine, by bulging so far out, see also to the sides.

CRITOBULUS: But whose nose is finer, yours or mine?

SOCRATES: Mine, if you grant that the nose is made to smell with. For your nostrils look down toward the ground, but mine are wide open and turned outward so that I can catch scents from all around.

And so on.

Interestingly, even in this self-parody, Socrates is deftly using his famed method. By interrogating Critobulus about his definition of beauty, Socrates reveals discrepancies, contradictions, and consequences that are unacceptable. If beauty is defined by fitness and function alone, then Socrates' features are beautiful, which they are famously *not*. This dialogue illustrates Socrates' notorious use of irony. By pretending to convince Critobulus that he is beautiful, Socrates has really been doing something else entirely: demolishing his erroneous definition of beauty.

titled *Teaching as a Subversive Activity.* "Question-asking is the most important intellectual ability man has yet developed."

If you took Professor Christensen's course in Corporate Strategy at the Harvard Business School, you might be surprised to find that he does not spend most of the class time teaching. Instead, he asks questions. "In taking this view of teaching and learning, we join a conversation which has been under way in Western civilization . . . since Socrates," according to *Education for Judgment* (Harvard Business School Press), the definitive book on this approach, which he co-authored.

These are the kinds of questions you would be asked in Christensen's classroom. Choose the ones that are most applicable to your current work situation and ask them of yourself or others.

Open-ended questions: What are your reactions to the General Motors case? What aspects of this problem were of greatest interest to you? Where should we begin?

Diagnostic questions: What is your analysis of the problem? What conclusions did you draw from these data?

Information-seeking questions: What was the gross national product of France last year?

Challenge (testing) questions: Why do you believe that? What evidence supports your conclusion? What arguments might be developed to counter that point of view?

Action questions: What needs to be done to implement the government's antidrug campaign?

Questions on priority and sequence: Given the state's limited resources, what is the first step to be taken? The second? And the third?

Prediction questions: If your conclusions are correct, what might be the reaction of the Japanese auto industry?

Hypothetical questions: What would have happened to the company if a strike had not been called by the union?

Questions of extension: What are the implications of your conclusions about the causes of the Boston bottling plant strike for executives of plants in other large cities?

Questions of generalization: Based on your study of the computer and telecommunications industries, what do you consider to be the major forces that enhance technological innovation?

 3. Use both "open" and "closed" questions.

As we saw in Exercise #1, Professor Christensen begins his dialogues with open-ended questions, including the most open-ended of all, "Where should we begin?" This points to the single most useful tool in using questions to stimulate thinking: orchestrating "open" and "closed" questions.

You can control the flow and pace of any conversation, interview, or meeting by using each kind of question at the right time.

- *Open questions* invite the other person to respond freely—and sometimes surprisingly. Some basic open questions are: "Please tell me more about that." "What are your thoughts on . . . ?" "Can you fill me in about . . . ?"

- *Closed questions* elicit specific information you want from the other person: "What's the budget for this project?" "Who else needs to be on the team?"

Obviously, each of these kinds of questions has a different function. For example, experienced trial lawyers try never to ask a witness a question to which they do not already know the answer. On the other hand, a management consultant coming into a new organizational situation will typically ask open questions to "get the lay of the land"—and to let people reveal their biases.

SOCRATES, CONSULTANT

History's first management consultant's report took the form of a dialogue between Socrates and some of his closest friends. Through their conversation, they analyzed a highly dysfunctional organization and prescribed what needed to be done to restore it to health. The organization they discussed had been taking a beating by its competitor. Their report called for sweeping changes and provided a mission statement and master plan for creating a new institution.

That badly beaten organization was the city-state of Athens. The competitor was the rival city-state of Sparta. The consultant's report is Plato's Socratic dialogue, the "Republic." The new organization that was proposed in the report and that lasted five centuries was Plato's Academy, which he set up years after Socrates' death.

Frame three "open" questions and five "closed" questions to use at an upcoming business, professional, or social occasion.

4. *Ask this most important question about your primary relationship.*

I like to think that the ghost of Socrates gave this great question to one of his carriers of the torch, psychotherapist Harry Dunne, Jr. It happened during a counseling session in which Dr. Dunne was stymied in his work with a troubled couple. Suddenly, he had a breakthrough. A great question occurred to him, one that has helped with hundreds of clients and that he has described in his book *One Question That Can Save Your Marriage*:

> The question came into my head as if it had been whispered in my right ear by some ghostly presence who happened to be passing through my consulting room, and it popped out of my mouth just as effortlessly. As it did, though, I wondered if The Question wasn't too direct, too probing. Therapists are usually more circumspect than this, their questions more carefully formed and considered, so it startled me that I'd been so impetuous.

Dr. Dunne has used the question for twenty years. It has proven to be one of those powerful "open" questions that can trigger a dialogue that changes a situation or relationship completely. The question is:

"What is it like to be married to me?"

Explaining how to use this question, Dr. Dunne notes some of the qualities of the best Socratic questions:

> It's realistic—it allows couples to work on the only element in their relationship which they do have the power to change. It's simple but provocative, easy to understand, but requiring an effort to look deep inside yourself. And it can be used by one or both partners, so that either one can start working on their own to improve things.

 ## 5. Create your own list of Great Questions.

Socrates obviously gave careful thought to the questions he wanted to ask, and the results were extraordinary. One biography of him is subtitled *The Man Who Dared to Ask*. We all can benefit from following in his path by creating our own Great Questions that reflect our deepest interests, highest goals, and most troubling concerns.

This exercise was first suggested by my friend and colleague Michael Gelb in *How to Think Like Leonardo da Vinci*. It's the kind of exercise that is easy to read if you're on the run and figure you'll do it "sometime when you have the time." For that reason, I'd like to share here the experiences of Roben Torosyan, one of the nation's leading scholars on "transformative learning," who actually did it. "I was inspired by Socrates," he says. "His courage in pursuing the truth gave me the intellectual stamina to keep going in this internal dialogue." Torosyan's experience will make clear what you might expect, and his insights will reveal how rewarding this exercise could be for you.

> I had the most interesting and strange experience last night. I thought I was hallucinating. It all started when I decided I

HOW IT FELT TO BE "SOCRATIZED"

By and large, Socrates' friends testified to the life-enhancing impact of their conversations with him. Their view was expressed by Phaedo as Socrates breathed his last: "He was the wisest, and most just, and the best of all men whom I have ever known." But Socrates' friends also acknowledged that his questioning could get on your nerves. One of them put it this way:

> Anyone who enters into conversation with Socrates is liable to be drawn into an argument; and whatever subject he may start, he will be continually carried round and round by him, until at last he finds that he has to give an account both of his present and past life. And when he is once entangled, Socrates will not let him go until he has completely and thoroughly sifted him.

If you find that Socrates' confrontational approach sometimes seems arrogant and overbearing, you are in good company. Through the ages, there have been some readers of the *Dialogues* who have admired his commitment and wit, while at the same time feeling the pain of the "gadfly's stings." One such critic, I. F. Stone, remarks in his spirited *The Trial of Socrates*:

> There is a touch of cruelty at the expense of his interlocutors. The most humiliating—and infuriating—part of the Socratic mode of interrogation was that *their* ignorance was

wanted to try the "Hundred Questions" exercise. The instructions, which turned out to be very important, read as follows:

> In your notebook, make a list of a hundred questions that are important to you. Your list can include *any kind of question* as long as it's something you deem significant: anything from "How can I save money?" or "How can I have more fun?" to "What is the meaning and purpose of my existence?" and "How can I best serve the Creator?"

shown to be real while they felt that *his* self-proclaimed ignorance was ostentatious and pretended. Behind his "irony," his veil of mock modesty, Socrates was laughing at them.

Fair enough—Socrates was, after all, so provocative to his fellow citizens that they eventually voted for the death penalty.

It should come as no surprise then that, in the wrong hands, the Socratic method can be abused, as exemplified by the tyrannical law professor in the film *The Paper Chase* who drives students to despair with his relentless and destructive questioning.

I recall meeting a real-life victim of such a professor, a personable but ill-educated young lawyer who, hearing that I was interested in the Socratic method but obviously never having heard of the historical Socrates, said: "Oh, yes, they used that method in my law school."

"Oh, what was it like?" I asked.

"Well, the teacher picked on one student each class period, made him stand up, and then asked him questions until he broke down."

But these are truly abuses, and Socrates was guilty of them himself only on rare occasions. Usually, his questioning was driven by a passion for understanding and a dedication to impelling his fellow citizens to think things through. He sought no profit in this work, nor even renown. He did it for his soul's sake and for the sake of the souls of his countrymen. As he correctly warned in his "Apology": "If you smite this 'gadfly' with your hand, you will go on sleeping til the end of your days."

The challenge for us, even if we find his approach occasionally arrogant, is to benefit from the powerful positive strategies that he uses to accomplish his goals.

Do the entire list in one sitting. Write quickly; don't worry about spelling, grammar, or repeating the same question in different words (recurring questions will alert you to emerging themes).

Why a hundred questions? The first twenty or so will be "off the top of your head." In the next thirty or forty, themes often begin to emerge. And in the latter part of the second half of the list, you are likely to discover unexpected but profound material.

I was especially intrigued to see if I'd arrive at anything "unexpected" or "profound" at the end, as I felt sure I already knew my questions (after all, I think about this stuff daily!).

Initially, I had questions like "How can I find what's 'right' for me?" and "How can I not be distracted as easily?" Many questions revolved around wanting to achieve "more balance and harmony." Another theme was how to "get beyond my own narcissism."

After filling a page with 20 questions, I was already a little tired. It was late (about 11:20 P.M. when I began), and I had to get up at 7:10 A.M. for yoga. I felt "I don't HAVE to do it in one sitting. Why should I?" But I liked the idea of following the directions as best I could, even if only to see what would happen if I did exactly what was intended—like a mini-experiment. So, I made a leap of faith, assumed the author probably may have really intended 100 questions for some reason, and kept going, hoping maybe I'd find out something in the end.

By question #47, I had a deeper than usual flash: "How can I probe deep within me, to live 'like a genius,' utterly unconcerned with others' judgments, only interested in the problem at hand?" Some nagging themes also repeated regularly, such as, "How can I respect myself enough to protect my time, to master it, so I'm less flung about and tugged to and fro?"

It got hard again after question #60, after I had filled four pages. I was exhausted and felt like I couldn't possibly go on. Again I reread the instructions, and looked for the part about what happens with the latter half of the 100. I decided that I knew I could stop if I wanted to, but that instead I WOULD stick it through—because, as I told myself, I really didn't know WHAT would happen if I did it all. Part of me didn't believe anything really profound or unexpected would come out of it.

Sure enough, from question 88 to 89 there was a sudden and very marked shift. I went from "What else matters besides the practical in life?" to "Where is the light, the source of power and divinity—the source and inspiration for all?" At the time I was writing this, I was also aware of a change in my bodily condition, as if I was tripping on a psychedelic drug or getting into some other state of mind. As I felt the pen press into the paper in my journal, it actually felt for a moment as if something or someone or some energy was driving the writing for me, moving my pen.

Looking back on that moment now, I think I may have been truly hallucinating—given my achy back and neck, and that I was so sleepy but was staying up nonetheless. I said to myself then in a blur, "This isn't me, right now—something's passing through me." I believe I may have had some form of an altered state of consciousness experience.

On reflection, it is interesting how the quality and kind of questions changed: from egocentric preoccupations, and other concerns about what I or we can do, to eventually a mystical transcendental state of mind entirely. Interestingly, I was aware of and could have written some so-called "profound" questions earlier, but they felt contrived at that point, without my having gone through the process. Yet later, I was immersed for a time in another world. The experience resembled what actors call "being IN it"—getting INTO a role so thoroughly that one is living it, and no longer outside it.

To me, this experience tells us what other role models have told me for years. When I once fancied a career in architecture, I met the great architect Frank O. Gehry and asked him what advice he'd give a budding student; he said with excitement and conviction, "Follow your obsessions! Find your obsessions and follow 'em!" The poet Rainer Maria Rilke too said to let your questions guide you through life. To me, such commitment resembles "Acting like a genius." Watch a "genius," or a child for that matter: they will get totally INTO it—whatever "it" is—center themselves around the problem itself, not giving a care about anyone or anything else for a time.

Ironically, after the fact, I felt almost scared the next morning to LET myself write this very article. To actually DO now the kind of committed work I was the night before only envisioning was a whole other challenge. So I said to myself,

"I'll just jot down messy notes of my thoughts and later put it together." But then I couldn't stop writing, and this piece flowed forth.

Fortunately, my job involves writing on and teaching these very kinds of life-transforming ideas. I run workshops, conferences and online ventures to promote clear and creative thinking in all aspects of life—personal, work, civic or otherwise.

For me, this all shows how incredibly important it is to let ourselves really get into any project, almost lose our self-consciousness and abashedness to get immersed in whatever we're doing, whatever we're exploring, to LET ourselves have each experience—beyond clichés, and breaking through detached coolness or mindlessness—as fully as possible. THAT seems to be "living," no?

 6. Ask "Why?" until you get to the truth.

Socrates never seemed to be satisfied with the first answer to one of his great questions. Nor with the second, third, or fourth. Once he had become involved in the search for an adequate answer to an important question, he simply did not give up.

As managers and professionals, we can benefit from being this persistent in seeking the "root causes" of organizational problems. One of the best ways to do this is to simply ask "Why?" until you get a satisfactory answer. This is the organizational counterpart of Exercise 3 in the previous chapter.

    a. Pick the symptom or problem you wish to explore and ask "Why is this taking place?"

    b. Repeat the process for each answer you get, asking "Why?" about each one.

    c. Continue asking "Why?" about each answer you get. The answers will soon begin to converge, as numerous separate symptoms are traced back to two or three basic sources.

Avoid fixating on blaming individuals or specific events. Probe for systemic causes—the ones that *truly* answer the question "Why?" When answers do focus on individuals, ask: "OK, but is that the only reason?" I used this technique with a client in New York's Silicon Alley—Manhattan's counterpart to Silicon Valley.

I have no expertise in computer technology, yet the partners in this dot-com found it profitable to have me ruffle their feathers every week or so. What I did for them was inspired by what Socrates did for the two generals.

That Monday morning, as I arrived for my regular visit, the elevator doors opened on a surprising tableau in the firm's reception area. One of the partners was standing in the middle of the reception room, looking as if he were undergoing a colonoscopy-on-the-run. Behind him, other executives were racing around, like extras in a Marx Brothers farce.

"Phil, what's wrong?" I asked.

"COMPLETE CLIENT MELTDOWN!" he muttered through clenched teeth.

"Is there anything I can do—except get out of the way?"

"No. We know what the problem is. See you after the holidays." (It was just before the Memorial Day weekend.)

I didn't even step out of the elevator. I just pressed "Ground," went downstairs, and walked back to my office.

The next morning, when the smoke had cleared, I learned what had happened. A crucial piece of the firm's proprietary software, on which its entire future hinged, had blown up in the face of a major client. But when I arrived at their offices to begin my inquiry into this debacle, I was immediately informed that the problem had been solved. My client explained: "It was all George's fault." Like Socrates' two generals, my client knew what he thought—and his view had spread throughout the company like a virus. Everyone agreed: "*It was all George's fault.*"

My job was to ask questions that challenged this assumption to try to get to the root causes of the problem. It took most of the day, as I trudged from one person's office to another. Here are excerpts:

Q: Why did the software blow up?

A: Because George didn't tell the client about X.

Q: Why didn't George tell the client about X?

A: Well, because . . . he didn't know about X.

Q: Why didn't he know about X?

A: Because Brian, the one in charge of that programming team, didn't ever tell George about X.

Q: Why didn't Brian tell George about X?

A: Er . . . I guess that would be because . . . Brian decided eight months ago that "George does not have the requisite IQ to be working here, and stopped talking to him."

I wish I could say that this solved the problem, but it didn't. We still had lots of work to do to get managers to share mission-critical information. (Socrates levels with us about this—hardly any of his dialogues come to a final conclusion.) But a start had been made. And, because they recognized the need to communicate better, during the next month two other meltdowns-in-the-making were averted because managers talked to one another.

Many top companies today see question-asking as basic to their success. For example, a series of "Why" questions was used to reveal the causes of a 1992 catastrophe at Sears, Roebuck. The company had lost 15 percent of its auto repair business nationally, and 20 percent in California, for a total estimated cost of $8 million. When the series of "Why" questions was raised ("Why have consumer complaints risen by 50 percent?" "Why are Sears repairmen overcharging customers?" etc.), the causes of the debacle became apparent.

 ### 7. Lead by asking questions and encourage questions from those with whom you work.

Socrates' greatest achievement was inspiring his friends and colleagues to develop their own question-asking capacity. Here, too, we can follow in his footsteps.

As a professional in your field, you can help build a "question-friendly culture" in your organization. "The Socratic method is an extremely ef-

SOCRATES TEACHES WITH QUESTIONS

In Plato's dialogue "Meno," Socrates models his way of teaching through raising questions rather than imparting information. We get our word *education* from his practice: Its Greek roots, *edu* and *care,* mean "drawing out."

He teaches a slave boy how to determine the sides of a square of a given area. "This knowledge will not come from teaching but from questioning," he declares.

Socrates starts by drawing a square in the sand with his staff; it is two feet long on each side, so its area is four square feet. Then, he asks how long the sides would have to be for its area to become eight square feet.

At first the slave guesses that the sides would have to be twice as long, that is, four feet. But Socrates draws another diagram that shows him that this must be wrong, since the area of that square is sixteen square feet. The slave, like so many of Socrates interlocutors, has discovered that his first opinion is not defensible, once Socrates starts raising questions!

"We have helped this lad toward finding the right answer," Socrates notes, "because now not only is he ignorant of it, but he will be quite glad to look for it." Socrates gradually leads the boy to figure out the solution for himself: A square with twice the area of the original one needs to have sides that are the length of a diagonal drawn across the original square—a version of the famed Pythagorean theorem.

fective technique for leaders," says top corporate consultant Michael Gelb. He explains:

> Effective leaders are skilled at asking carefully worded questions, guiding people to greater understanding of issues and problems until appropriate solutions become obvious. By guiding people to think things through for themselves, the (Socratic) leader encourages shared pride and ownership of the solutions generated.

Ed Bassett, a senior vice president at DuPont, testifies to these principles in his work as an executive:

> The secret of leading in a rapidly changing environment is to be committed to living the examined life oneself. Leaders

must learn to be flexible and creative in tactics, and adaptable to shifts in culture and style, while holding to guiding principles of vision and ethics as though they were Platonic ideals.

Here are five rules for turning your team into a question-friendly one. You may think that your colleagues already understand some of these, but you're probably wrong! It never hurts to reaffirm them regularly, to make sure everyone has gotten the message.

- Lead by asking questions that focus people on what matters and get them thinking about solutions.

- Tell your employees and coworkers that questions are welcome.

- Always respect a question, even if it seems "stupid" or has been covered before.

- Give full attention to the person who asks a question, if at all possible.

- Practice "active listening" by repeating back what you have heard. After doing that, feel free to ask your own questions to clarify the context and issues involved. ("WHY do you need an extension of the deadline?" "Are there any steps we can take to get the project back on track?")

 8. Change attitudes with positive questions.

Some carriers of the torch in our time have used Socrates' question-asking approach very differently from the way he did. They have discovered that the right questions enable you to channel thinking in a more positive direction. You can sometimes change people's attitudes by asking rather than by telling.

One of the best practitioners of this approach is Tom Heck, one of the nation's foremost "personal coaches." Here are some specific instances where Tom used the power of positive questions to focus clients and coworkers on becoming part of the solution rather than the problem. Each of them has clear applications in any business situation where you need to work with other people.

Questions Direct Our Focus.

One evening, as parents were picking up their children from our after-school care program, a mother demanded to "speak to someone in charge." This mother was upset because her young daughter's jacket had been ripped on the Ping-Pong table.

The first question I asked was "What can I do to make things right?" The woman paused. One simple question had redirected her focus from looking at the problem to looking for a solution. Within moments we had solved the problem, and the mother left happy that her daughter was in our program. Help yourself and your members by asking questions that focus on solutions.

Questions Change the Way We Feel.

Last week I was on my way to teach a snorkeling class for our Earth Service Corps program when one of the members stopped me to complain about all of the mess caused by the almost-completed renovations to our YMCA. As he continued with his complaining, his mood grew worse. I knew it was time for a good question.

"What are you excited about?" I asked.

"Excited? Nothing," he replied.

"Well then, what could you be excited about if you wanted to be?"

This was the key to the door. Suddenly he looked around and began to see things differently. He was, as it turned out, excited about the new weight room. He was excited about the new cardiovascular workout circuit that was almost complete.

It was a question that refocused this member's mind and thus how he felt. You and I can change the way we feel in an instant, just by changing our focus.

Questions Change Our Resources.

In 1993 I had been working for the YMCA for two years, and I was ready to begin the process of getting my senior director certification program. When I proposed this to my supervisors, their response was "There isn't enough money in the budget this year."

At first I began to ask questions like "Why is there never enough money to spend on training?" and "Will I ever get my senior director certification?" But then I caught myself. I knew these types of questions would only bring defeat. I decided to ask questions that would serve me. I replaced the old questions with "Who can help me raise the money I need?" and "Who can I call to help me?"

With these new questions, I began to get new answers. The result: In one day I found the people who helped me raise the $700 registration fee. If I had gotten stuck on disempowering questions, I would never have found the money for the training program. The interesting aspect is that the money I used to attend the program had been available the whole time. It was there for the asking. My questions allowed me to access the resources. I believe that as long as I continue to ask any question, I will receive an answer. Sometimes it's like playing *Jeopardy!*: The answer you want may already be there; all you have to do is come up with the right question.

Tom has developed a five-step process for asking problem-solving questions that, more often than not, lead to solutions:

- Be specific.

- Ask someone who has the ability to help.

- Offer something to the other person first.

- Ask with congruent belief.

- Ask and ask again.

Be specific. Instead of asking "How will I ever find some volunteers?" ask "Where can I find ten volunteers right now who have a great attitude and have the desire and ability to make a difference in the lives of kids?" Clarifying your questions will increase the likelihood of receiving answers that are useful.

Ask someone who has the ability to help. I recently built several indoor high ropes course initiatives in our two gyms. The initiatives required the attachment of safety cables to the gym rafters. At first I asked the facility manager if the rafters could handle the extra stress, but he was unable to answer my question. Eventually I tracked down the architect, who located the original blueprints, and he gave me an answer. Have you been looking for answers from sources that are unable to help?

Offer something to the other person first. At the beginning of last school year I had approached one of the county elementary schools to see if school officials there would like to participate in our in-school team-building program for fifth-graders. After discussing the benefits of the program, the principal decided to decline the offer.

This year, when I approached the principal, I offered him one free program and requested that he allow us to work with the class that was having the greatest difficulty getting along, He took us up on the offer, and when he witnessed the results we achieved with the first class, he immediately signed up his other five fifth-grade classes.

To achieve this result, I asked myself, "How can I deliver this high-quality program to this school?" By approaching the question from the standpoint of offering something to the other person first, I was able to find an answer to my question.

Ask with congruent belief. When some people ask a question, you can tell that they don't really expect a very good answer. Their body language tells you what type of answer they are expecting. Imagine your membership director asking the following question in a hesitant voice while shaking his or her head from left to right: "You wouldn't want to be a member of this YMCA, would you?" This question would not work!

When you ask a question, it is important to be congruent in your tone of voice and your body language. Believe in your desired quality outcome when you ask a question.

Ask and ask again. Three years ago, the main computer in our branch suddenly died one Monday afternoon. We needed a new computer fast, but we did not have the money to purchase one. As I left work that day, I turned to the office manager and said, "I will find a free computer within the week!" I did not know how I was going to do this, but I decided to follow this five-step process with an emphasis on the fifth step. I asked everyone (and I mean everyone) if he or she had or knew of a computer that could be donated to the Y. Finally, on Thursday night, I happened to see a friend who is a doctor. I mentioned our need for a computer, and he said, "I've got one I don't need any more and you're welcome to it. In fact, I have an extra printer, too, if you would like to take that." Ask until you find a solution. Do not give up.

Tom Heck can be reached at his website: www.tomheck.com.

 9. What is the one best question to ask about your organization?

The ghost of Socrates that visited Dr. Harry Dunne (Exercise 4, above) may have also dropped in on Professor Michael LeBoeuf, a management consultant who came up with another of those Great Questions.

"The next time you have trouble understanding why people behave the way they do," says LeBoeuf, "just ask [this] question and things will come quickly into focus."

What is really rewarded in this organization?

Please formulate in your own mind your answer to this question about the organization you now work for, even if it's your own! Now, to get a feel for the possible usefulness of this approach in your organization, just consider how things might be different if what got rewarded were

- Solid solutions instead of quick fixes

- Risk taking instead of risk avoidance

- Smart work instead of busywork

- Quietly effective work instead of squeaking joints

- Quality work instead of fast work

- Working together instead of working against

Can you formulate your own "best question" to ask about your work situation?

Leaders and top performers in different industries and professions as diverse as salesmanship and academic counseling have developed the question-asking approach in more detail for their fields. For example, Kevin Daley, CEO of Communispond, the largest training company in personal communications skills, has developed "Socratic Selling." "Its roots lie in Socrates' method of talking less and listening more," Daley explains. "By their own admission, most salespeople talk too much. Too few 'Socratically' help customers draw the logical conclusion. I count on genuine dialoguing to join strengths to work together towards the common goal of meeting the customer's real needs."

In higher education, Socratic feedback has been highly successful in helping black students at the University of Michigan to succeed in their studies by building self-confidence. Rather than getting the programmed feedback that is the norm in academia, these students were involved in ongoing dialogues that helped them stay focused on doing their best work. They were spared the discouragement of early "failures" until they had built up real mentor relationships with their professors. The result was that these students did far better in their freshman year than did other black students.

 ### 10. *Learn from television's carriers of the flame.*

If Socrates were alive today, he would love to host a talk show on PBS. He'd relish bringing in the most accomplished, brilliant, and informed minds from anywhere in the world. He'd enjoy the play of ideas, the spontaneous interchange, and the blend of wit and profundity. And he'd delight in the challenge of asking the right questions that get to the heart of a problem or issue—or person!

So it's no wonder that you can get some fine lessons in question-asking by watching our contemporary masters at work: Charlie Rose, Ted Koppel, and National Public Radio's incisive Terry Gross (no relation). As you enjoy them, why not add their strategies to your repertoire.

In addition to prime-time network fare, there are other programs that feature a dialogue format. These are genuine conversations focusing on one topic in depth for at least thirty minutes, guided but not dominated by a real Socratic figure. Such programs on the air as of this writing are:

The Open Mind, with host Richard Heffner

Think Tank, with host Ben Wattenberg

Like It Is, with host Gil Noble

Uncommon Knowledge, from Stanford's Hoover Institution

Booknotes, with host Brian Lamb

 11. Question what you read, see, and hear.

By asking questions, you will get much more from your reading (starting with this book) and from what you see or hear in the media. When reading or studying, for example, don't just highlight important points you want to remember or review later. Query the text in the margin or on a separate sheet of paper. Highlighting puts you in the role of passively "absorbing" someone else's ideas. Framing your own questions, on the other hand, involves you in a dialogue with the author.

Set yourself the goal of coming up with one good question for each section of the text. You will be amazed at how much more your mind is engaged.

 *12. My own list of the most powerful questions
    a professional can ask*

Here are the thirteen questions that over fifteen years I have found to be the most effective for business and professional people. Use them as "starters," and you will soon be adding others more specific to your field and your personal style:

- What is our challenge here?

- Why is it worth tackling?

- How do we feel about it?

- Do we have the facts we need?

- Are we asking the right questions?

- What results are we really seeking?

- What's the worst that can happen?

- Why are we having this problem?

- Can you explain that further?

- What if we do nothing?

- Have we explored creative approaches?

- What do you propose?

- What can I do to help?

3

THINK FOR YOURSELF

> Do not be convinced by me, Agathon.
> Be convinced by the truth.
>
> SOCRATES, IN PLATO'S "SYMPOSIUM"

Wʜᴀᴛ ᴡᴏᴜʟᴅ ʏᴏᴜ ᴅᴏ if you received a message from on high about what you should do with your life? Socrates found himself in that position. The way he handled it displayed one of his basic principles: Think for yourself.

To fifth-century Greeks, the place to go for advice on how to live your life was the Oracle at Delphi, as Euthydemus did in Chapter 1. This temple, perched on a peak overlooking the Mediterranean, is impressive even today. In the fifth century, it must have been an extraordinary experience to trek up to the sacred precincts, enter the shadowy portico, make your offering to the gods, immerse yourself in the hypnotic music and odor of the incense, and receive the advice intoned by one of the priestesses.

It was the ultimate source of wisdom for most Athenians. But not to Socrates. He insisted, as we have seen, that even when we receive opinions from the most authoritative sources, we owe it to ourselves to determine that the source is, indeed, entirely reliable. We must also ask whether the advice is relevant to *us,* given our character, situation, and goals.

Here's how Socrates judged for himself on an occasion that would determine the course of the rest of his life. The incident is reported in the "Apology," the dialogue by Plato in which Socrates defends his life and work to the jury that will decide his fate.

Among Socrates' earliest companions was Chaerephon, a skinny, pale, awkward fellow who followed him around everywhere. Chaerephon believed that Socrates was the wisest man in Athens, and possibly in all the world. To prove it, Chaerephon made a journey to Delphi to consult the Oracle.

"Is there any man wiser than Socrates?" Chaerephon asked.

And the priestess replied, "There is no man wiser than Socrates."

Socrates was baffled and greatly disturbed when Chaerephon returned to Athens with his tidings. Chaerephon had taken the oracle's answer at its face value. Obviously, he argued, Socrates was the wisest man in the world!

Socrates himself was not so sure. "What can the god mean by this riddle?" he asked. "I know very well that I am not wise, even in the smallest degree. Then what can he mean by saying that I am the wisest of men?"

It could not be that the oracle had lied, because the oracle spoke with the voice of Apollo, and gods did not lie. For a long while, Socrates was at a loss to understand the meaning of the oracle. Then he thought of a way to fathom the mystery. He decided to look for a man who was obviously wiser than he was. When he had found him, he would go to Delphi and point out the oracle's mistake, saying, "You said that I was the wisest of men, but this man is wiser than I am."

Socrates went first to an Athenian politician who was famous for his wisdom. He questioned him on many subjects. "When I conversed with him," Socrates said later, "I came to see that, though a great many persons, and most of all he himself, thought that he was wise, yet he was not wise." Socrates tried to prove to the politician that he was not really wise but only imagined himself so. Naturally, the man quickly became angry, since Socrates was publicly exposing him as a fool.

"I am wiser than this man," Socrates thought as he took his leave. "Neither of us knows anything that is really worthwhile, but he knows nothing and thinks that he knows; I neither know nor think that I know. At any rate, I seem to be a little wiser than he is on this point: I do not think that I know what I do not know."

He went on to another man, and another, to those who were most highly esteemed for their wisdom. The same thing happened each time. The so-called wise man was always sure of his wisdom at the beginning of the conversation. But as Socrates went on asking questions, the "wise" one became confused and started to contradict himself. Then he grew angry and stalked away from the man who had shown him up.

After he had talked to a great many of Athens' political leaders, Socrates began to see a disturbing pattern: "I found that the men whose reputations for wisdom stood highest were nearly the most lacking in it, while others who were looked down on as common people were much more intelligent."

Socrates now began to see what the oracle had meant. "No man is wiser than Socrates," the oracle had declared. The man who knew he knew nothing was the wisest of all, because he was not deluding himself.

Then, if none of us is wise, what could a man do? He could go on asking, and trying to learn.

We must, like Socrates, judge for ourselves (even when we are given advice by the highest authority). We must do our own thinking to confirm or refute what we have been told. Interestingly, the Oracle at Delphi itself proclaimed this principle. Though considered the ultimate in wisdom and prognostication, the priests of the Temple at Delphi warned that each supplicant had to make his or her own judgment about what the oracle told them. Failure to do so could be disastrous.

The most famous example was when Croesus, king of Lydia, asked the oracle for advice on whether or not to go to war with Persia. He was told that "If you fight the Persians you will bring down a mighty empire." He went to war, but the empire he destroyed was his own.

But Socrates goes even further than merely trying to construe the correct *interpretation* of the oracle. He undertakes to *judge it for himself* through logical examination and discussion with others. We, too, must think deeply, on occasion, in order to interpret our world correctly and act wisely. Socrates' *process* can help us to do this. Specifically, let's list the seven steps that we will be exploring in the rest of this chapter:

1. Socrates only begins this process because *he thinks of himself as a thinker.* He has the deepest trust in his capacity to judge for himself.

2. He *acknowledges his intuition.* The oracle's declaration does not sit right with him, and he accepts his uneasiness as a challenge to be addressed by using his mind.

3. Socrates *takes time to think.* He is willing to be patient, even dogged, in obtaining the information and insights he needs.

4. Socrates *adopts a strategy,* in this case an empirical one, of searching for evidence for and against the oracle's statement. He does not just stew on the challenge; he attacks it systematically.

5. Socrates *reaches out to involve others in his thinking process.*

6. Socrates *comes to a surprising but well-considered conclusion.* It is a "eureka" moment—a *creative insight* that sheds new light on the oracle's statement and makes it understandable and compelling. (We now call these "paradigm shifts.")

7. Socrates *acts on his conclusion.* He uses his thinking to propel his life in a productive direction.

SOCRATES' SPIRIT IN OUR TIME

Socrates' determination to think for himself has no nobler exemplification in our time than Richard Feynman's investigation of the Challenger space shuttle disaster. Feynman discovered that he could do his duty as an American only by bucking the Establishment and making his own independent judgment. He was a heroic carrier of the flame.

The Challenger space shuttle exploded shortly after its launch in January 1986, taking the lives of several astronauts, including the beloved schoolteacher-turned-astronaut Christa McAuliffe. Feynman, a Nobel laureate in physics and a legendary teacher at the California Institute of Technology, was appointed to the Rogers Commission by the president to investigate the disaster and ascertain its cause.

Feynman was already widely known as a gadfly. He had called his Nobel Prize "a pain in the neck," because he hated any kind of ceremony and pomposity, and felt that the process of thinking together with colleagues and students was what was important in science, not awards and prizes. His bestselling book was titled *Surely You're Joking, Mr. Feynman.*

As the Rogers Commission pursued its work, Feynman came to the conviction that he and the other members of the commission were being manipulated toward preconceived conclusions and away from a real inquiry into the causes of the accident. There was great pressure to expedite the proceedings, to trust the "experts," and to "go along" with what "everyone knows." But Feynman had doubts and felt the same patriotic duty as Socrates: to find the truth of a matter that meant so much to his countrymen.

So Feynman began his own personal inquiry. Significantly, he found himself acting just as Socrates did in testing the Delphic Oracle's dictum. The result was a "eureka" experience for other commission members—and for the entire nation.

This Socratic approach was evident in a key incident at the headquarters of the supplier of some of the key components of the shuttle. When Feynman arrived for a briefing, he was ushered into an ornate conference room and presented with three leather-bound, gold-stamped books titled "Briefing for Dr. Feynman." Then, several top executives began to hurry him through their presentation.

After listening for a while, Feynman said, sounding much like Socrates,

"Gentleman, if you don't mind, I'd like to slow down a bit. I have a few questions." He opened the first of the volumes to page one, read the first paragraph, and asked a penetrating question. In response to the answer, Feynman framed another two questions, probing beneath the surface to get at the logic and the facts that he needed.

After an hour of this dialogue, Feynman had only gotten to the middle of page three. But he was beginning to expose the real causes of the accident, which was just what his hosts wanted to avoid. "Dr. Feynman," said one of the company executives, "at this rate this process will take a lot of your valuable time. Wouldn't you like to hear the rest of our presentation and be able to get back to your important work at the university?"

Feynman replied quietly but firmly, "No, gentleman, I would not. There is nothing that could possibly be more important to me than to do my duty for my country in finding the real causes of this tragedy. I will take as long as is required to do that. I trust you feel the same way. Let us proceed."

Feynman's independent investigation did not please the chairman and other members of the Rogers Commission, and he came under powerful pressure to desist. But, like Socrates pursuing his mission to question, reason, and probe, he was indefatigable.

The culmination of Feynman's work came at a dramatic public meeting of the commission. Feynman presented his theory that the disaster's physical cause was that the shuttle had been launched in severely cold weather and that the temperature caused the failure of key components. His ideas were derided until he dramatically dunked a piece of the rocket booster's O-ring material into a glass of ice water and revealed to everyone that the material lost its needed resiliency.

Let's look more closely at how Feynman's work in this situation highlights the Socratic strengths that we must all learn to use.

First, Feynman had confidence in his capacity to judge for himself— he trusted himself as a thinker. Despite being surrounded by experts on matters in which he had little expertise, he believed that he could rely on his intelligence and intuition to conduct his own inquiry.

Second, he took the time to think things through, refusing to be hurried by the pace of others, by social pressure, or by his own impatience.

Third, Feynman had developed a repertoire of thinking strategies and tools appropriate to his field and to thinking in general.

Fourth, Feynman called upon others to provide him with crucial input. He consulted with colleagues and friends who were knowledgeable about every aspect of the relevant science and technology.

Fifth, Feynman approached his task creatively, opening himself to insights from unlikely places.

Finally, Feynman devised a way to make his thinking clear and convincing to others. Rather than relying on his own authority and expertise, he designed a demonstration that communicated his unique perceptions to others.

We will explore these core competencies in the remainder of this chapter.

CHALLENGES, EXPLORATIONS, AND APPLICATIONS

 1. Think of yourself as a thinker.

As we have seen, Socrates begin his inquiry of the oracle's pronouncement by trusting in himself as a thinker. He is puzzled and challenged, but he knows that he must use his own intelligence to resolve the situation.

In this exercise you will write two one-paragraph descriptions of yourself as a thinker: the first reflecting honestly how you typically think, the second describing the ideal toward which you would like to move.

(a) Currently, I would describe myself as a thinker this way.

As to my *confidence* in myself as a thinker, I . . .

_____

_____

_____

_____

Strengthening Your Socratic Spirit

- Do you think of yourself as a thinker and relish using your mind? (Exercise #1)

- Are you truly open-minded? (Exercise #2)

- Do you regularly challenge your mind to go beyond facts to analysis, synthesis, and judgment? (Exercise #3)

- Do you take the time to think for yourself by acknowledging that a problem or question requires extended thought and giving yourself the needed time? (Exercise #4)

- Do you think fluently not only with words but also with numbers and time frames? (Exercise #5)

- Do you have a handy way to spark yourself and others to generate new, positive ideas on any situation or issue? (Exercise #6)

- Do you know how to refine your thinking to take account of constant change? (Exercise #7),

- Do you have a "mental toolbox" of ways to orchestrate your thinking? (Exercise #8)

- Are you an independent scholar—a self-directed and productive investigator and thinker in the areas that matter most to you? (Exercise #9)

As to *control* of my thinking process, I . . .

_____

_____

_____

_____

(Continued)

As to my *enjoyment* of the process of thinking, and the *value* I place on it, I . . .

———————————————————————

———————————————————————

———————————————————————

———————————————————————

As to having *tools and strategies* for thinking that work well for me, I . . .

———————————————————————

———————————————————————

———————————————————————

———————————————————————

As to *using* my thinking to guide my decisions, I . . .

———————————————————————

———————————————————————

———————————————————————

———————————————————————

(b) As a thinker, I would like to move in the following directions.

As to my *confidence* in myself as a thinker, I would like to . . .

———————————————————————

———————————————————————

———————————————————————

———————————————————————

As to *control* of my thinking process, I would like to . . .

_____

_____

_____

_____

As to my *enjoyment* of the process of thinking and the *value* I place on it, I would like to . . .

_____

_____

_____

_____

As to having *tools and strategies* for thinking that work well for me, I would like to . . .

_____

_____

_____

_____

As to *using* my thinking to guide my decisions, I would like to . . .

_____

_____

_____

_____

2. Cultivate an open mind.

Socrates' fellow-Athenians prided themselves on having open minds. As Pericles declared in his paean to the citizenry, "Each Athenian, in his own person seems to have the power of adapting himself to the most varied forms of action with the utmost versatility and grace." Socrates tested that vaunted openness and frequently found it lacking. When he challenged his fellow citizens to justify their fundamental beliefs, they usually stuck by their convictions even when it was apparent that they had no solid foundation in logic, knowledge, or experience.

We, too, pride ourselves on being "open minded." But are we really? Do we truly expose ourselves to ideas that challenge our basic assumptions, our most cherished values? Socrates did not find that to be the case, and neither have I.

Most people, whether their sympathies are "liberal" or "conservative," do not really listen when they are confronted by opinions that directly challenge their deepest convictions. On the rare occasions when we do engage in "debate" about such issues, most of us seek solely to win over our opponents rather than to learn something. Even when a person is bested in a discussion, he will often continue to insist on his point of view rather than try to learn something from the power of the other person's reasoning.

Our culture encourages such a posture. We all have been brought up and educated with the "adversarial" model for resolving disputes. This model, based on our legal system, assumes that the truth will emerge through the most vigorous *combat* between advocates of opposing positions. If each of us fights for our own opinion as ruthlessly as possible, then the one left standing when the smoke clears must be right.

Regrettably, this model obscures the truth as often as it helps us discover it. The adversarial model favors the bigger, stronger, louder champion, regardless of his or her views. Even worse, it distracts us from looking for creative ways to reconcile conflicts by finding new perspectives that accommodate differences or mediate opposing positions.

    a. Think of the last time you engaged in a knock-down-drag-out argument over a matter of principle. Was the experience really rewarding and gratifying? If so, in what ways? If not, can you think of any ways the occasion could have had a better outcome?

b. Think of a friend or colleague who has a view on an important issue, problem, or situation that is diametrically opposite yours. Consider how you might approach him or her for a discussion in which your goal is to learn something that might induce you to modify your position in ways that are acceptable to you.

The next time you find yourself in a situation where someone confronts you with an opinion with which you violently disagree, resolve that you will respond, if appropriate, by saying something like:

> I'm really interested in your opinion on that. Could you fill me in on why you hold it? What are the facts or the logic that you find compelling? It's an opinion I don't share, so I'd really like to learn more about why you hold it, to consider modifying my position.

 ### 3. Challenge your mind to make significant judgments.

To Socrates, the capacity to judge for ourselves was the expression of our human dignity. No oracle, no law, no assumed belief, no unanimously held opinion was exempt from our examination of its validity.

Many contemporary psychologists agree. They see our capacity to judge for ourselves as the apex of our mental functioning. Notable among them is Professor Benjamin Bloom of the University of Chicago, who created the most widely used hierarchy of thinking processes.

1. *Remember.* Recall bits of information, terminology, techniques, usage, etc.

2. *Understand.* Comprehend what you read or hear, so that you can summarize or explain it.

3. *Use.* Apply what you've learned in concrete situations.

SOCRATES SAVES FORTY-NINE DRACHMAS BY THINKING FOR HIMSELF

In Plato's dialogue "Cratylus," Socrates is approached for advice by two young friends. His response is a witty appeal for self-reliance in intellectual matters:

> If I had not been a poor man I might have heard the fifty-drachma course of the great Prodicus, which is a complete education on this subject. Then, I should have been able to answer your question. But, regrettably, I have only heard the single-drachma course, so I do not know the truth about such matters. However, I will be glad to assist you in investigating them and finding the truth ourselves.

This insistence on self-reliance "illustrates the attitude peculiar to Socrates among all the great teachers of the world," notes Edith Hamilton in *The Greek Way to Western Civilization.* "He will not do their thinking for the people who come to him."

4. *Analyze.* Break a subject down into its components, so that you can see how they fit together and spot any logical gaps where you might need more information to understand the subject better.

5. *Synthesize.* Put all the pieces back together in a new, personal way that combines information from many different sources and creates new insights and ideas about the subject.

6. *Evaluate.* Judge the value of material for a given purpose.

Use this diagram to identify the ways you are using your mind on a major problem or issue you face right now. Simply work your way up the pyramid, asking the following questions:

a. Have I done my "homework" on this function?

b. Have I done *too much* in this area, and if so, do I need to move up to the next area of exploration?

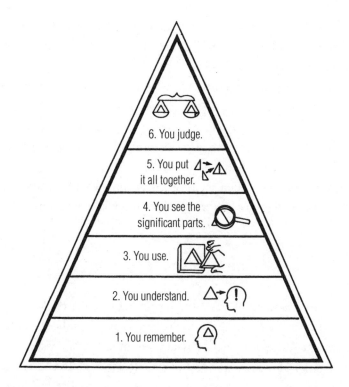

6. You judge.

5. You put it all together.

4. You see the significant parts.

3. You use.

2. You understand.

1. You remember.

c. Have I neglected any of these areas in the process of thinking through this issue, problem, opportunity, or situation?

d. What additional work do I need to do to get to the point of making a judgment?

e. When would be the best time to make this judgment?

REEVALUATE YOUR BELIEFS AND CONVICTIONS

Are your beliefs consistent with the religious or spiritual label you would put on yourself? Which major philosopher's views best express your views on major ethical issues? You can get a bracing philosophical workout by exploring these questions on the website www.Selectsmart.com. Among a wide range of self-scoring questionnaires are two, The Religion Selector and The Ethical Philosophy Selector.

The first will reveal whether there are discrepancies between your basic beliefs and the creed you identify yourself with, whether it be Eastern

Orthodox Christianity or Secular Humanism. After you have indicated your position and how strongly you feel about it, the site produces a list of twenty-six religions and belief systems prioritized according to their consistency with *your* opinions. Then, you can click on any of those to get more information about that belief system.

The Ethics site will enable you to match your moral opinions with those of thinkers ranging from post-Socratics like the Cynics and the Epicureans to Spinoza and Jean-Paul Sartre.

Both sites offer a bracing exercise in deciding where you stand on basic issues and finding out how these viewpoints jibe with your professed ideology.

 4. Take the time to think for yourself.

Socrates was a slow thinker. At the beginning of most of the dialogues, he lags way behind the other participants. Typically, others would have a fast answer to the problem or issue presented for discussion, like the "sound bytes" offered by our politicians at news conferences. Socrates would explain that he was not as quick as everyone else but needed to back up and proceed more slowly. "I'm just an ignorant man in this field," he'd say. "Help me to understand what you are saying, and why."

Of course, when his friends tried to explain the basis of their strong opinions, they usually discovered that they lacked the logical or evidential basis for them. It turned out that their fast answers had no validity.

We usually think too fast, or to be more exact, we truncate the thinking process too early and think we have finished when we have really only started. Perhaps this comes from our school and college training, when it was important to get the right answer *fast,* whether in class discussion or on a timed examination. To judge for yourself, you have to take the time to find out what YOU really think. But most of us, most of the time, simply accept whatever pops into our head when we first begin thinking, and often it's not even our own idea but something we have accepted uncritically from someone else.

When you feel the need the take your time to think something through, think of what you're doing not as "slow" but as "thoughtful," "leisurely," "exploratory," "comprehensive," "thorough," or "profound."

HOW SOCRATES "CENTERED" HIMSELF

Socrates would often *prepare* to judge for himself, by "centering" before engaging in a dialogue. He would often take time to get in touch with what he really thought and felt about the subject. Socrates' way of doing this is portrayed at the beginning of Plato's "Symposium." (A Greek *symposium* was not an academic colloquy but a small dinner party at which the guests were entertained and conversed on compelling subjects.) At the start of this party at the home of the playwright Agathon, Socrates, the eagerly awaited guest of honor, is conspicuously absent. A servant is dispatched to look for him in the neighborhood, in case he's lost his way.

"He's up the street, standing under a neighbor's awning, and doesn't wish to come in yet," the servant reports.

"How strange," says the Agathon, the host. "But go on calling him."

"No," interjects Socrates' friend Aristodemus, who is acquainted with his habit. "Leave him alone. He has a way of doing this. Sometimes he just goes into a trance before an event like this. He'll come in presently. Let him be!"

When Socrates does enter, he is well prepared to be at this best. (We will pick up what happens later at this party, in Chapter 5.)

Take Time to Consider a Problem or Issue

Identify a problem or issue that you have faced in the past month on which you have the feeling that you may not have taken as much time to think through as you should have.

a. Why did you curtail your thinking process? (Impatience? Anxiety? Pressure of other matters? Inadvertence? Or . . . ?)

b. If you had taken more time to think about the problem or issue, how would your thinking have improved or led to a better decision?

c. When will you next face a comparable situation? How can you plan to take more time to think it through? (Work with a colleague or friend to help you slow down? Use one of the techniques presented later in this section? Set a more realistic deadline? Other . . . ?)

 ### 5. *Improve your thinking by using the three "filters against folly."*

In virtually every one of the dialogues, Socrates put some opinion or belief on trial for its life. To test these convictions, he used the filters of logic, experience, and common sense, all of which are still relevant in our time. And we also can benefit by using two other "filters of folly"—numeracy and ecolacy.

Do you recognize this common experience? You watch a television interview with a renowned expert on a certain subject, who uses powerful facts and logic to explain why a certain public policy is desirable. Then, two days later, you read an article by an equally renowned expert in the same field, who contends with equal persuasiveness that the same policy would be disastrous.

We are surrounded by such contradictory authorities, and we need to judge among them. Garrett Hardin, the distinguished scientist, ecologist, and carrier of the flame, says that we can judge for ourselves if we master the filters against folly that enable us to look critically at the statements of experts.

To make our own appraisal when we hear the "experts" speak (our equivalents of the Delphic Oracle!), we need:

Literacy—the ability to understand and interpret the words

Numeracy—the ability to understand quantified information and to interpret it intelligently

Ecolacy—a new skill needed to take into account the effect of complex interactions over time.

"No one filter by itself is adequate for understanding the world and predicting the consequences of our actions," says Hardin. "We must learn to use all three."

Numeracy consists of "the art of putting numbers to things," of probing such factors as the rate of change, proportions, and ratios. Ecolacy is the ability to see long-term results and is characterized by the question "And then what?"

If you need a crash course in using these tools to judge for yourself, then Hardin's book is a superb place to start. In it, he shows how to use them on such topics as health insurance, nuclear-reactor safety, food and drug safety, global warming, and foreign aid.

 ## 6. Experiencing "Eureka!"

The Greeks loved the story of Archimedes' "eureka experience." The great mathematician had been challenged by his patron, King Hieron II of Syracuse, to devise a method for ascertaining whether a crown, which the King had been given as a gift, was made of pure gold or alloyed with silver. Since the crown was impossible to measure exactly because of its elaborate design, Archimedes was stumped for quite some time. Then, after giving up on trying to solve the problem, he was relaxing in a bath when he noticed that as his body sank into the water, the water rose until the tub overflowed. He realized in a flash that the weight of the water it displaced would reveal its specific gravity and thus its composition.

Archimedes was said to have been so exhilarated by this "a-ha!" experience that he leapt out of his tub, raced out the door of his house, and ran naked in the street shouting "Eureka!"

Plutarch interpreted Archimedes' spirited reaction as an expression of the unique delights of having "Aha!" breakthroughs: "We have never yet heard of a glutton who exclaimed with such enthusiasm, 'I have eaten,' or a lady's man who cried abroad, 'I've made love.'"

One of the most powerful ways to think for yourself is to "go creative." When you come up with ideas that only YOU could think of, you know you are bringing your unique perspective to the situation.

Here is my favorite method for sparking your own "eureka" moments. It's a seven-step process that you can use on your own or with others. If you like the technique, you can enlarge the diagram and the script, print it on Day-Glo yellow stock, and pin one on your corkboard or refrigerator. Then, you can conduct an ad hoc, do-it-yourself creativity session whenever you like.

Here's how it works. Picture yourself working with people in your organization on a knotty problem or planning a major family occasion at home. Everything's going smoothly—*too* smoothly. Everything that's being suggested is sensible but uninspired. You're having that feeling of "déjà vu all over again," as Yogi Berra put it. Your gut tells you that there must be some new ideas, new approaches. But no one is coming up with anything really fresh or exciting. What to do?

You reach above your head to the corkboard behind you on which there is a glowing yellow placard in the shape of a light bulb (pictured below). It's a simple, anytime-anywhere formula for getting any group to think creatively.

The illustration shows one side: the basic process. On the other side is a very simple script with the exact words you say to the group to spark some creative thinking. You might start off by saying: "Our ideas seem sound, as far as they go. But how about going beyond what we've done before. I have the feeling we can be more creative." Or: "Let's devote the next half-hour to a 'creative pause.' Let's generate some fresh, new ideas."

Three topics are proposed, and you start with the first one. "Let's just brainstorm to start things off. Please, no criticisms or negative comments. Listen and see if you can each 'leapfrog,' using every idea as an inspiration to generate others. Go for quantity at this point."

The flow is slow at first, but within minutes the pace picks up. The group's off and running. Pretty soon, people begin laughing, but warmly, at each other's "far-out" ideas and finding some possibilities in some of them. Rather than criticizing each other, they're now building on each other's contributions.

Subsequent phases of this process lead to the choice of the most interesting ideas, the refinement of some of them, and the decision to look further into the most promising. The brief creative pause has yielded from one to five ideas that were not "on the table" when you started, though they may have been lurking in the minds of some people who didn't feel comfortable expressing them. Not only that, people feel "up."

1. PAUSE

Say: "Let's take time out to think about this
in some fresh ways."

2. FOCUS

Say: "I'd like to generate some fresh approaches to capitalizing on our strengths."

"Let's look together at the area of _____ to come up with some new ideas."

3. QUESTION

Say: "How could we make it possible to _____?"

"What factor could we play with to change the picture here?"

4. CREATE

Say: "Let's hear new ideas—without criticism or judgment."

"Let's build on each other's wild ideas."

5. CHOOSE

Say: "Which of these many ideas is worth looking at more closely?"

6. REFINE

Say: "How can we use what's valuable about this idea?"

7. ACT

Say: "How can we test this safely, easily, and economically?"

They have joined with each other to use their imaginations and stimulate each other.

Can you get new ideas from just such a simple process? Absolutely. It works every time. Will you always come up with wonderful, usable innovations? Not a chance. That's not the point. You can't guarantee results—no one can, when it comes to creativity. All you can do is to invite, permit, encourage, and reward the *process*. But the more you do that—the more occasions on which you let people know that you *want* fresh thinking—the more good results you will get. Those who have new ideas will be encouraged to share them rather than stifle them because everyone seems satisfied with the old chestnuts.

7. *Avoid misjudgments by practicing "Heraclitean" thinking.*

One of the pre-Socratics from whom Socrates learned so much was Heraclitus, the sage who wrote the familiar dictum "You can never step into the same river twice." Heraclitus is the first great exponent of the idea that the nature of our world is change—a school of thought that reaches its apogee in contemporary science, which tells us that the atomic, biological, and cosmic worlds are in a constant state of flux. "Nothing is, everything becomes; no condition persists unaltered, even for the smallest moment; everything is ceasing to be what it was, and is becoming what it will be."

Socrates was very aware of the constant change and differences that characterize our world. That is why he was impelled to continually point out how absolute statements could be easily refuted by specific instances.

Today we all know on an abstract level that we live in a world of constant change. On every level of our reality, things are constantly changing: from the molecular through the biological through the social to the global. Yet we often err by not applying this principle to our everyday lives. Our language makes it easy to judge poorly. The words and concepts we use imply constancy, not change; identity, not diversity; and definitiveness, not open-endedness.

Consider the kinds of statements often heard some years back and how they violate these truths about reality:

TWO WHO THOUGHT FOR THEMSELVES: SOCRATES AND BUDDHA

Judging for themselves was a driving force shared by Socrates and Buddha, who were contemporaries. Religion scholar Karen Armstrong notes that both men found themselves compelled to reject the beliefs that their society thrust upon them. Both of them rejected their most important teacher because they had to find their own way.

Both Buddha and Socrates felt a deep spiritual need to judge values and divinity for themselves. So strongly does she feel this kinship that Armstrong describes Buddha as "an Indian Socrates."

- *The Japanese are competitive.* (Which Japanese? When?)

- *She is an overcontrolling manager.* (As perceived by whom? In what circumstances?)

- *I never get the breaks.* (In what areas of life? For what period of time?)

- *Marriages don't work.* (For whom? When? For what kinds of people? With what exceptions?)

The best techniques for avoiding these mistakes, and for using language itself to spur us to sounder thinking, are those suggested by the discipline of general semantics. These immediately usable techniques provide ways to ask "Which?" "When?" and other clarifying questions:

"Index" your statements to make clear that they apply only to specific cases. We use indexes all the time in everyday life to differentiate between things that are superficially "the same": seats in a theater, room numbers in a hotel, telephone numbers. Picture the index as a small subscript number under the subject you are discussing to remind you that it is a specific instance. Thus, in talking about "teenagers," do you mean:

Teenager (1)—the honor student

Teenager (2)—the athlete

Teenager (3)—the computer hacker

Teenager (4)—the gang member

Instead of asserting that "the Japanese are competitive," you might say:

> The twenty Japanese businesspeople whom I met while doing a project in the field of financial management behaved in ways that seemed highly competitive to me, in that they insisted on personal acknowledgment for each of their contributions to the project.

"Date" your statements to make clear when they were true. Dating statements is a tremendous contribution to judging their usefulness. Here, we simply add or imagine a little date as a subscript to the statement.

> "The president's position on defense spending . . ." (during the presidential campaign)
>
> "The president's position on defense spending . . ." (after one year in office)
>
> "The president's position on defense spending . . ." (after midterm elections in which his party lost control of the Senate)
>
> "The president's position on defense spending . . ." (after leaving office and becoming a humanitarian)

Consider how dating would add to your capacity to judge the statement about Japanese businesspeople.

> "That project on which I worked with twenty Japanese businesspeople took place fifteen years ago, at a time when competition between American and Japanese businesses was at its most intense in the postwar period."

Use "etc." to remind yourself and others that there is more to be said that might alter the conclusion. Here's where we interpolate or imagine a tiny "etc." after every statement to remind us that our statement covers only part of the truth.

> I should add that the firm for which I was working was in merger talks with the Japanese firm, that I myself was very eager to get the maximum credit for every aspect of the project, and that my Japanese counterparts actually did tremendously effective work on the project.

Now, apply these three techniques yourself. Imagine that a friend comes to you and says one of the other statements mentioned at the start of this section:

> "I have an overcontrolling manager."

> "I never get the breaks."

> "Marriage doesn't work."

How would you respond, using the techniques suggested above?

 ## 8. Seven thinking strategies

Reading the *Dialogues,* one is constantly struck by Socrates' resourcefulness in steering the inquiry. At one point, he will press forward relentlessly with logical precision. Then, suddenly, he will switch ground to approach the issue from an entirely different direction. Or he will introduce an evocative metaphor or dramatic experience. Clearly, he is orchestrating a set of thinking strategies: different ways of analyzing any problem or issue. Mastering such strategies can endow us with some of the same resourcefulness.

These seven tools of thinking will enable you to focus on any problem or issue in a productive way. They were developed by Dr. Edward de Bono, who has carried the flame of robust, independent thinking in our time. He has used these tools to spark creative and critical reflection in millions of people and thousands of organizations.

Pick the one that intrigues you most, and find a way to use it right

SOCRATES AND THE "IMPIOUS" EURIPIDES

Socrates' independence of mind was mirrored by one of the greatest playwrights of his time, Euripides. Both of these men challenged, shocked, and ultimately alienated their fellow Athenians.

Euripides was one of the three tragic dramatists, each of whom ranks with Shakespeare or Ibsen, who thrived during Socrates' lifetime. Aeschylus, the eldest, had forged theater out of the inchoate dance to Dionysus. Sophocles, author of *Oedipus Rex,* developed the mature tragic form from which Aristotle drew the principles of the art. But Euripides, who wrote tragedies that debunked the gods and heroes, criticized the cruelties and injustices of war, and championed the needs and rights of women, was the one most closely associated with Socrates.

Both Socrates and Euripides combined sharp-witted skepticism with an intense moral sense. In *The Trojan Women,* Euripides portrays the way in which women and children are the chief victims of war and conquest. In *Iphigenia at Aulis,* he portrays the generals who led the Greeks in the Trojan War as poltroons, egotists, and cowards who will offer one of their children as a sacrifice to keep the war machine going. In *Medea,* Euripides shows the rage that mistreatment and injustice can evoke in a woman.

Socrates' contemporaries, like Aristophanes, himself a playwright, acknowledged the connections between the two great skeptics and moralists. According to an Athenian quip, "Socrates lit the kindling for Euripides' bonfire." We can only imagine what went through Socrates' mind when, seven years before his own trial at the age of seventy, the Athenians drew weary of Euripides' criticisms and exiled him for "impiety."

now on something you need to think more about this week. You will find that these tools enable you to generate your own unique thoughts and then to judge for yourself what course of action is best for you.

PMI: Plus, Minus, Interesting

Benjamin Franklin suggested that when you need to make a decision, you list the pro's and con's on a pad, then tote up the two columns. But that system, while often helpful, leaves out new, creative thoughts that don't elicit a "yes" or "no" response. PMI invites you to broaden your thinking by considering not just the positives and the negatives but what's "interesting" about any idea or proposal.

Consider this one: At the birth of every child, every family should receive a stipend that could accumulate interest as the child grows up and would then be at the young person's disposal when he or she reached the age of eighteen—for higher education, starting a business or family, or some other purpose. Think about three positive aspects of this proposal, then three negative ones, and then three "interesting" implications, consequences, or related ideas.

CAF: Consider All Factors

This tool challenges you to make your thinking about any problem or issue more complete. If you're considering buying a house, for example, you probably have certain questions and factors in mind: location, commuting, schools, recreational facilities. But focusing and discussing ALL factors will yield some you might otherwise overlook. How about noise, pending changes in the neighborhood, asbestos, etc. The use of checklists can be a tremendous help in creating your CAF.

C&S: Consequences and Sequel

The essence of "environmental" thinking has been defined as always considering "what comes after THAT." It's a powerful principle. C&S urges that we be more systematic about envisaging the consequences of our actions.

In considering taking a new job, for example, most people tend to focus on the immediate prospects. But if you are considering the position as a long-term commitment, it's important to direct your thinking very specifically to where you will be in five years, even ten years, and in some cases twenty-five years. Business organizations think in terms of "succession planning" over two to three decades and know that they must identify the likeliest candidates for the best jobs that far in advance if they are to be ready when the time comes. So should you.

AGO: Aims, Goals, Objectives

Simply formulating your reasons for doing what you are doing can often clarify your thinking. We tend to settle for the first or uppermost goal without realizing that there are other objectives in the back of our mind.

For example, a colleague of mine was having tremendous difficulty in studying for an important examination she had to pass for advanced accreditation in her field. She was completely focused on "passing the exam" as her goal. During a conversation about this, I asked her whether some of the material she needed to learn would really help her do a better job for her clients. Instantly, she realized that it would and that by bringing that other goal to the forefront, she could jump-start her motivation to get involved with the material. She returned to her studying that evening with a much-improved attitude.

FIP: First Important Priorities

We all have learned the need to prioritize in terms of actions, rearranging our TO DO lists so that the most important items are uppermost, not merely the most urgent. But the principle applies to our thinking, too.

After we have used tools like CAF or AGO, it's important to prioritize the many ideas we have come up with. In thinking about your investments, for instance, a major first step many people neglect is to consciously determine what your investment goals are (taking risks for large gains, slow but steady growth, income, etc.). Similarly, when we are considering getting involved in a new relationship, we are generally awash with different considerations about the other person. It's often very important to step back to think through what we really value and seek in the relationship.

APC: Alternatives, Possibilities, Choices

APC introduces the purely *creative* dimension into your thinking. Here's where you are invited to brainstorm, use your intuition, and come up with "far-out" ideas. We have explored this strategy in detail in the section "Experiencing Eureka!"

OPV: Other Point of View

Most of us rarely focus our thinking specifically on empathizing with others. But in any situation where you need to relate effectively, it's an invaluable thinking tool. Often when working on a personal relationship problem at work or outside the workplace, I'll have each person explain how the situation feels "in their shoes," and then really LISTEN to how the *other* person feels "in their shoes." This simple exchange of points of view will often resolve long-standing difficulties.

 ## 9. *Become an independent scholar.*

The Athenians believed firmly that "each man must himself be a research worker in truth if he is ever to attain any share in it," writes Edith Hamilton in her classic *The Greek Way.* "If the Platonic dialogues point to any one conclusion beyond another, it is that the Athenian did not want someone else to do his thinking for him." This theme has been a pillar of American intellectual life ever since Ralph Waldo Emerson proclaimed it in his Phi Beta Kappa address at Harvard: "The Scholar Should Be Man Thinking."

Socrates is the model for today's independent scholars, men and women for whom the pursuit of knowledge and understanding is a passion, not a profession. These are serious scholars, scientists, social activists, artists, and others who pursue their inquiries outside of academe. Vincent Kovaloski, a carrier of the flame who is an independent scholar of the history of the Great Books movement, has described these inquirers this way:

> The Socratic amateur is the classical antithesis to the professional purveyor of knowledge. Socrates distinguished himself from the Sophists of his day, who set themselves up as possessors of knowledge, and would teach students whatever they wanted to know, for whatever purpose, good or bad.
>
> Socrates insisted that he did *not* have wisdom—that he merely loved it, and hence should be called not a sophist but a *Philosopher,* a mere lover of wisdom. The Socratic amateur

SOCRATES—LIFELONG LEARNER AND INDEPENDENT SCHOLAR

Socrates learned all the time from everyone about everything, and so did his fellow Athenians. The result was an unprecedented flowering of thought and creativity in all fields. As Alexander Eliot explains in his book *Socrates*:

> During Socrates' lifetime, immense advances were made in practically all the main branches of human knowledge. Yet none of these advances was the work of scholars or researchers in the modern sense. This may well be the most alien thing about ancient Athens from our point of view. We sit and study, whereas Socrates and his contemporaries were athletic in habits of thought. They created their own studies.

Socrates' circle of friends included most of the people who were making intellectual history in his time. He considered his philosophizing as a search through the world of knowledge and experience—an unending but gratifying journey all along the way. "Not I but the city teaches," he liked to say. And from his beloved Athens, he learned all he needed to know.

isn't afraid to be a generalist, and tackles the biggest and most complex problems without reducing them to techniques, seeking to share and spread understanding, rather than to control and possess knowledge.

The tradition was exemplified by the wandering scholars of the twelfth century whose allegiance was to learning, not to any temporal power, and by the medieval universities, which arose out of the struggles of such scholars and their students with the Church.

Later, when the universities which they founded had in turn become moribund and "academic," once again it was independent scholars—in this case, the founders of modern science like Galileo, Kepler, and Boyle—who founded "learned societies" outside of the universities, to explore new ideas and new ways of knowing which the universities refused to entertain.

Independent scholarship always arises as a challenge to the dangerous myth that serious thinking only goes on in established, orthodox institutions, and that learning is the exclusive possession of the professoriate. In our own day of excessive bureaucratization and professionalism in learning, the Socratic amateur is an urgently needed voice.

You can become a leading expert yourself in virtually any field or on virtually any issue to which you are willing to devote the requisite time. That's a bold assertion, but I've documented its validity in two books about people who did it, how they did it, and how you can do it too: *The Independent Scholar's Handbook* (Ten Speed Press, 1993) and *Independent Scholarship: Problems, Promise, and Prospects* (The College Board, 1983).

In the *Handbook,* which is available at most public libraries, you will find specific guidance on every aspect of becoming an independent scholar, including

- research methodologies

- getting help from others, ranging from mentors to research assistance

- intellectual craftsmanship

- sharing your work through teaching, publishing, and nontraditional means

- organizing for mutual support

The most enlightened professors have themselves urged their best students to look beyond the authority of their professors, to judge for themselves in intellectual matters. These academics are true carriers of the flame as they convey this spirit to young people. For example, here's what Frank Turner, John Hay Whitney Professor of History at Yale University, told a group being initiated into Phi Beta Kappa. (Turner was, of course, echoing Emerson's oration cited above.)

You have immersed yourselves in the ideas your professors set before you, mastered those ideas and, to some extent, fed them back to your teachers who wished anything other than to have their own ideas returned to them. Deference to professorial authority would seem to be one of the almost inevitable by-products of undergraduate and sometimes even graduate academic achievement. Excessive deference to professorial authority, however, can lead to a moribund culture and to the death of both the mind and the imagination.

People who have achieved membership in Phi Beta Kappa have deferred long enough to the authority of professors. Therefore I urge you to resist deference to the academy.

After evoking the contributions of three independent scholars who did just this—Descartes, Tocqueville, and Darwin—Professor Turner concluded by challenging these young people, and us, to think for ourselves.

I encourage you to think about these three men and other people you may know in other fields of investigation and from other cultures. I encourage you to emulate the skepticism that Descartes directed against the schools of his day, to find a great thinker with whom you may have a lover's quarrel as Tocqueville did with Montesquieu, and finally to set out on your own voyage of discovery to your own Galápagos.

Voyage beyond the shores of your professors—explore and risk the shoals of new discovery and the achievement of your own intellectual and moral self-confidence.

CHALLENGE CONVENTION

When one is freed and gets on his feet and turns
his head and walks toward the light—
all he has seen till now was false and a trick,
but now he sees more truly.

SOCRATES, IN PLATO'S "REPUBLIC"

I
T IS A SUN-DRENCHED DAY in Athens as people begin to assemble in the agora for their daily shopping and socializing. The sunlight floods every corner of the marketplace: glistening on the burnished bodies of the athletes strolling among the vendors, falling on the fresh produce and the rich fabrics and jewelry being sold, reflecting off the soaring columns of the Parthenon high on the hill overlooking the marketplace.

Strangely, the sunlight seems to make Socrates think of its opposite, as Plato recounts the incident in the "Republic." Socrates is speaking to his young friend Glaucon, and as we join them he is conjuring up a vivid image of a strange place that is the opposite of everything around them:

"Imagine a group of people living in a long underground cave, facing the back wall.

"They have been here since their childhood. Their legs and necks are chained so they cannot move. They can only see straight ahead of them because the chains prevent them from turning their heads towards the opening, behind and above them.

"Behind them is a fire blazing at a distance, and between the fire and the prisoners there is a raised way. And you will see, if you look, a low wall built along the way, like the screen which marionette players have in front of them, over which they show the puppets."

"I see," murmured Glaucon, contemplating the imaginary scene Socrates had conjured up.

"Now please imagine," Socrates continued, "men passing along the wall carrying all sorts of statues and figures of animals made of wood and stone and various materials, which appear over the wall."

"This is a strange image, and these are strange prisoners," said Glaucon.

"Yes," said Socrates, "strange indeed. The prisoners see only the shadows of the puppets, or the shadows of one another, which the fire throws on the back wall of the cave."

"True," said Glaucon, "for how could they see anything

but the shadows if they were never allowed to move their heads?"

"And if they were able to talk with one another, would they not suppose that they were naming what was actually before them?"

"Very true."

"To them," Socrates said, "the truth would be literally nothing but the shadows of the images."

"That is certain."

"Now," Socrates said, "imagine that one of the prisoners is freed. Suddenly his bonds are removed, and he is allowed to stand up and turn around, and walk toward the light. How do you think he would feel?"

"I think that at first he will suffer sharp pains, and the glare will distress him," replied Glaucon. "He will be unable to see the real objects of which, while a prisoner, he had seen only the shadows."

"Yes," agreed Socrates. "But then his vision would clear. Though dazzled by the light of the real world, he would gradually grow accustomed to it. The pain and irritation would pass away. He would be able to distinguish among shadows, and reflections in water, and real objects."

"I can see that would be true, Socrates," said Glaucon.

Socrates continued: "Then he will gaze upon the light of the moon and the stars and the spangled heaven. Last of all, he will be able to see the sun, and not mere reflections of him in the water.

"He would come to realize that the sun was the source of heat and light. And he would think of the cave, and the prisoners there, and how they had had to form all their ideas about the world simply on the basis of shadows against the cave wall. And he would pity them."

"Yes," Glaucon agreed.

"Suppose now," Socrates continued, "that this man, after having had a glimpse of the sunlit world, were brought back into the darkness of the cave and chained once again. He would be unable to see in the cave until his eyes again became accustomed to darkness.

"The prisoners who had never left the cave would think him blind. Men would say of him that up he went and down he came without his eyes, and that it was better not even to think of going up. And the prisoners in the cave would say that if anyone tried to free them and take them up to the light, they would refuse to go."

Now Socrates explained his strange parable of the cave: "Sometimes a man is allowed to go up into the higher world and see reality as it actually exists. While he is there, he pities the poor prisoners in the cave. But when he comes back, he is dazzled by the light of the higher world, and returns groping and uncertain, to be laughed at by the prisoners of the shadow world."

Whenever we think of our intellectual progress as a movement from the darkness toward the light, we are using imagery that started with Socrates' allegory of "The Cave." It was his way of dramatizing our journey toward understanding.

Note that there is *pain* involved in the ascent from the world of shadows to the world of valid knowledge. And there is comparable pain—as well as danger—in returning to the cave with one's new awareness. This danger goes well beyond being laughed at, as Socrates explains in the passage directly following the one you have just read, in which he prophesies his own fate at the hands of his fellow Athenians.

SOCRATES: And if their way was to reward those who were quickest to make out the shadows as they went by and to note in memory which came before which as a rule, and which together, would he care very much about such rewards? And, if he were to go down again out of the sunlight into his old place, would not his eyes get suddenly full of the dark?

And if there were to be a competition then with the prisoners who had never moved out and he had do his best in judging the shadows before his eyes got used to the dark—which needs more than a minute—wouldn't he be laughed at? Wouldn't they say he had come back from his time on high with his eyes in very bad condition so that there was no point in going up there?

And if they were able to get their hands on the man who attempted to take their chains off and guide them up, wouldn't they put him to death?

GLAUCON: They certainly would!

Thinking people in every generation have applied the story of "The Cave" to their specific circumstances. Through the centuries, philosophers and theologians as diverse as Saint Augustine, Rousseau, Spinoza, Hegel, and Freud have evoked "The Cave" to dramatize the difficulties of seeing through our delusions and fantasies, to find truth.

A charming modern version of this allegory is *Flatland,* the mathematical fantasy by Edward Abbott in which he evokes what life would be like for creatures confined to two dimensions and then portrays what happens when one of them has the astonishing experience of breaking out of that "cave" into our world of three dimensions. Suddenly, he can see and experience things that are beyond the understanding of his fellow creatures still confined to a flat surface.

SOCRATES' SPIRIT IN OUR TIME

Socrates' allegory "The Cave" is used to challenge applicants to Bard College's early-admission unit, Simon's Rock College. The outstanding young people who apply are asked to interpret it in terms of their own lives.

Imagine what would happen if those students actually met Socrates when they arrived on campus. On a brisk September evening on the campus in Rhinebeck, New York, such a meeting did occur, but with Socrates' stand-in.

"Our students want to meet Socrates because they recognize that freeing themselves from the cave is the first step in their true higher education," said the young professor who invited me to the campus. "This is their first opportunity to critically examine the culture in which they have been raised as young people. If they wish, they can see how their family, their community, and the media have shaped their minds. And they can start to think for themselves."

Socrates confronted these bright American youngsters much the way he had challenged the youth of fifth-century B.C. Athens. He posed basic questions: "What do you believe?" "Why are you here?" "Where do you want to go?"

The students rose to the challenge. They identified some of the "shadows on the wall" that they felt had shaped their minds and that they wanted to examine critically. Among those cited by this particular group were:

- "A family culture, in which there was always just one right way to think about anything that came up, and everyone was expected to accept it."

- "The 'politically correct' viewpoint of my community that businessmen were antisocial, poor people all had hearts of gold, those in prison were victims of oppression, and government runs things better than profit-making organizations."

- "Commercials every twelve minutes during my favorite TV shows, pushing crap that I don't need."

- "Political campaigns waged by slogans and posturing by the candidates instead of discussions of real issues."

- "Local TV news that fills thirty minutes with stuff from the police blotter."

- "Song lyrics that are inane."

- "Some of what our parents tell us about how to live our lives."

In absentia Socrates has had over a hundred such dialogues with young people throughout the country over the past several years. Invariably, there's a thrilling sense of minds awakening to the need, and the promise, of being freed from the cave, and of beginning to think for oneself.

Most people today point to the media and cyberculture environments as especially powerful "caves" in which we live most of our lives. Instead of "prisoners chained in place," we are couch potatoes melded to our "remotes." Instead of the shadows of puppets, we spend our time viewing commercials or web pages. We are fed a constant diet of hype and propaganda, images and messages designed to instill new desires, fears, and anxieties. Whole books have been devoted to exploring this danger, with titles like Neil Postman's *Amusing Ourselves to Death*.

It's not just young people who express this. Socrates spends most of his time engaging in dialogues with those well beyond their college years: professionals, businesspeople, parents, community leaders. And they, too, share a vivid and unsettling sense of needing to free themselves from the cave.

Here's the best expression of the way many people seem to feel by an especially articulate observer, David Denby, essayist and movie critic at *The New Yorker*. Do you recognize any of these feelings in yourself?

> Like many others, I was cast into the modern state of living-in-the-media, a state of excitement needled with disgust. . . . I no longer knew what I knew. I possessed information without knowledge, opinions without principles . . . I sensed my identity had softened and merged into the atmosphere of representation, and I couldn't quite see where it ended and I began.

My own memories were lapsing out into the fog of media life, the unlived life of the spectator.

I was beginning to be sick at heart of living my life inside that immense system of representations and simulacra, the thick atmosphere of information and imagery and attitudes that forms the mental condition and habits of any adult living in a media society in the late twentieth century. I was uneasy in that vale of shadows, that frenetic but gloomy half-life filled with names, places, chatter, acts, cars racing, gunshots, experts talking, daytime couples accusing one another of infidelity, the sheer busyness of it all, the constant movement, the incredible activity and utter boredom . . .

In the "Challenges, Explorations, and Applications" section following, you will acquire the skills you need to participate in this kind of campaign to penetrate the shadows of illusion in our society.

CHALLENGES, EXPLORATIONS, AND APPLICATIONS

Socrates' cave represents the world of our "received beliefs." Each of us harbors a myriad of ideas, attitudes, and opinions that have been "programmed" into us by our upbringing, schooling, culture, and social and media environment. The "chains" that bind us to these ideas are our understandable desire to please others, to be accepted, and to save ourselves the effort of thinking things through ourselves.

Such acceptance is not entirely bad. In most cases, these ideas, opinions, and attitudes are quite serviceable. We should not have to think through everything ourselves. We do not need to challenge everything. But we do need to know how to conduct such a self-examination of our beliefs when it is required. Otherwise, we will live our lives as unwitting intellectual puppets. The uneducated man who has strong opinions but has never examined any of them is merely the ventriloquist's dummy of some obsolete philosopher or of the latest media hype.

In some of the Challenges, Explorations, and Applications in this chapter, I will be asking you to really question your own "received ideas"

Strengthening Your Socratic Spirit

- Are you aware of the "caves" from which you have escaped already in your intellectual and emotional development? (Exercise #1)

- Can you empathize with the "caves" in which others find themselves? (Exercises #2, 3, and 5)

- Have you examined the "conventional wisdom" you imbided from your parents and family to see whether it makes sense and conforms to your experience of life? (Exercise #4)

- Are you aware of the impact on your point of view of your occupation, your friends, your media diet, and your religious and spiritual background? Is your "information diet"—your ongoing sources for knowing and understanding what is going on in the world beyond your immediate circle—sufficiently broad, diverse, and challenging? Or is it dominated by a few sources that are most convenient and comfortable? (Exercise #6)

- Do you use your Socratic spirit to avoid being brainwashed by television? (Exercise #7)

- Are you ready to put one of your basic beliefs "on trial for its life"? (Exercise #8)

- Do you cultivate a critical and skeptical attitude to protect yourself against being bamboozled? (Exercise #9)

- Do you have a simple system in place for formulating a sound opinion on a challenging issue when you need to, so that you can defend your position with logic and evidence? (Exercise #10)

- Do you know how to use experts wisely and avoid being misled by false expertise? Do you have your own "kitchen cabinet" of experts in the fields and areas in which you need to think well and make good decisions, on whom you can call for advice and counsel? (Exercises #11 and 12)

- Can you function effectively as a gadfly when you need to? (Exercise #13) at the deepest level. It's always easy to see the speck in someone else's eye. It's a lot more painful to discern our own blind spots.

 ### 1. Revisit a "cave" from which you have freed yourself.

Visualize a time in your life when, looking back, you now realize you were in a "cave." (You were living your life according to how someone else thought you should without your even being aware of it.)

> a. "Feel" your way into and around that state of mind. (Why was it comfortable, etc.)
>
> b. Recall how it felt when you realized that you needed to question that viewpoint.
>
> c. Recollect what enabled you to free yourself.
>
> d. Reflect on whether you could or should have gone back into the cave to help others free themselves.

 ### 2. Enter the cave of an "opinion shaper."

Think of a person in public life whose opinion(s) have struck you as shocking, offensive, wrong-headed, destructive, etc. (a politician, pundit, or bigot perhaps). Now ask yourself: What experiences could this person have had that could have led them to espouse this viewpoint (especially experiences you have *not* had). Second, ask yourself: Is there at least one aspect or facet of what they are saying from which I could learn something?

 ### 3. Experience "The Cave" via video.

Want to experience what it's like to become aware that you are living your life in "The Cave"? Three compelling films available on video evoke that experience powerfully: *The Matrix, Wag the Dog,* and *The Truman Show.*

PRISONERS IN A REAL CAVE

Socrates' allegory "The Cave" and its prisoners may have been inspired by a real-life situation. In his time, the island of Sicily was renowned for its wealth and luxurious style of living. When Plato visited it, he noted that the citizens typically participated in not one but two banquets a day as well as other indulgences. He concluded that it was no wonder their minds were not keen enough to philosophize!

One source of Sicily's wealth were the mines at Cimmer. Many of the workers in these mines spent their entire lives underground, never seeing the light of day. Socrates would likely have heard about this, and the image may have grown in his mind as a symbol of mental imprisonment.

4. *Explore the cave of prefabricated thoughts.*

We each have a head full of "shadows on the wall" that illustrate the fallacy of accepting hand-me-down thoughts and prefabricated ideas. These "shadows" are the proverbs we heard from our parents and others, such as:

> All that glitters is not gold.
>
> Many hands make for light work.
>
> Out of sight, out of mind.
>
> He who hesitates is lost.
>
> You can't teach an old dog new tricks.
>
> Better safe than sorry.

Sound good? Of course they do, unless you stop to *think* about them. When you do, it's not hard to think of exceptions, extenuating circumstances, and other factors that qualify their usefulness. In fact, every such

proverb you can think of actually has a *contrary matching proverb*!
Just reconsider those above with these hints about their contraries:

- All that glitters . . .   Never look a . . .

- Many hands . . .   Too many cooks . . .

- Out of sight . . .   Absence makes . . .

- He who hesitates . . .   Look before . . .

- You can't teach . . .   It's never too late . . .

- Better safe than sorry . . .   Nothing ventured . . .

Now, try to think of contraries for these:

- Variety is the spice of life.

- The pen is mightier than the sword.

- Silence is golden.

- Clothes make the man.

- A miss is as good as a mile.

- A bird in the hand is worth two in the bush.

- If at first you don't succeed, try, try again.

- Opposites attract.

- Faith will move mountains.

- We'll cross that bridge when we come to it.

- There's no fool like an old fool.

- Blood is thicker than water.

- All work and no play makes Jack a dull boy.

- There's safety in numbers.

Join with a friend in playing this game. Then go on, if you wish, to discuss these questions:

- What do these contradictions in proverbs and other "conventional wisdom" mean?

- What do they teach us about how to find wisdom for living?

 5. Talk to a fellow "prisoner."

Do this exercise with three different people: a member of your family, a personal friend, and a person you know through your work. In each case

a. Identify an important belief or opinion of this person with which you disagree.

b. Then stretch yourself to identify the reasons why that person might have come to the belief or opinion with which you disagree.

c. Finally, consider whether your analysis yields any ways of finding "common ground" for agreement or of helping him or her see why you differ.

 6. Examine some images on the wall of your cave.

In this exercise, you will explore the "shadows on the wall" of the "cave" that are created by these four dimensions of your life.

- Your occupation

- Your family

- Your friends

- Your media environment (reading, television viewing, radio listening, etc.)

For each of these, I'm going to ask you to articulate some of the beliefs and points of view that have been with you for so long that you take them for granted. You may have difficulty putting them into words, but only by doing so can you see them clearly and decide how you feel about them at this point in your life. Here's some help in describing them.

"A CITIZEN NOT JUST OF ATHENS . . ."

There was no prouder Athenian than Socrates. He enjoyed and benefited from Athenian citizenship for his entire life and rarely wished to even visit elsewhere. When Athens went to war, he served creditably in the front ranks.

At the end of his life, when offered the opportunity to save his life by fleeing into exile, he chose to abide by the laws of his home city. Yet this supreme Athenian said, "I am not just a citizen of Athens, nor even just a Hellene. I am a citizen of the world."

All of us spend a major part of our lives in the "cave" of our occupation, profession, or job. As a result, we tend to see the world through the selected perspectives of that profession. For example:

- Psychotherapists see professionally only those people with psychological problems. After they spend up to ten hours a day intimately involved with people with pathologies, it is natural that many of them tend to see mental illness all around them—in their mates, children, and friends.

- People in law enforcement spend their workday with people involved in criminal activities, and as a result many of them have the opinion that criminal impulses are so pervasive that only stronger law enforcement will keep them in check.

a. Your Occupation: What attitudes, beliefs, and points of view have been instilled in you by *your* job, profession, or occupation?

Do the same exercise with:

b. Your Circle of Friends and Acquaintances: What attitudes, beliefs, and points of view do you have mainly because they are the dominant ones among your friends and acquaintances?

DR. SOCRATES

Socrates' contemporary Hippocrates revolutionized the practice of medicine by using Socrates' questioning approach. He found Greek medicine dominated by the priests of Aesculapius, a deified hero inherited from the days of Zeus and Aphrodite. Temples dedicated to this God dotted the Attic landscape.

If you were ill, you were likely to take yourself to one of these temples, where you would sleep before the statue of the God, frequently in the presence of supposedly healing snakes (hence the snakes coiled around the staff of Aesculapius, a symbol still associated with doctors).

"It was Hippocrates who brought about a drastic reform in this temple cult of healing," writes Howard W. Haggard in *Mystery, Magic and Medicine*. "His great accomplishment was to relieve the gods of their responsibility for the prevention and the treatment of disease and to place that responsibility where it belonged—squarely upon the shoulders of man."

Key Question: Do you have any close friend whose opinions on political, social, and cultural issues are radically different from your own? If so, how do you or could you use that friendship to test your own convictions? If not, how come? What would be the advantages of having such a friend?

c. Your Family and Upbringing: What attitudes, beliefs, and points of view do you have mainly because they were inculcated by your upbringing and education?

Key Question: Is there some important area of your belief system that is radically different from that of your family? If so, how did you come to frame a different position? If not, how come? Are there any beliefs you adopted from them that you have never questioned but feel you should question?

d. Your Media Diet: What attitudes, beliefs, and points of view do you have mainly because they are reinforced by your regular diet of newspapers, television, radio, and magazines?

Key Question: Do you maintain a critical stance when receiving information or ideas from the media? ("How do they know that?" "Do they have a bias?" "What's the source?" "What evidence have they presented?")

e. Your Religious/Spiritual Belief System (or lack thereof): What attitudes, beliefs, and points of view do you have mainly because they have been part of you from an early age?

Key Question: Are there basic axioms of your religious/spiritual belief system you have never questioned? If so, are you satisfied with your reasons for not examining them critically?

One final, essential point: Freeing ourselves from our blind belief in ideas we have never really examined does not imply any particular political or cultural persuasion. "Knee-jerk liberals" are just as guilty of this as "hide-bound conservatives."

A person like myself, raised and educated in a secular, humanist tradition, may harbor just as many of these unexamined beliefs as a Christian, Hindu, or religiously observant Jew. In my own case, for instance, I have at various points in my own life had to critically examine the following beliefs and convictions, which I had accepted from my parents and my schooling:

- Government programs to alleviate poverty are desirable and generally effective.

- Religion is not a necessary and beneficial part of one's life.

- The free market is detrimental to democratic values and works against the interest of a large part of the population.

- Education is the most effective means of social progress and development of individuals.

In some of these cases, I found that I could not defend my beliefs adequately and needed to change my opinion. In others, I was able to reaffirm my convictions with real confidence.

The point is that reexamining these basic beliefs was painful, sometimes agonizingly so. It was *not* a purely intellectual effort, but involved some of my deepest emotions. It challenged my sense of myself, since I had closely identified some of these beliefs with who I was and what I stood for.

7. *Watch television with Socrates.*

You can transform television commercials from annoying interruptions to fuel for your Socratic scrutiny. It's a great game to play with other adults or with your kids. Just keep a pad and pencil beside you as you watch and jot down the major "appeal" of each commercial (e.g., fear, sex, health, physical attractiveness, aging, status).

After you've captured at least two dozen such appeals, examine them and group them into major categories. Print these in large type on a shirt board and post it adjacent to the TV screen. Now, on subsequent stints in front of the set, your challenge is to refine your initial list until it adequately covers ninety percent of the commercials you hear.

You may need to regroup, create more comprehensive categories, and otherwise jiggle in order to get the best "taxonomy." Along the way, you will be creatively heightening your awareness of the appeals being used right now in television commercials.

Share your product of this inquiry with friends.

- What does it reveal about the American viewing public? About our values as a society? About the psychology of you and your fellow citizens?

- In what ways are you different from the kind of person to whom the advertisers seem to be appealing? Are there appeals that attract you but that you feel you should resist?

8. *Put one of your basic beliefs on trial for its life.*

In this exercise you will select one of your beliefs and critically examine how and why you have adopted it. Make sure the belief you choose is so

SOCRATES' LOVE OF THE LIGHT

Socrates loved the light in every sense, starting with the unique quality of the Aegean sunlight that visitors to Greece have so often noted. Thinkers, artists, poets, and visionaries have been drawn to this area because of the brightness, the clarity, the exhilarating quality of the sun on the sea, on the stark hills, and on the glistening buildings.

Socrates associated this inspiring sunlight with the Athenian quest for truth and understanding. "This has been our genius—a genius for light, for open hearings, for the uncovering of secret things," as the playwright Maxwell Anderson has Socrates say in *Barefoot in Athens*.

> Athens is driven and made miraculous by the same urge that has sent me searching your streets! It is the Athenian search for truth, the Athenian hunger for facts, the endless curiosity of the Athenian mind, that has made Athens unlike any other city. Shut out the light and close our millions and we shall be like a million cities of the past that came up out of the mud, and worshipped darkness a little while, and went back, forgotten, into darkness.

meaningful in your life that coming to understand it better will be well worth a generous amount of thinking time.

Plan to proceed through the following steps over at least two weeks. This will provide time for various kinds of critical examination: introspection, reflection, self-inquiry, conversations with others, recalling and consulting sources of opinion or facts, etc.

The result may well be the confirmation and indeed deepening of your commitment to your belief, as you remind yourself of the compelling reasons behind it. Or it may reveal that the sources of the belief are not as convincing as you once assumed. Either way, you will understand much better how you come by your convictions and how you might develop them in the future.

   a. Select one of your beliefs, such as . . . (examples from areas including physical/mental health, religion, politics, child rearing).

b. Identify the prime source, or more than one if appropriate, of this belief. ("I have come to this conviction because . . .") Write down the reasons, evidence, and experiences that have led you to this belief. (Another useful exercise to do here is "The Whys," on pages 31–32.)

c. Using this set of criteria, assess the reasons, evidence, and experiences for their accuracy and strength:

- Authorities

- References

- Factual evidence

- Personal experience

d. Rate the validity of the source or sources you identified on a scale of 1–4:

1. *Unquestionable validity:* Belief must be true, valid, and relevant to my present circumstances.

2. *Excellent validity:* Belief is supported by considerable evidence; it is logical and relevant to me now.

3. *Moderate validity:* Belief is supported by substantial evidence but should be reexamined to see whether changed conditions require that it be modified.

4. *Low validity:* Belief cannot be supported by convincing evidence and should be reformulated.

Now, if you rated the belief lower than "1" (Unquestionable validity), formulate the opposing or alternate belief of each of the those you listed in step 2 above. For example, you might list the following as an alternate to the first belief, "Career success depends primarily on hard work . . .":

Career success depends primarily on contacts and connections in your field and socially.

e. See the other side: Describe the point of view of the opposing view, and identify some of the reasons and evidence that might encourage someone to hold that belief. Consider modifying it if you are convinced by this reexamination.

f. Evaluate your new position on this belief according to the following criteria and any others you feel are relevant in this case:

- How well is your belief supported by the evidence and by sound arguments?

- How well does your belief explain the facts?

- Is your belief consistent with your other beliefs about the world?

 ### 9. *Cultivate skepticism as a virtue.*

In this exercise you will upgrade what Professor Neil Postman of New York University calls your "crap detector." The term is from Ernest Hemingway, who said that it was one of the writer's most important tools.

Each day, keep an eye peeled for the most telling instance of lying, deceiving, and distortion or concealment of the truth. This will take no extra time at all, since these messages and images are thrust at you continually, unless you live in a cabin at Walden Pond without a television set or computer. For example:

- Billboards

- Advertising flyers

- Newspapers

- Commercials on radio or TV (and sometimes the newscasts!)

- Opinions thrust on us by other people.

For the top choice each day, identify the technique of deception or distortion being used. (It's going to be a hard call!) Share your examples with friends and colleagues, and invite their comments and observations.

 ## 10. *Craft a sound opinion on a current issue.*

In this exercise, you'll do what Socrates did on those 364 days each year when his conversations in the agora did *not* reach the level that warranted being reported as one of the dialogues! On those days, he listened. Often, he professed ignorance and positioned himself as "seeking to learn from those who know more than I do." (This was one of the expressions of his famed Socratic irony.)

He identified in his own mind the questions and issues that needed clarification. He considered how those issues might best be formulated for profitable discussion. He asked questions to enrich and deepen his understanding. The reason Socrates did all this preparatory work is that it was immensely rewarding. It sharpened his mind, and it enabled him to formulate, discuss, and resolve issues.

Critical thinking is not merely a negative activity. Its ultimate purpose is to cut through the crap and develop sound opinions that impel intelligent, effective action.

In this exercise, you will formulate your own well-tested viewpoint on a current issue. It will be an issue that is being widely discussed this week or month, so that you will have plenty of opportunities to use these techniques in conversations with friends and colleagues.

The entire process will take roughly two weeks, but, like Socrates, you will be learning in a rewarding way throughout the process. And by the end, you will have formulated your own position in a way you may never have done before.

The difference will be that you will *not* be following the pattern that most of us fall into in discussing such current issues. We choose a position prematurely, then defend it vigorously rather than benefiting from really hearing the opinions of others. Rather, you will be quietly pursuing another strategy, one that is likely to win you fresh recognition as a good conversationalist, as well as upgrade your thinking.

SOCRATES' LEARNING

Socrates immersed himself in the cutting-edge intellectual work of his day, then transcended it. He took advantage of the fact that the most exciting thinkers in the Western world were drawn to Athens. He sought them out, learned what they had to teach, then challenged what he had learned to enhance his own understanding.

As a young man, Socrates was impressed by Anaxagoras, brought to Athens by Pericles and dubbed "The Mind." He became notorious for speculating, after examining a meteorite, that the sky was populated not by gods but by celestial objects and that the sun was a great fiery orb and the moon shone by its light.

Socrates was impressed by this daring thinking and also, one must assume, by the fact that the Athenians eventually grew intolerant of Anaxagoras, brought him up on charges of impiety, and exiled him!

The opening of Plato's dialogue "Protagoras" portrays how avidly the Athenians welcomed visiting sages. Socrates describes how a friend comes rushing to his house before dawn:

"Early this morning he gave me a tremendous thump with his staff at my door; someone opened to him, and he came rushing in and bawled out: 'Socrates, are you awake or asleep?'

"I knew his voice, and said: 'Hippocrates, is that you? Why have you come at this unearthly hour?'"

"I bring the best news," he exclaimed. He drew nearer to me and said: 'Protagoras is come.'"

Whereupon Socrates and his friend make their way to the home of Callias, where Socrates goes toe-to-toe with the famed sophist visiting Athens from Thrace. They argue about the nature of virtue, and it's one of the all-time heavyweight matches in the history of philosophy. At the end Protagoras declares graciously: "I cannot but applaud your energy and your conduct of the argument." You can read their dialogue and decide for yourself how well Socrates did, in Plato's "Protagoras."

By the age of thirty-five, Socrates had transcended his teachers. He invented his own field and method of inquiry. Socrates realized that his own calling was not to understand the physical world, like Anaxagoras, but to probe the human one. Athenians began to say that he had brought philosophy down from the heavens and into the affairs of men and women. To explore this new realm, he needed a new method—asking questions—which revealed people's motivations, values, and ideas about human nature.

You will use a five-step process, by asking questions and listening for clarification of the following steps. Each step must be over one day in duration, in order to permit you to "sleep on it."

Days 1–3: LISTEN without judgment and with an open mind as people express themselves on the issue. Note particularly how the way people *frame* an issue signals their whole point of view, e.g., "pro-life" versus "pro-choice."

Days 4–5: ACKNOWLEDGE the different points of view on the issue by expressing them in your own words, reflecting them back, and getting feedback on the accuracy of your paraphrase.

Days 6–8: EVALUATE the soundness of the arguments for each point of view on the basis of evidence, logic, relevance, and other appropriate criteria.

Days 9–10: Consider the CONSEQUENCES of each position.

Days 11–14: EXPRESS your own opinion and listen to the feedback, criticisms, and reactions.

 11. Use "experts" wisely.

Socrates started his lifelong quest by going to the experts, as you will recall from page 136. He went to Athens' foremost political leaders, poets, philosophers, and businesspeople, each of whom had definitive answers to his questions. However, when Socrates questioned them about the reasons or evidence for their views, it became apparent that they did not know what they were talking about.

We, too, live in a world of purported experts. We are bombarded with authoritative judgments and opinions. We, like Socrates, need the tools to judge among them.

Our world is too complex for us to examine the evidence on every issue in which we need to make up our minds. So we need to find and use experts we can trust—individuals and organizations that have demonstrated to us that they have the expert knowledge, the objectivity, and the integrity to provide reliable guidance.

For example, I rely on such organizations as Consumers Union for advice about products and services, Scientists in the Public Interest for interpreting research on nutrition and the environment, and various programs on PBS and National Public Radio for information about subjects ranging from brain research to media integrity.

THE SOCRATIC TRAVELER

Socrates felt about Athens much the way Thoreau felt when he said, "I have traveled much in Concord." Like Thoreau, Socrates could travel much in his home city because the outstanding people of his time were drawn there. By seeking them out for his mental adventuring and growth, he obviated the need for travel.

In our world, however, we must often leave home to find diversity and stimulation. When we do, we can get the most from our travels by being a "Socratic traveler." Here's how:

1. Be a Socratic traveler by freeing your mind from preconceptions about your destination so that you can see it with fresh eyes.

2. Be a Socratic traveler by asking good questions about the places and people you visit before, during, and after your trip.

3. Be a Socratic traveler by seeking out *experiences,* not just things to buy.

4. Be a Socratic traveler by looking for the *values* that motivate the people you visit.

5. Be a Socratic traveler by asking what you can learn about *yourself* in the particular places and among the people you meet.

6. Be a Socratic traveler by seeking out the most interesting range of different people and places.

7. Be a Socratic traveler by coming home with your soul strengthened by your travels.

We'll start, as Socrates did, by identifying the pseudoexperts. You will go on a safari, a big-game hunt in which your prey will be to bag a "pseudoexpert." Bagging one of these critters will be a bracing reminder that you can defend yourself against such beasts.

In the second part, you will assemble your own "kitchen cabinet" of individuals and organizations whom you have learned to trust and rely on for forming your opinions on issues you care about.

Part One: The Pseudoexpert Safari

You will evaluate a significant "scientific" opinion in a field of importance to you. These criteria come from the superb field guide *Trust Us, We're Experts!*, written for the Center for Media and Democracy by Sheldon Rampton and John Stauber.

First, select a research report on a topic meaningful to you. For example, the top websites on medical and health matters provide on-line access to scientific papers on the findings they report. Examine the report using the following tools of inquiry:

Margin of error

Our general respect for scientific findings is well founded. Scientists have developed a system of detecting errors that is more effective than those of most areas of inquiry. There are standards of evidence, review processes, and a "culture" that supports—and even applauds—people who make a compelling case against the conventional wisdom. However, most scientific findings have a margin of error. In fact, one of the fastest ways to ascertain a researcher's scientific integrity is to ask: "Are there any possible flaws in your study?" An honest investigator will always acknowledge possible flaws. Other questions to ask are:

- Is there enough information to warrant the conclusions?

- Was the study submitted to peer review? (Was it published in a reputable scientific journal?)

- Are the results consistent with those from other studies performed by other researchers?

- Is there a consensus among other experts in the field?

- Who disagrees with the findings, and why?

Follow the Money

Research costs money, and it is always smart to ask where the money is coming from. Where did the funds for the study come from? Who employs the researchers? Are there any disclosures in the study about the researchers' connections as consultants or advisors to organizations with a vested interest in the findings?

A great deal of medical research these days is funded by pharmaceutical companies with a powerful vested interest in the results. Such research is usually reliable if it appears in "peer-reviewed" journals where it has been critically examined by independent researchers. However, investigators who receive such funding often must agree that their findings will not be published unless approved by the corporate sponsor.

The Mask of Neutrality

Many organizations with hidden political agendas operate under names that conceal or belie their mission. "Front groups" sponsored by corporations and industries, as well as politically oriented "think tanks," like to fly under flags that sound neutral.

Here are some examples of groups that despite their names are actually advocates of corporate interests:

The Advancement of Sound Science Coalition

Citizens for Sensible Control of Acid Rain

Citizens for Sound Environmental Policy

Council for Solid Waste Solutions

Foundation for Clean Air Progress

National Environmental Policy Institute

National Wilderness Institute

Science and Environmental Policy Project

On a somewhat loftier but no less pernicious level are the political and cultural think tanks that abound, particularly in Washington. Often they have a decided political bias, and sometimes they are shameless fronts for intellectualizing the interests of their corporate sponsors. Yet you will see these "resident scholars" or "senior fellows" on TV as pundits, and read their op-ed pieces or columns in newspapers and magazines.

Think tanks like this may lean to the Right or the Left, but there are twice as many on the conservative side, and they are much better funded. The authors of *Trust Us, We're Experts!* write: "So much money now flows in that the three leading conservative think tanks—Heritage, the American Enterprise Institute, and the Cato Institute—took in more contributions during the 1997–98 congressional cycle than all the so-called 'soft money' contributions to the Republican National Committee."

PART TWO: RECRUITING YOUR "KITCHEN CABINET" OF RELIABLE AND TRUSTWORTHY EXPERTS

We can't investigate for ourselves each issue on which we need to make a decision. So we need to identify those experts in each area whom we *can* trust. Recruit your "kitchen cabinet" of reliable and trustworthy experts by:

- Keeping an eye peeled for experts on issues of concern to you who write objectively, understandably, and credibly; then continuing to benefit from their views through their regular writings or websites.

- Identifying newsletters and magazines that provide fair, clear, up-to-date analysis of your major issues.

- Getting involved with a study group or activist group on one of your chief issues. The interchange with other intelligent people who are tracking the issue can greatly help clarify the conflicting points of view.

12. Is the campus a fortress of free thinking?

We like to believe that our college and university campuses are bastions of unfettered thought and speech. Certainly, most academics and intellectuals believe they should be. Professor Edward Said of Columbia University, for example, contends that the role of the university is basically Socratic: "to unsettle and oppose, to test all orthodoxies, to offer routes by which young minds may travel from one culture or value system to another." But the limitations on free speech on our campuses was revealed by a provocative experiment conducted by a pair of activist-intellectuals.

David Horowitz, a conservative, initiated the experiment by seeking to purchase a full-page ad in campus newspapers on a dozen campuses considered liberally oriented, among them Harvard and Columbia. The ad opposed the idea that America should consider paying reparations to African-Americans to compensate them for the depredations and economic costs of slavery. His ad was refused by all the papers he approached. Horowitz was seeking to demonstrate that American campuses were practicing a liberally oriented "political correctness."

But David Maizell, a liberal professor, gave Horowitz's provocation an additional twist. He submitted an ad arguing that a certain passage in the Old Testament portrays God as encouraging abortion. He submitted his ad to a dozen conservative schools, not just Christian ones but a number of state schools and private but secular colleges. Only one school agreed to run his ad.

Maizell's point was that, taken together, Horowitz's provocation and his own did not reveal a *liberal* bias. Rather, the two actions revealed that resistance to unpopular or heterodox views is the rule on ALL college campuses, despite the fact that these institutions are considered to be the prime venues for free, unfettered discussion of basic issues and values.

 ## 13. Be your own gadfly.

At least once a month (perhaps on a plane flight where you have a wide choice of free magazines), purposely spend a half-hour reading a magazine with a viewpoint completely contrary to your own. Or listen to a television or radio discussion program of that kind. For example, if your orientation is liberal and progressive, then read respectfully and openly *National Review* or a similar conservative journal. If you are conservative yourself, choose *The Nation* or one of its liberal cousins. When you come across an opinion or argument that really rattles your cage, ask yourself these questions to test the validity of the belief of yours that it challenges:

- Where and when did you adopt your position?

- What evidence or logic would you use to support your belief, and is it *really* more compelling than what you are reading?

- Are any facts or arguments being presented that you have not really taken into account before?

- Can you appreciate why the argument being presented could be convincing to the person presenting it and to the many readers who find it convincing?

- Can you develop any facts or insights that would make you or the author you are reading change position?

- Are there any circumstances or situations that would make the position in the magazine more acceptable or understandable?

- Are there any ways in which the view you are reading could be reconciled, even partially, with your own?

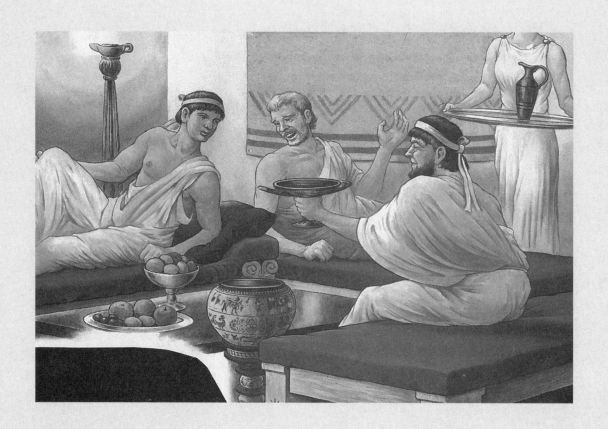

CHAPTER

GROW WITH FRIENDS

When a group of friends have enjoyed fine conversation together, you will find that suddenly something extraordinary happens. As they are speaking, it's as if a spark ignites, passing from one speaker to another, and as it travels, it gathers strength, building into a warm and illuminating flame of mutual understanding which none of them could have achieved alone.

SOCRATES, IN PLATO'S "CRITIAS"

THE GUESTS ARE STARTING to arrive for a dinner party at the start of Plato's dialogue, the "Symposium." The host, the playwright Agathon, had carried off the top prize at the annual festival of new plays at the Theater of Dionysus. To celebrate his triumph, he has invited a diverse group for the unique blend of supper and socializing that the Athenians called a "symposium."

The food and wines are superb, of course, and they are served by a staff of highly attractive young people, to the delight of the guests who lie on couches as they dine, talk, and flirt. What more could one ask of an evening?

Plenty, when Socrates is one of the guests. He was invited to dinner practically every evening, because once he arrived the conversation always crackled with energy, relevance, and wit.

As soon as he arrives, Socrates makes some comments about why he enjoys and benefits from such occasions and how he gets the most out of them.

AGATHON: Socrates! Over here. Sit next to me. You're looking marvelous!

SOCRATES: Delighted to see you, Agathon, and congratulations on your triumph last week. I've never had such success myself in pleasing the crowd!

AGATHON: Thank you, my friend. But I didn't pull you over here to get complimented. I know our topic for this evening is a favorite of yours, and I'm eager to hear what you have to say, before the others. Can you tell me your position?

SOCRATES: I would if I could, Agathon, but I'm afraid I can't. Even if I did have the answer, there's no way I could pour my understanding into your mind, like a full glass dumping into an empty one. Only trivial notions can be conveyed that way.

AGATHON: Understood, Socrates. It's just that you always seem to have given such careful thought to our topic of the evening at one of these symposia that I assumed you'd have the answer all worked out.

SOCRATES: I appreciate that, Agathon, and of course I have prepared well for our dialogue. These discussions are my main way of becoming the best Socrates I can be. But if I just wanted to speak my own thoughts out loud, I could talk to a mirror, without the bother of leaving my house.

I've come here because I'll only be sure I've done my best thinking, when I hear others, and submit to the exhilarating discipline of the dialogue. All of us are smarter than any of us.

For Socrates and his friends, conversations like this were one of the chief ways to live well. They enjoyed and benefited from them in several ways that we, too, might find rewarding.

First of all, the participants were willing to rise above the level of ninety-nine percent of everyday conversations. "We descend to meet," Thoreau observed sharply. Socrates and his friends saw conversation, dialogue, meeting together as important and energizing, so they made it so!

Second, their dialogues clarified the values by which they lived. These conversations stimulated them to express their own opinions and have others fully hear and respond to them. Then, they listened fully to alternative views and were challenged to correct their own lazy or fallacious concepts.

Third, the process of engaging in such conversations honed their minds, whatever the topic. Today, mental health experts proclaim the necessity for just this kind of interaction for the robust development of our brains, from infancy to old age. "Use it or lose it" has become a commandment for mental well-being, and one of the most readily available and powerful ways to do that is by putting "more thought in your talk."

SOCRATES' SPIRIT IN OUR TIME

We all need our Socratic friends and mentors just as Socrates and his friends needed each other. We all have felt the impact of those who made us realize that we were not fulfilling our potential, who raised challenging questions about what we were doing with our life. But in our time these friends and mentors take different forms and have different names. We often call them "consultants," "executive coaches," "trainers," "motivational speakers," . . . or "therapists."

This last label should be no surprise: Therapists play much the same role in our lives that philosophers did in Socrates' Athens. We tend to think of philosophers as cloistered academics with little to tell us about how to live our lives. But in Socrates' time, they were robust and influential gurus to those seeking advice about success, happiness, and fulfillment. So it should be no surprise that a wonderful example of a Socratic friend and mentor should involve two psychiatrists.

The first of them, Arnold Beisser, was a lot like one of the fifth-century Athenians whom Socrates confronted in the streets of Athens. "From the standpoint of the outer world," Beisser recalls, "I was doing pretty well. I had become the director of a training program for psychiatrists, I have a lovely wife . . . So I kept my mouth shut, did my work . . . and that was that! But I was miserable. This is not who I really am, I thought."

Beisser had good reason for satisfaction with what he had achieved. He could justly be proud and pleased at having graduated from medical school and found the love of his life, despite the fact that he is paralyzed from the neck down from polio. Beisser responded to his inner turmoil by intentionally seeking the kind of teacher, friend, and mentor who could change his life. And this quest culminated with his finding himself inviting into his own home a modern-day Socrates!

Beisser's job gave him the opportunity to bring colleagues to his facility from throughout the country. "I would invite these men and women to stay with us, so that I not only participated in their daytime teaching activities, but I also had them to myself in the evenings. I did my best to learn all I could. Although it was not conscious, I think I was secretly seeking my own salvation."

It came in the form of a Socratic figure, a man with "an unconventional lifestyle, disrespect for authority, and [a] strongly held belief in fostering and supporting individual freedom and choice in all he encountered." This Socratic figure was Fritz Perls, founder of Gestalt therapy in the United States. Perls had other Socratic traits, such as blunt candor. On first meeting Beisser in his wheelchair, Perls's first question was "What happened to you?" "He said it with such childlike innocence and wonder that I did not take offense," recalls Beisser. "His refreshingly candid reaction showed nothing more than honest interest. It was a relief."

As they got acquainted, Perls listened and questioned in true Socratic style, fixing on key terms and showing Beisser how he had accepted stock meanings that now needed to be questioned. "He listened carefully, and using my own words, showed me what I had said. This made my words stand out, so even I could see that I had choices I had not seen before."

Like Socrates, Perls was unique for his intimate approach and the consistency of his convictions. "Our relationship was different from the impersonal ones I had known before when I was in analysis," Beisser reports. "With Fritz, everything was personal, and there was no way to avoid what was real. I saw him under many different circumstances, and he was always the same person. Since he was living in our house, I saw him at dinner, at work, on awakening, and when retiring. He loves all of life equally—each person was unique and yet the same for him. He lived as he believed."

Like Socrates, Perls had no interest in or concern for posterity, or for creating disciples or institutions to convey his ideas. The Gestalt therapy centers that sprang up around the country received little or no support from him. "He lived as he believed," concludes Beisser, "in this elusive moment as if it were forever."

What had this latter-day Socrates done for Beisser?

> There comes a time in middle life when it becomes necessary to find a means of integrating who you were when growing up with who you really want to be. Most of us need a guide to help us find our way . . . Fritz was mine, and in the process opened me to finding others too. He was my first spiritual guide (although he would never have used those words). He sought the love and truth and beauty that lay beneath all that was mundane and seamy. He was loving without being possessive, and he was wise in the ways I needed him to be.

CHALLENGES, EXPLORATIONS, AND APPLICATIONS

 1. Discover what you value most in conversations.

Socrates did not have a single goal for his encounters with his friends. He enriched his life through conversation and dialogue in a wide variety of ways. Our encounters, too, can yield a multitude of delights and benefits, ranging from the enjoyable and exhilarating to the deep-reaching and profound. For example, here is the view of psychologist Herbert Otto:

> One of the most important things is to surround yourself with people who help you to validate the reasons for your existence or help you to explore the basic existential questions: What are you here for? What's life all about? And to help you to clarify whether your behavior is consonant with your values.
>
> Of course, it goes without saying that [these friends] offer you caring, love, enhancing of your self-esteem, giving you the

Strengthening Your Socratic Spirit

- Are you keenly aware of the things you value most in conversations with your friends? (Exercise #1)

- Can you spark an interesting conversation with virtually anyone in any situation? (Exercise #2)

- Do you know how to turn any social occasion into a "symposium"? (Exercise #3)

- Are you aware of the basic structure of a good conversation? (Exercise #4)

- Would you like to launch your own "Socrates' Café"? (Exercise #5)

- Would you like to engage in great conversations on-line? (Exercise #6)

- Do you use significant conversations as a way of upgrading your workplace? (Exercise #7)

- Do you participate in "democracy as discussion" to help create a better world? (Exercise #8)

strokes that you don't get anywhere else. And they should stimulate your creativity. Surrounding yourself with people who turn you on will stimulate you creatively. When it comes down to doing it, being with people who do this for you, or with whom you are experiencing this together, that's where I think we're fantastically short in our culture.

Think of the three best conversations you have had over the past month. Recall high points from them, or the overall atmosphere that made them so enjoyable or powerful for you. Now note three qualities of each of these conversations.

Here are some of the qualities that people in my workshops frequently come up with:

- Originality

- Tolerance

- Tact

- Sincerity

- Wit and humor

- Relevance

- Brevity

- Clarity

- Concreteness

- Charm

Which ones do you value in talking with other people?

 2. Engage in dialogue with anyone, anywhere.

Socrates demonstrates that lively and valuable conversations can occur with anyone, anywhere, anytime. They do not have to take place in formal surroundings, on weighty topics, or among "special" people. Quite the reverse: Such conversations can often elicit the extraordinary in any time, place, and person.

Following in Socrates' footsteps, Maurice Berger, a cultural historian and critic, hops aboard a bus in Manhattan and sparks fascinating dialogues. "I call these my back-of-the-bus conversations," he explains.

When I board the bus, usually at a stop near the New School University where I work, I'm in the heart of Greenwich Village, an area of upper-middle-class, mostly white professionals. By the time I get off the bus, a block from my apartment at Ninety-sixth Street and West End Avenue, many of the passengers are black and Hispanic, the residents of Har-

SOCRATES ON FRIENDSHIP

"Good friends," Socrates said, "give me greater satisfaction than other men get from good horses or dogs or game-cocks. If I have anything good, I teach it to my friends, and I place them with others from whom I think they will make some gain. There is no possession more valuable than a good and faithful friend."

lem, Washington Heights, and Inwood north of Ninety-sixth Street.

I sit in the back of the bus, where passengers sit facing each other rather than in tight rows. New York is a place where people rarely look each other in the eye, let alone talk to each other about things that matter. I find that direct address can be disarming. It can soften people's defensive posture.

Most people are not used to being asked questions. They don't think their answers matter. Yet, here I was asking questions that mattered, looking these people directly in the eye to hear what *they* think. Almost everyone I spoke to—tourists, workers from the suburbs, native New Yorkers—responded. Before I knew it, I'd have these wonderful group conversations.

I have found that even as a white person, I'm regularly able to dialogue with people of color. Most New Yorkers, fearful of rejection or untrusting of people who are different from them, stick to people from their own communities. Yet, I have observed that to ask a stranger a question directly and kindly is more often than not the way to get an answer in this city.

As this final comment suggests, Berger's back-of-the-bus conversations have more than personal significance. They are his way of doing something vitally important for our social and political future: bridging the gap between "different" people in our society. His acclaimed book *White Lies: Race and the Myths of Whiteness* (Farrar, Straus & Giroux, 1999) is a masterly exploration of this theme, and from his position as senior fellow at the Vera List Center for Art and Politics at the New School University, he exerts national influence among those working for a truly compassionate society.

 3. Turn any social occasion into a "symposium."

Socrates found an opportunity every day to shift his conversations onto more interesting, exciting, important ground. We can follow in his footsteps, as does Douglass Cater, the noted writer on politics and culture. He uses a bold strategy for elevating the conversation at dinner parties.

After people have run through their small talk, Cater politely broaches whether the group might want to devote a few minutes to an issue or problem that everyone should find of interest. If the group is agreeable, he poses the question or issue and solicits initial responses from each person, round-robin fashion. After everyone has expressed himself or herself on the subject, Cater encourages an interchange sparked by the variety of views. This turns what might otherwise be a mundane evening into one that is enjoyable and often profitable. It just requires that someone take the lead in inviting people to focus on one interesting topic for some "big talk."

Another way to lift the level of conversation is to hone in on the special reason or purpose that has brought people together. Oddly, you will frequently find that no one is actually honoring that reason or purpose, but they are delighted to when asked.

For example, here's what I did at a little opening of an exhibition of paintings by local artists in my community. You would think that the reason or purpose of such a gathering would be to appreciate the artists' paintings, yet from previous experience, I knew that little of that actually occurs. Quite the contrary. People mostly stand around ignoring the paintings, after a cursory "Oh, that's very nice." So I made myself a brightly colored button to wear on my lapel that read:

> Please help me
> to appreciate
> your painting

WHAT HAPPENED AT AN ATHENIAN SYMPOSIUM?

The Athenian symposium was a males-only evening of eating, drinking, conversing, and enjoying intimate entertainment. When you arrived for a symposium at the home of a well-to-do Athenian, you were greeted by a servant who relieved you of your cloak and sandals, then gave you a bowl to wash your hands in, before you reclined on a couch with the other guests. You might be wreathed with leaves or flowers.

Before the drinking began, the guests thanked Zeus by pouring libations of wine on the ground. Then the slaves offered each man a glass of fragrant wine, *propoma*. Later came the food, served on clay or metal plates. You would eat with your fingers (there were knives and spoons, but no forks) and wipe your hands on the bread, which was tossed to the dogs.

The second glass of wine was diluted with water, the amount of which was determined by the host, the symposiarch. Fruits, nuts, and sweetmeats were served with the wine.

All the while there was singing to the accompaniment of the flute, played by a girl, or a recital of poems. The lyre was passed from one to another so each guest had a chance to play. The wealthier hosts invited musicians, singers, and dancing girls.

The conversation gathered momentum, ranging over a variety of subjects, from gossip to philosophy. Guests vied with one another to display their wit, education, and profundity.

In the course of an hour, nine different artists were delighted to show me their painting and tell me what they were trying to do, how it delighted them, why they chose it to exhibit, and how it related to other paintings in the show. They helped me see in their paintings things like:

Layers—for me the interest is in how I can create the sense of density, of levels beneath levels, which is how I feel our minds are . . .

The balance of colors and forms—and notice how no matter how you turn the painting, it's still satisfying that way—like this sculpture over here, that you can walk right around, and it looks great from any angle.

I wanted to express in these two faces how much each person is involved in their own feelings, and yet they are a couple; they connect with each other in ways which they might not even realize, like the way the shapes of their heads and the look in their eyes is similar.

Socrates did this all the time: At the potter's he asked about what made a good pot; at the gymnasium he inquired about what made a beautiful body; at the sophists' lectures he questioned what made a good argument. From these conversations he learned more than technical information; he gathered the grist for speculating on what made for excellence in any area of human activity.

 ### 4. Recognize the drama of a good conversation.

Socrates had an innate sense of the drama of a good conversation. We can acquire such a sense ourselves and use it to orchestrate our discussions with friends.

A good conversation has the same shape as a good movie, play, or musical composition: a beginning, a middle, and an end. One of the reasons so many conversations are boring is that they do not have any shape or progression: They are like dull, mechanical work—the same at each point in the process.

In a good conversation, as Mortimer Adler tellingly put it,

> *the beginning* should set the stage by focusing on the theme— the problem, the question, the subject to be discussed.
>
> *The middle,* which should run a longer time, should be devoted to exploring the problem, the question, or subject and should elicit all the differences of opinion that are relevant to it, with support for these opinions.
>
> *The end* should bring the conversation to a conclusion— a decision reached if the conversation has a practical purpose, a position agreed upon if the matter is theoretical. If agreement is beyond reach, then the conclusion may involve suspended judgment and the tabling of the matter in question for further conversation, and perhaps resolution, at a later time.

That last, by the way, is the ending of almost all of Socrates' dialogues, so I would give it more prominence than Adler does. Rather than being a second-best option, you should regard it as the natural outcome of most such conversations. The point is not to make a decision or even reach a consensus but to explore different perspectives, deepen understanding and sympathy, and perhaps stimulate imagination and creativity.

Such a pleasingly shaped conversation can be a unique joy, as Adler describes: "An hour of good conversation is like an hour of good amateur sport. It can be more than simply pleasurable; it can be hilariously amusing, especially if the participants observe good manners and there is an equal give and take."

 ## 5. Launch your own Socrates Café.

"Socrates models for us philosophy in practice," proclaims Chris Phillips, who is a kind of Johnny Appleseed for groups throughout the country. "For him, philosophy is a way of living, something that any of us can do. The Socratic method is a way to seek truths by your own lights; it is a system, a spirit, a method, a type of philosophical inquiry, an intellectual technique, all rolled into one."

The Socrates Café is a popular form of Socratic dialogue vigorously championed by Phillips in his book of the same title. The purpose is to "bring philosophy back to the people," to give "ordinary people" the opportunity to show how extraordinary they can become when challenged with meaty issues in a supportive environment. Hundreds of Socrates Café groups launched by Chris or inspired by his book meet regularly in bookstores, senior centers, and other venues to engage in lively conversations about "big questions": Who are we? What is truth? What is a friend? What is "home"?

The story of how Socrates Café started is a stirring tale of Socratic self-examination and high purpose. A decade ago, Chris Phillips found himself at a turning point in his life. He had left behind him a meaningless job and a failed marriage. "I decided to start asking forward-looking questions, questions that would help me make a radical transformation in my life," he recalls. "I began asking questions like 'What calling will make me feel that I am getting the most out of my mortal moment?'"

When the answer came, it was an epiphany: "I wanted to be a philosopher on the model of Socrates! I wanted to hold Socratic dialogues!" That

"HE SEEMS TO SEE INTO MY SOUL"

What did it feel like to be a friend of Socrates? Here is the most famous description, spoken by Alcibiades at the dinner party portrayed in the "Symposium."

It's not that I haven't heard gifted speakers before, but none of them, not even Pericles, moved me this much. I recognized that they spoke well, but they didn't have Socrates' insight. When he speaks to me he speaks just to *me*. Under his searching questions, I realize that I'm not living true to myself, and that I need to do something about it.

When I am in conversation with him, I'm so moved by the power of his ideas that I feel it in my body: my heart beats faster, and tears will well up in my eyes. I've seen the same thing happening to others.

Don't deny it, Socrates. Right now, at this moment, I know that if I let you start asking me your questions, the same thing would happen to me again. That's why I want to keep talking and stay drunk: it's the only way to avoid your demonstrating that I need to get control of myself!

vision launched him on a five-year trek throughout the United States, starting Socrates Café groups at bookstores, churches, and other venues. His book *Socrates Café* relates this wonderful adventure and gives comprehensive instructions for those who wish to start their own group.

Chris suggests the following steps, which you can read about in more detail on his website, www.philosopher.org.

1. Ask the participants to propose questions for discussion. Jot them down, and when everyone has had a chance to contribute, take a vote on which one the group wants to tackle first. (You can come back to the others eventually.)

2. To start with, let the discussion flow freely.

3. When appropriate, begin to probe one of the most interesting

statements by asking for concrete examples of an abstraction or for the facts or logic behind a statement.

4. Once points of view are explained, ask Socratic questions like:

  • Is there another side to this?

  • Are there alternative viewpoints?

  • Are there assumptions built into this statement, or implications that we should discuss?

  • Are disparate items being lumped together?

  • Are there logical inconsistencies?

5. Keep bringing more new people into the discussion.

To illustrate these principles, Chris cites a person in one of his sessions who asked, "How can we overcome alienation?" Among the questions Chris would ask to explore this topic are:

  • Do we always *want* to overcome alienation? Could it be productive and stimulating, intellectually or artistically?

  • What do we really *mean* by "alienation"? What does it mean to overcome it?

  • Are there different *kinds* or *degrees* of alienation?

Chris's final piece of advice on facilitating a Socrates Café is "Just keep asking yourself: 'What would Socrates do?'" By that he doesn't mean you should mechanically ply people with questions. As he explains:

It wasn't wasn't merely that Socrates presented himself, or posed, as a perplexed inquirer—he *was* a wonderfully perplexed inquirer. And it wasn't just that he was trying to show us that we know far less than we think we do, but rather, that he was stressing that knowledge is hard-won, that perhaps we

are always ignorant to some degree (perhaps to some great degree), but that through a certain type of inquiry we can become less and less ignorant.

So Socrates wasn't feigning ignorance to lead others to
recognize their own ignorance, but rather, as a perplexed soul,
he inspired other perplexed souls to inquire with him, so that
together, in this collective inquiry, together they might become
less and less perplexed.

There are other kinds of conversational groups you might find rewarding, such as great books groups, study circles, and "councils." A
good source of basic information about them is *The Joy of Conversation*
by Jaida n'ha Sandra, who describes "salons" that have emerged around
the country.

A salon encourages "big talk"—conversation that goes beyond the
usual trivialities of weather, sports, shopping, TV, and movies (though it
can include provocative, thought-provoking "takes" on even those familiar topics). "When the coffee's strong and the chemistry's right," says
Sandra, "our conversations seem to tap directly into the zeitgeist. One
person's ideas inspire another's and another's. Salons are fun, they're
glamorous. And yet they're simple to produce."

Here are the simple steps to launching your own Socrates Café or salon in your neighborhood:

a. *Recruit your partners*. Decide on several other people to form
   your team to launch the group. You can do it with just one
   other person, or more if you're blessed that way, but not more
   than four in addition to yourself. You want a group that can
   easily and quickly agree on the why and what you are up to.

b. *Plan your group*. Have one meeting at which you discuss the
   following things, and get your consensus down on one sheet
   of paper:

   • Who else—and what other kinds of people—do we want
     to invite?

   • What kinds of topics will we discuss?

- Where should we meet?

- When should we meet?

- Any ground rules at the start?

- What should we name our group?

- How should we promote the group?

- How should we handle "chairing" of the meetings?

- When and where will the first meeting be?

- How should we announce the first meeting?

c. *Announce the first session.*

d. *Hold the first session.* Have some refreshments available for free or for purchase if possible. To warm up the room have music playing when people arrive. Lapel badges with just first names in big bold letters can be helpful to everyone, if it suits your group's style.

Here's one agenda you might use:

1. Initiate personal introductions all around with any "twist" you like.

2. Introduce the topic. A good one for a first session is "What makes a great conversation?" (See #1 above.)

3. Make sure everyone speaks who wants to.

4. If you like, ask the group for suggestions on some of the major questions the planning group discussed (above), e.g., what the group should be called, what's the best day and time to meet, ideas about venue, etc.

5. Discuss possible topics for future sessions.

6. Announce the time and place for the second session and if possible the topic.

SOCRATES AND THE SILENUS

Socrates' homeliness tended to put people off, since the Athenians esteemed physical beauty so highly. So when his friends wanted to introduce someone new to him, they had a little trick to assure that his appearance wasn't an obstacle.

They explained that Socrates was like the little statues of the Silenus, which Athenian craftsmen sold in the agora. These plaster figures portrayed an ugly, drunken, dissolute, paunchy figure. But *inside* some of these little figures, the sculptors imbedded a lovely golden figurine. The problem was that to discover the possible prize within your Silenus you had to be willing break it open, smashing through the external mold to get at the inner treasure.

Getting to know Socrates was like that, his friends observed. You needed to be willing to get past the external appearance, to appreciate the soul within.

6. *Dialogue in Cyberspace*

Socrates would have enjoyed discussions in cyberspace. He was constantly reaching out to talk with new people, but he was confined to face-to-face encounters. We now have an electronic agora—a public space for significant conversations that spans the globe. You can easily find, participate in, and launch computer-based conversational groups.

Sound good? It can be if you find the right venue for you. But it will take some work to do that. Much of the "chat" that goes on in cyberspace is low-grade stuff: "flat, stale, and unprofitable." (A great deal of it is also very often pornographic—the dirty little secret about the tremendous success of the services offering "chat" is that much of it used for sexual purposes.) Moreover, the anonymity of the conversations via computer seems to encourage frivolity and even offensiveness—the so-called flames in which people speak crudely and even violently to each other. So you need to exercise care in seeking out the right "communities" for yourself. But when you find them, they can be immensely rewarding.

People who participate in such conversations as a regular part of their lives are known as Netizens (the on-line version of "Citizens"). They often join on-line communities like The Well, based in San Francisco; Echo, based in New York; or smaller ones, such as The Cellar, headquartered in the back room of Tony Shepps's home in Collegeville, Pennsylvania. ("If the Internet is the world's biggest mall," says Shepps, "we're the friendly coffee shop down the street.")

"What I like is that it's open all hours," said a member of The Cellar, a nurse with two daughters, to writer Dinty Moore, who portrays this group in his delightful little book *The Emperor's Virtual Clothes: The Naked Truth About Internet Culture*. The nurse, with the lovely name Bronwyn, continued: "But you don't have to go anywhere or have anyone over. You don't have to clean the floor, you don't have to stock the fridge, you don't have to worry about a babysitter. You can access it anytime. People are perfectly willing to slap you across the face and say 'you're wrong, wrong, wrong, wrong, wrong, your logic is flawed, everything about this is faulty.' But having said that, though, they are forced to back it up. 'Here's where your logic is flawed.' There is a delightful ability to bat something back and forth until all the meaning is wrung out of it."

This begins to sound, to me, a little like people trying to do what Socrates and his comrades did so nobly in the streets of fifth-century Athens. They engage in high talk about every kind of intellectual topic. They brainstorm and problem-solve together. They criticize one anothers' creations. They pose questions, get answers, and thereby cope more effectively.

The computer makes such conversations global. Joseph Traub, a Columbia University professor, reports: "When I wake up in the morning I turn on my machine and there typically are messages from Japan, China, then from the previous day from Germany, Kiev, Moscow, and so on. When I remember what we used to go through to communicate with, say, Warsaw or Moscow, the 'connectivity' is extraordinary."

Another computer-based conversationalist is Pamela McCorduck, wife of Professor Traub (the two are colleagues of mine at Columbia University), who says: "I spend an hour a day in front of my machine just chatting with people. My social life is infinitely more varied than my parents'. Mainly it has to do with the fact that I meet people on-line who then I want to meet in person."

SOCRATES, "MY MAN!"

A Socratic figure can turn up anywhere, anytime, wherever and whenever people start to talk honestly about things that really matter. The novelist Walter Mosley has portrayed one in several books featuring his hero Socrates Fortlow. When asked how he got that unusual first name, Fortlow explains: "We was poor and country. My mother couldn't afford school so she figured that if she named me after somebody smart then maybe I'd get smart."

Here's the beginning of a typical dialogue between this contemporary Socrates and an Athenianlike African-American who sits next to him at a lunch counter:

Socrates asked, "What kinda work you do, Wilfred?"

"I'm self-employed. I'm a businessman."

"Oh yeah? What kinda business?"

Wilfred smiled and tried to look coy. "What you think?"

"I'd say thief," Socrates answered. He speared a hot yam and pushed it in his mouth.

Wilfred's smile widened but his eyes went cold.

"You got sumpin' against a man makin' a livin'?" he asked.

"Depends."

"'Pends on what?"

"On if it's wrong or not."

"Stealin's stealin', man. It's all the same thing. You got it—I take it."

"If you say so."

"That's what I do say," Wilfred said. "Stealin's right for the man takin' an' wrong fo' the man bein' took. That's all they is to it."

That's just the start. By the time Socrates is through with Wilfred, the young man, like one of Socrates' Athenian friends, has realized that his quick and sure opinion is doubtful at best. You can read the complete dialogue in Mosley's novel *Always Outnumbered, Always Outgunned*.

7. Foster productive conversations at work.

This chapter has purposely focused on the joys and benefits of great conversation in our lives outside of work. But the power of conversation is being rediscovered in the world of work, too.

"Before there were presentations," writes Ian Parker in *The New Yorker,* "there were conversations. . . . I think that we as a people have become unaccustomed to having real conversations with each other, where we actually give and take to arrive at a new answer. We present to each other, instead of discussing."

Leaders in management are recognizing the need to foster genuine conversations in the workplace. For example, HRDQ, one of the most progressive organizations in the field, has developed a series of programs on "Performance Management Through 5 Key Conversations" and "Encouraging Innovation Through 5 Key Conversations." In the first of these, managers learn to develop high-performance employees through collaborative and productive dialogue. They engage employees daily in meaningful, performance-related conversations, and thereby build relationships and get results in a collaborative atmosphere. In the program on Innovation, the focus is on exploring possibilities beyond conventional thinking, encouraging people to stretch their creative abilities, to invite risk taking, and to collaborate on the best ways to navigate through organizational boundaries.

 8. Engage in "Democracy Is a Discussion."

There is one more realm in which the power of conversation is being rediscovered. As democracy sweeps across the world, an extraordinary program called "Democracy Is a Discussion" is promoting deeper understanding of its principles. This project uses the Socratic model of citizens engaging in dialogue about the basic issues of their society—the model that was pioneered in the West's first attempt at a democratic society. It offers each of us the opportunity to launch our own powerful conversation about our way of living together.

Conceived and directed by Sondra Myers in Washington, D.C.,

CONTINUING SOCRATES' "GREAT CONVERSATION"

Socrates' dialogues with his friends set the pattern for our entire Western intellectual tradition. This fact is reflected in the title *The Great Conversation*, which Robert Hutchins gave to his introductory volume in the Great Books of the Western World series, published by Encyclopædia Britannica. Here is how Hutchins expressed the conviction that the Western tradition is embodied in one continuing dialogue initiated by Socrates.

> Whatever the merits of other civilizations in other respects, no civilization is like that of the West in this respect. No other civilization can claim that its defining characteristic is a dialogue of this sort. No dialogue in any other civilization can compare with that of the West in the number of great works of the mind that have contributed to this dialogue. The goal toward which Western society moves is the civilization of the *Dialogue*. The spirit of Western civilization is the spirit of inquiry. Nothing is to remain undiscussed. Everybody is to speak his mind. No proposition is to be left unexamined. The exchange of ideas is held to be the path to the realization of the potentialities of the race.

My personal favorite example of this kind of dialogue is a group that meets monthly at Columbia University in New York City. It is one of eighty-odd University Seminars that, taken together, may be the hardiest revival of the Socratic dialogues in our time. The University Seminars were launched after World War II by Margaret Mead and other radical intellectuals who wanted to bring university-based learning to bear on major world problems.

The seminars are frankly based on the Socratic model. "Long before I went to college, I was enchanted with Plato's *Dialogues*," said founding director Frank Tannenbaum. So he was probably the ideal person to devote his life to reviving Socratic conversations as a new way to address the major problems of our world.

The seminars bring together those who think, research, and theorize with those who get things done, set policy, and provide goods and services. There are no lectures, no credits, no examinations, and no diplomas. There is just learning through conversations that are serious but not solemn, learned but passionate, knowledgeable but biased toward action. Their purpose is to enhance the lives of the participants and to help create a better world.

Democracy Is a Discussion provides materials for conversations in informal groups, community and civic organizations, voluntary associations, and academic programs. "We believe that small discussion groups are the very essence of the democratic process," says Myers, who has championed the idea both in the United States and in emerging democracies around the world.

The *Democracy Is a Discussion Handbook* of reading materials and discussion guidelines has been used throughout the United States and distributed in eleven languages courtesy of the U.S. Information Agency. Over 100,000 copies have been distributed worldwide.

More information about this important program is available from Sondra Myers at 1232 22nd Street, NW, Washington, D.C. 20037.

CHAPTER

SPEAK THE TRUTH

It has been my fixed principle
to speak the truth.

SOCRATES, IN PLATO'S "APOLOGY"

IT IS TWO HOURS into the trial of Socrates on an April afternoon. The jury of five hundred is growing restless on their stone benches. They have been harangued since noon by a "tag team" of the three plaintiffs, Meletus, Anytus, and Lycon, who have accused the seventy-year old defendant of "introducing new gods and corrupting the youth."

Now, suddenly, the pace picks up. Socrates begins to speak and lifts the whole debate to a new level. Beginning with his famed "Socratic irony," he summarizes the charges against him, reviews his lifelong mission, and affirms his commitment to the role he created: gadfly to individuals and to the State. For him, this was the supreme act of patriotism: showing one's loyalty not by conformity to the majority but by acting on the highest principles of the community.

Plato's "Apology," in which we find Socrates' speech, is the *locus classicus* for freedom of thought and expression in our Western tradition. It is also a call to each of us to speak the truth in our personal lives, at work, and as citizens.

Well, I don't know how you gentlemen may feel after hearing my accusers. For myself, I must confess that I was rather carried away at times. Not that anything they said was true, you understand!

I think the most impertinent lie Meletus told you was that I'm a clever speaker. I say "impertinent" because you'll soon discover for yourselves what a whopper that was.

He warned you to beware of my presumed eloquence, to watch out for my tricks. Rubbish! You've little to fear on that score from so transparent an old fellow as myself. I'm not an orator—unless the word has come to mean someone who speaks the truth.

And you know, although I'm seventy years old, this happens to be the very first time that I've been brought to court. The usage here is utterly new to me. I couldn't extemporize in courtroom style if I tried. That's why certain eloquent well-wishers offered to compose a defense for me to read aloud. I didn't take them up on it, however. I asked myself whether or not it would be proper for someone of my age and reputation, such as it is, to offer you a set piece like some schoolboy seeking approval. And I decided that it would not be proper.

Instead, I'm going to talk to you just as I always talk. I aim to say whatever comes into my head today. If a foreigner addressed you in his own dialect, not knowing Attic speech, you'd surely excuse his ignorance, his uncouth delivery. Please set yourselves to tolerate, in just that way, an untutored old man's tongue. Disregard my manner, gentlemen, and address your minds to the matter of what I tell you. Remember, that's your job.

I'll begin with the earliest charges brought against me, in times long past. "There's a certain sly fellow named Socrates," people used to say, "who pokes into secrets far beneath the earth and above the heavens. He's a cultist, an atheist, and a born confusionist—a past master at turning sensible conversations inside out. Beware of Socrates! That man can make sheer nonsense appear to outshine plain truth!"

Well, such were the lies told about me by a playwright or two, and repeated ever since by a good many nameless, faceless folk. To tell the truth, I fear these old lies more than anything. I know they must have influenced your minds when you were young and pliable. And I rather despair of helping you to shed your firmly rooted prejudices against me.

Still, the law compels me to defend myself. I hope for all our sakes that I'll succeed, although it does seem hoping against hope.

What, in a nutshell, is the present charge? As I read it, the indictment merely repeats the same old gossip regarding my occult researches on the one hand, and my curiously sinister conversational habits on the other.

I say the gossip lies, and I suggest you put true gossip in its place. A good many men amongst you, gentlemen of the jury, have personally conversed with me in the past. Still more have overheard conversations in which I took part. Now I ask those of you with personal knowledge to tell your companions whether or not you ever heard me discussing sorcery or esoteric science from an insider's viewpoint.

Again, I ask you to declare openly whether or not you ever heard me advise anyone on how to get away with murder in debate. You haven't, have you?

The fact is, I know nothing about such matters. One reason why I've consistently refused to take any money for teaching is that I have no specialties, no secrets, no tricks to impart.

Yet I realize that some of you here may object and say, "Well, Socrates, we have been taught that where there's smoke there's fire. We guess there must be something back of all this rumor and resentment that beclouds you. And, Socrates, you'll make our job much easier for us if you will kindly just confess right now and tell us what the trouble is. What exactly HAVE you done to set half, or more than half, of Athens bitterly against you?"

That would be a reasonable question, it seems to me; a fair request. Therefore I'll do my best to comply with it. The trouble comes down to this: I do in fact possess an extremely peculiar and disturbing sort of wisdom. You'll think I'm joking, perhaps, when I tell you that this wisdom of mine is the true cause of my present troubles. Especially when I go on to reemphasize the fact that my kind of wisdom has nothing sinister or supernatural about it. Anyone who says I traffic in strange powers lies. No, my wisdom is, above all, human, down-to-earth, here-and-now.

I am that gadfly which the gods have sent to sting you Athenians.

Our state, my friends, is like a great steed—powerful and impressive, but lazy and dim. Without the constant provocation by the gadflies, it would grow even more unwitting and unfit.

In the course of the last thirty years, I have not spared anything or anybody, myself included. I have devoted my life to providing this service to my city. I have neglected the things which most men value, such as wealth, military commands, and political appointments.

While I live, I shall never stop showing how things really are in Athens.

It has been my fixed principle that the uncovering of truth could do no harm. I have believed that speaking the truth could injure only what is false among workmen, businessmen, Sophists, statesmen, or gods.

The air of a democracy is only healthy when inquiry bites constantly at the heels of every proposal and every project, even at the foundations of our way of life.

Socrates' commitment to tell the truth had three aspects, as he notes in the "Apology": personal, social, and political. He felt the need to confront individuals who were deluding themselves, social practices that needed scrutiny, and political issues that were misunderstood. As a result, Socrates has always been a mentor for men and women who have felt the need for honesty, personal and public. His name has been invoked from their jail cells by Thoreau, Gandhi, and Martin Luther King, Jr., each imprisoned for acts of civil disobedience. Such dissenters are often recognized in retrospect as having upheld the highest values of their society and culture.

We need our gadflies, whether we call them dissidents, whistle-blowers, mavericks, or even revolutionaries. Every organization, every society, rots from the top when it suppresses or ignores criticism. Healthy organizations as well as healthy societies thrive on what Socrates calls "their freedom, their willingness to look at all the evidence in the search for truth." But this role of challenging the status quo cannot be left to others. Each of us must be a gadfly of sorts, from time to time, in our own way, in our community and organizations, if not on the national level.

Marian Wright Edelman, founder of the Children's Defense Fund, has put it eloquently in her own Socratic "Apology," *The Measure of Our Success*:

Do not think that you have to make big waves in order to contribute. My role model, Sojourner Truth, slave woman, could

THE TRIAL OF SOCRATES

Any citizen or group of citizens in fifth-century Athens could bring charges against another citizen, as Socrates' three accusers did. Wracked by decades of war with Sparta, which had recently resulted in humiliating defeat, the Athenians were looking for scapegoats. Increasingly, Socrates' constant questions came to be seen as a corrosive irritant. His trial took place in a witchhunt atmosphere.

There was no judge in such a trial, nor were there lawyers, which was why training in persuasive speaking by the sophists was so popular. Any citizen might be faced at any time with the need to defend his life, on his feet.

The plaintiffs and the defendant each presented their case to a jury of five hundred fellow citizens chosen by lot. They also had an opportunity to cross-examine each other. The jury voted by placing stones in urns, then the stones were counted. If a verdict of guilty was announced, the defendant had the opportunity to himself propose an appropriate penalty for consideration by the jury.

In Socrates' case, the jury voted closely for guilty: Had thirty-one votes gone the other way, Socrates would have been acquitted. Asked to propose a penalty, Socrates stunned the jury by declaring that since his only "crime" had been to serve the city to the best of his ability as a needed gadfly, he should be "punished" in the same way as Olympic champions or victorious generals: with free food and lodging at the expense of the city for the rest of his life.

Of course, the jurors were aghast at Socrates' arrogance. They had expected him to propose exile, which was what his accusors were probably after. Immediately, Socrates' friends leapt forward to offer to pay a handsome fine. But Socrates would have none of it.

On a second vote, the jury turned against Socrates, decreeing his death by a sizable majority. As Socrates was taken out of the courtroom, a friend exclaimed: "Socrates, I can't bear that you are sentenced to death so unjustly." Socrates quipped back: "Be comforted, my friend. Would you prefer that I had been *justly* sentenced to die?!"

Within days of Socrates' death, the Athenians realized what a tragic mistake they had made. A period of mourning was imposed, and many of the gymnasia and schools were closed. Meletus, one of the prosecutors, was condemned to death, and the other, Anytus, was banished. Later, a statue of Socrates was erected on the Sacred Way, the road leading from Athens to a famed temple.

Plato provides a complete account of the entire trial, including Socrates' cross-examination of his accusers, in the "Apology." Two other dialogues portray what happened subsequently. "Crito" recounts the conversation between Socrates and his oldest friend, who had visited him in his prison cell the night before his death to beg him to acquiesce in a foolproof plan to escape into exile. "Phaedo" portrays the scene in the the prison cell as Socrates took the hemlock.

neither read nor write but could not stand slavery and second-class treatment of women. One day during an anti-slavery speech she was heckled by an old man. "Old woman, do you think that your talk about slavery does any good? I don't care any more for your talk than I do for the bite of a flea."

"Perhaps not," snapped back Sojourner Truth. "But the Lord willing, I'll keep you scratching."

"A lot of people think they have to be big dogs to make a difference." Edelman observes. "That's not true. You just need to be a flea for justice, bent on building a more decent home life, neighborhood, work place, and America. Enough committed fleas biting strategically can make even the biggest dog uncomfortable and transform even the biggest nation. Be a flea for justice wherever you are and in whatever career you choose in life and help transform America."

SOCRATES' SPIRIT IN OUR TIME

Socrates' willingness to endure the negative reactions that often come with telling the truth can be an authentic inspiration for us. One person who experienced the full force of this inspiration is the philosopher Alain de Botton, director of the graduate philosophy program at London University. He describes vividly how he had his revelation on a bitterly cold winter day in New York, in a deserted gallery on an upper level of the Metropolitan Museum of Art. He found himself standing in front of Jacques-Louis David's painting *The Death of Socrates,* which is on the cover of this book.

> If the painting struck me so forcefully, it was perhaps because the behavior it depicted contrasted so sharply with my own.
>
> In conversations, my priority was to be liked, rather than to speak the truth. A desire to please led me to laugh at modest jokes like a parent at the opening night of a school play. With strangers, I adopted the servile manner of a concierge greeting wealthy clients in a hotel—salival enthusiasm born of a morbid, indiscriminate desire for affection.
>
> I did not publicly doubt ideas to which the majority was committed . . .
>
> But [Socrates] had not buckled before unpopularity . . . He had not retracted his thoughts because others complained. . . . Such independence of mind was a revelation and an incitement. It promised a counterweight to a supine tendency to follow socially sanctioned practices and ideas.

As de Botton notes, the challenge to speak the truth will confront most of us in much less dramatic and visible ways than in the case of Socrates. It may occur anytime with any of our friends or colleagues. But that can be just as daunting as having it happen in a public forum. It can start with challenging statements of prejudice or bigotry instead of quietly pretending we didn't hear that reference to " those people" or "foreigners" or even more offensive terms. Or in our work lives, it may involve speaking the truth even when it is uncomfortable for ourselves or our coworkers because it is of vital importance to the health of our organization or to its impact on our clients or customers.

For example, at the Kaiser Permanente health facility in Denver, Dr. Michael Leonard spoke the truth to several colleagues but discovered that his act of Socratic honesty had potentially lifesaving implications. As reported in *The New York Times* (Dec. 5, 1999), Dr. Leonard was operating on a cancer patient when he made a serious mistake. But to his tremendous credit, he learned something from that mistake.

Dr. Leonard, an anesthesiologist and chief of surgery at KP, had reached into a drawer for a medication. Inside were two vials with yellow labels and yellow caps: one was a paralyzing agent that he had correctly administered to keep the patient immobile while he was operating; the other one was an antidote to reverse the paralysis. "I grabbed the wrong one," Dr. Leonard said. "I used the wrong drug." Fortunately, the drug wore off and the patient was not harmed.

Most doctors would keep quiet about their mistake, but not Dr. Leonard. He immediately talked about the mistake with the surgeon, the scrub nurses, and the hospital pharmacist. He was shocked to discover that his telling others about his mistake was rare behavior. For example, when he told his five medical partners about it, "Four of them said, 'I've done the same thing.' And one of them said, 'I did the same thing last week.'" Dr. Leonard concluded, "I've been chief of this department for five years, and I'm the chief of surgery. But nobody had ever said to me: 'We have this problem.'"

Within seventy-two hours, steps had been taken to ensure that this mistake would not recur. The vials were relabeled and repositioned so that it was impossible to reach for one blindly and pick the wrong one.

What Dr. Leonard did was so important that it has been institutionalized at many hospitals in "Near-Miss Programs." Practitioners are encouraged and rewarded for reporting and dealing aggressively with mistakes that almost got made so that the actual mistakes can be averted before they happen!

CHALLENGES, EXPLORATIONS, AND APPLICATIONS: SPEAK THE TRUTH . . .

- To yourself and others

- In your organization or·profession

- As a "public citizen"

Strengthening Your Socratic Spirit

• Are you able to tell the truth to your friends, family, and colleagues when doing so is uncomfortable? (Exercise #1)

• Do you think that the organization you work in would function better if people were more truthful about the challenges and problems you face? Do you feel that you tell the truth as often as you really should? Do you have a clear test to use when you can't decide whether or not to tell the truth? (Exercise #2)

• Do you actively resist when your organization, institution, or profession is engaged in what you know is lying to the public? Have you ever spoken up when you disagreed with what everyone else was saying, in your organization, community, or social group? Do you work with others to advance the truth and act on it in your community or nationally? (Exercise #3)

As we have seen, Socrates functioned as a gadfly in two ways: privately and publicly. Privately, he "went about trying to persuade you, young and old, to make your first and chief concern . . . the highest welfare of your souls." Publicly, he was a gnat on the hindquarters of the State, that lazy, complacent creature that needed constant needling if it was not to become hopelessly complacent.

The challenges, explorations, and applications that follow cover this same ground, starting with telling the truth in our intimate relations, then in interactions with professional associates and people we meet socially (the kinds of interactions that de Botton and Dr. Leonard described), and finally, with becoming more active in goading our society about its need to change.

 1. Speak the truth to yourself and others.

Socrates challenged his fellow Athenians by rejecting their easy answers to his questions. He insisted on probing for what they really thought, and he criticized them, sometimes mercilessly, about their self-delusions.

Brad Blanton is a contemporary carrier of the flame known for his candor who practices and teaches "radical honesty." Some of his methods challenge his clients and students in much the way that Socrates' assaults discomfited his fellow citizens. "Tell the truth," Blanton declares simply.

As in Socrates' case, his approach is so powerfully effective that it has offended many, but it also has won him a loyal following of people whose lives he has changed dramatically.

Here's a typical example of how Blanton's advice can work wonders if you've got the courage to use it. Paul La Fontaine was a thirty-three-year-old project manager at Bertelsmann Music Group (MSG) when he started practicing radical honesty. "I would tell vendors precisely what my budget was and exactly what I was willing to spend," he recalls. "I would interrupt meetings to ask people if they were angry."

His colleagues started calling him "the honesty guy." Then came the acid test:

"I was called in by a VP who asked me if I was happy with my job," re-calls La Fontaine, who had become a devotee of radical honesty.

"'No!,' I answered."

"He was shocked. He turned red and screamed."

"I said, 'You don't give me enough responsibility, latitude, or money.'"

"Well, he didn't fire me. We had a conversation, and within three months I had more responsibility, latitude, and money."

Blanton is a psychotherapist based in Washington, D.C., who writes books, gives workshops, and spearheads a worldwide movement to prompt people to tell the truth. "Radical honesty is a kind of communication that is direct, complete, open, and expressive," he explains. "It's an authentic sharing of what you think and feel."

Another Socratic theme echoed by Blanton is our need to acknowledge that we are surrounded by lies and ignorance (see "The Cave," pages 116–119). "We all need to question authority and to recognize that you ultimately are the authority on your own life, period."

Blanton is willing to start with himself. Here's how he tries to tell the truth about why he wrote his major book, *Radical Honesty*:

I'm writing this book because I want a lot of people to know
my name, now and after I die . . . I want to be thought of
as smarter than everyone else. I want to make money from
writing this book. If you are looking for a book that wasn't
written by an asshole, you've got a long search ahead of
you. Every asshole who writes a book is a megalomaniac just
like me.

So how do you start being "radically honest" with yourself first, then
with others? Blanton suggests that you gather some good friends or colleagues and agree to experiment with telling the truth, including the
truths about your anger and resentments, as a method of mutual support.
Agree that for ten days, all legitimate resentments may be expressed.

Blanton offers these guidelines for telling these truths in the proper
way:

- Talk face to face to the person with whom you are angry.

- Start your sentences as often as possible with the words "I
  resent you for . . ."

- Speak in the present tense.

- Eventually, get specific; don't stop with general descriptions
  or judgments.

- Focus on what happened instead of on what didn't happen.

- Stay in touch with your experience while you talk.

- Stay with the person beyond the time it takes to exchange
  resentments.

- After you both have fully expressed your specific resentments,
  state your appreciation of each other the same way.

- Keep it up.

SOCRATES ON THE SOCIAL FUNCTION OF TRUTH

In the "Apology," Socrates used the witty metaphor of the gadfly to dramatize the need for truth telling. Only the constant bites of the gadfly keep the State alert enough to avoid disastrous mistakes by those in power.

> If you kill me you will not easily find a successor to me, who, if I may use a figure of speech, am a sort of gadfly, given to the state by God.
>
> The state is a great and noble steed who is tardy in his motions owing to his very size, and requires to be stirred into life. I am that gadfly which God has attached to the state, and all day long and in all places am always fastening upon you, arousing and persuading and reproaching you.
>
> You will not easily find another like me, and therefore I would advise you to spare me.

2. *Speak the truth in your organization or profession.*

Sissela Bok is a carrier of the flame who has sounded the alarm about a crisis in American life of which all of us are aware but that has yet to be added to the public agenda. Her ongoing campaign started in the wake of the scandals ignited by the government's deception vis-à-vis Watergate and Vietnam. In response to the shock we all felt over having been lied to and manipulated, Bok published a book with a simple but powerful title: *Lying*. Morever, she expanded our awareness to encompass the broader picture of a society virtually addicted to deception.

She expressed quiet outrage at the way in which so many professionals were lying, day in and day out, to the public, to each other, and to themselves. In business, government, law, medicine, and every other field of endeavor, she easily showed, "deception is taken for granted when it is felt to be excusable by those who tell the lies and who tend also to make the rules." She explained:

Government officials and those who run for elections often deceive when they can get away with it and when they assume that the true state of affairs is beyond the comprehension of citizens. Social scientists condone deceptive experimentation on the ground that the knowledge gained will be worth having. Lawyers manipulate the truth in court on behalf of their clients. Those in selling, advertising, or any form of advocacy may mislead the public and their own competitors in order to achieve their goals. Psychiatrists may distort information about their former patients to preserve confidentiality or to keep them out of military service. And journalists, police investigators, and so-called intelligence operators often have little compunction in using falsehoods to gain the knowledge they seek.

I call Bok's book "prophetic" because in the years after she published it, we have experienced continuing revelations of such deception from every quarter: from Wall Street investment firms to TV evangelists, from Iran-Contra to Enron. Bok envisions the far-reaching impact of these deceptions,

the many ways in which deception can spread and give rise to practices very damaging to human communities. These practices clearly do not affect only isolated individuals. The veneer of social trust is often thin. As lies spread—by imitation, or in retaliation, or to forestall suspected deception—trust is damaged. Yet trust is a social good to be protected just as much as the air we breathe or the water we drink. When it is damaged, the community as a whole suffers; and when it is destroyed, societies falter and collapse.

To help us combat this cultural riptide toward lying, Bok offers us three Socratic questions we can ask ourselves every time we find ourselves tempted to lie. Answering them will help us discern whether this is an occasion where we can, should, or must speak the truth.

Must I Speak the Truth?

- Are there alternative courses of action that will resolve the difficulty without the use of a lie?

- What might be the moral reasons to excuse the lie (such as self-defense or lifesaving, or extreme triviality)?

- What would a group of reasonable people say about the lie?

Consider a recent instance in your own life when you have lied and apply Bok's questions to them.

   a. Were there alternatives available to you?

   b. Are there moral reasons to excuse the lie?

   c. What would reasonable people say about your lie?

Now, envisage, if you can, an occasion that could develop in the immediate future that would tempt you to consider lying. Again, apply these three questions to examine your decision.

HOW TO SPEAK THE TRUTH: LOGOS, PATHOS, AND ETHOS

When you speak your truth, you must express yourself as well as you can. Socrates and his fellow Athenians had a very clear idea about what that entailed. They saw three principles at work when a speaker successfully conveyed his truths to others. As later codified by Aristotle, they are just as valid today as they were 2,500 years ago:

    LOGOS—your ideas, concepts, logic, and language

    PATHOS—your emotional connection to your audience

    ETHOS—your character and integrity

These three criteria reveal the immense success of some of today's top speakers. For example, Tom Peters, the speaker most sought after by the nation's business and professional groups, is a geyser of ideas (logos) drawn from his uniquely broad consulting and writing experience. He can draw just the right concepts and examples from the worlds of business and organizational life. But he also makes an emotional connection (pathos) with his audiences as he strides up and down the center aisle to literally reach out to every attendee. He displays his own passions; he acknowledges the apprehensions and fears that we may feel in trying new ideas; and he reveals much about his own struggles and reversals of fortune.

To complete the picture, Peters displays his character and integrity (ethos) by speaking out about issues that might offend many of his clientele, such as inequities in the workplace and the need to give more dignity and meaning to the "cubicle-workers."

- When you share your truths, how would you estimate your effectiveness in terms of these three aspects? Are you strongest with your logos (ideas), your pathos (emotional connection), or your ethos (integrity)?

- What steps might you take to bolster the one on which you rate yourself as least powerful?

- Think of the most effective truth teller you know, personally or as a public figure. How would you evaluate that person on these three criteria?

 ### 3. Speak the Truth in your community, nation, and the world.

Socrates was essentially a "loner," despite his cadre of devoted friends and champions. He was not associated with any movement, group, enterprise, or institution. In the Athens of his day, he could make his maximum impact as an individual. The free citizens of Athens numbered only 40,000, and you could walk across the entire city, from the docks of the Piraeus to the Gate of Aeghistus, in a few hours. But in our mass society,

SOCRATES' ATHENS AND OUR AMERICA

Socrates saw the essence of his society in its commitment to the pursuit of truth through free inquiry—as we do. Here is how the playwright Maxwell Anderson has him express it in *Barefoot in Athens*:

> Truth will make and keep us free, Lycon. You have made me realize something which has never been clear to me before. Athens has always seemed to me a sort of mad miracle of a city, flashing out in all directions, a great city for no discoverable reason. But now I see that Athens is driven and made miraculous by the same urge that has sent me searching your streets! It is the Athenian search for truth, the Athenian hunger for facts, the endless curiosity of the Athenian mind, that has made Athens unlike any other city.

it is usually necessary to join your voice with others to protest effectively or to agitate for change.

To activate this aspect of the Socratic spirit in you, here is a seven-step program for working collaboratively on behalf of a cause that means something to you. It's simplistic, of course; I merely want to suggest the broad outlines of what's involved. I have listed the best books of advice and support in Appendix B.

- *Choose a problem, issue, or cause* that you would like to address in your community, in the organization in which you work, or in our world. Don't just grouse about things in general; pick an issue you would really like to work on now.

- *Contact other people* or an activist organization working on that issue to determine if its priorities match yours. If not, take the initial steps yourself and pick up comrades along the way.

- *Learn more* about how to effect the change, so that you become as expert as possible in all its aspects. Have others elsewhere tackled this issue and come up with strategies and tactics you can learn from?

- *Decide on the best role you can play* in light of your interests, circumstances, abilities, and style. If you act on an appropriate scale, you can get the ball rolling.

- *Be willing to confront* when that becomes necessary. When you challenge the status quo, you are going to provoke opposition. Be prepared to deal with it flexibly, intelligently, and creatively.

- *Spread the word* about your effort. The new communications media offer unprecedented opportunities to inexpensively and effectively rally support. And by all means, let the Giraffe Project (see next section) know what you're doing.

Make a point of challenging one thing you hear in conversation this week that you regard as prejudiced, bigoted, or unreasonable. Afterward, note how you felt about doing it and the result.

RECOGNIZING GADFLIES: THE GIRAFFE PROJECT

There are people like Dr. Leonard all over our country and indeed throughout the world, people who speak up and make things better. Many of them are identified and recognized by the Giraffe Project, whose admirable motto is "Stick Your Neck Out." Based on an island in the state of Washington, and funded in part by the Kellogg Foundation, the Giraffe Project identifies, supports, and promotes people who take a stand for the truth, usually at considerable personal and professional risk. "We honor people for questioning conventional wisdom, challenging authority, and championing the common good—the very things Socrates spent his life doing for Athens!" says Ann Medlock, a cofounder of the Project.

Among recent "giraffes" are:

- Veteran USDA inspector William Lehman, who has, on occasion, rejected up to 80 percent of the Canadian meat that comes to his border inspection station because it smells putrid and contains bone fragments, metal fragments, blood clots, pus, and abscesses.

GADFLIES IN OUR TIME

Socratic gadflies—dissenters who sting us by challenging conventional wisdom or established ways of doing things—frequently pay a high price—the kind exacted from Karen Silkwood, Andrei Sakharov, or Nelson Mandela. The best account of these contemporary gadflies is *Speaking Truth to Power: Human Rights Defenders Who Are Changing Our World* by Kerry Kennedy Cuomo, which chronicles the lives and accomplishments of fifty-one men and women from thirty-five countries and five continents who have put their lives at risk, as Socrates did. The pantheon includes well-known names like Elie Wiesel, the Dalai Lama, and Desmond Tutu as well as other Nobel Prize winners, but the book also includes interviews with lesser-known activists like Juliana Dogbadzi of Ghana, who has organized national resistance to the practice of consigning young girls to sexual slavery by priests.

Cuomo's book was the subject of a theatrical production at the Kennedy Center in Washington that featured Glenn Close, Edward James Olmos, and Sigourney Weaver as well as a PBS documentary. "You cannot kill an idea, you cannot imprison freedom," said Nelson Mandela about the book, using words that applied well to Socrates. "The lives of the common women and men in this book, heroes every one, inspire all who believe in liberty and justice. This book is proof of the capacity of one person of courage to triumph over overwhelming evil."

Pressured by the USDA to pass more Canadian shipments, he stood up for the truth. Despite physical threats, maligning by Canadian officials, and punishment by his agency, he not only persisted, but "upped the ante" by pressing for a GAO audit and going to the media.

- Gay Jervey became a "giraffe" when she discovered that the Oregon Department of Transportation was quietly reactivating a rock quarry and asphalt plant in her town of Mosier. She and her husband mounted organized opposition to the dirt, noise, dust, pollution, and negative economic impact of "the pit," and did studies showing that it could contribute to landslides, contaminate groundwater, and threaten the salmon stream. Using their own money and time, they formed the Mosier Alliance to fight the state, provoking threats and vandalism from some business interests.

When they won in court, it "sent shock waves through state agencies all the way to the governor's office," according to local coverage. Then, using the community activism they'd built, the Jerveys started a dozen projects to transform the town in positive ways, from turning a slimy bog in the center of town into a scenic little lake, to building a new marina on the river to accommodate fishing, windsurfing, and swimming. For a decade of pioneering work, Jervey was eventually selected as Mosier's Woman of the Year.

· Twelve-year-old Danny Seo gathered a handful of kids and founded Earth 2000, an environmental and animal rights group that blossomed into a 20,000-member force of tenacious teenage activists. Based on his experiences, and to share what he learned with others, he wrote and published *Generation React: Activism for Beginners* (Ballantine, 1990). Jane Goodall calls it "a wonderful book, chock-full of innovative ideas, tips, and solutions to make changing the world a lot easier."

a. Identify someone you know personally or admire as a public figure who functions as a Socratic gadfly.

b. List three qualities this person displays that enable him or her to make a contribution.

c. How could you strengthen these qualities in yourself?

ELDERS AS GADFLIES

Socrates reached his peak as a gadfly in his late sixties, and if he had lived longer, he would clearly have been at the top of his form for another ten to fifteen years. One's sixties and seventies offer unique opportunities to function as a gadfly. In fact, it could be argued that it is a natural and healthy "life task" of those years.

"Generativity" is the name that Erik Erikson, the pioneer of Life Stages theory and research, gave to the challenges of one's mature years.

He believed that taking positive steps on behalf of the next generation was a healthy way to use that period of life.

Many older people in our society also have unique resources for operating as a gadfly, namely:

- *Time:* If you are retired or semiretired, you have time to devote to good causes of your own choosing.

- *Skills and capabilities:* A lifetime of professional work has likely given you strengths to contribute, ranging from serviceable skills like management, technical knowledge, or the ability to communicate.

- *Security:* You do not have to be as cautious and prudent as you may have had to be when controversial or activist actions could have damaged your career and your livelihood.

- *Wisdom:* You have the worldly experience to judge which causes are most important and how they can best be helped.

You can also prepare your grandchildren to be the gadflies of their generation. Start by reading to them early and often "The Emperor's New Clothes," and if appropriate, suggest that they be on the lookout for examples of people around them who refuse to say or even see that "the emperor is naked." In some cases it may be best not to let your grandchildren's parents know you're doing this!

7

STRENGTHEN YOUR SOUL

We should strive to gain more intelligence,
arrive at more knowledge of truth,
and develop finer character.

SOCRATES, IN PLATO'S "APOLOGY"

W E HEARD SOCRATES DEFEND his truth telling in the open-ing dialogue of the last chapter. But there was a second great theme to his "Apology"—the need for each person to strengthen his or her own soul.

Men of Athens, I am your friend, I love you. But so long as the breath and the power are in me I will not cease the practice of philosophy. I will exhort anyone I meet, saying:

O my friend, why do you, who are a citizen of the great city of Athens, care so much about laying up the greatest amount of money and honor and reputation, and so little about wisdom and truth and the improvement of your soul?

We should not be concerned about winning fame or polit-ical honors, but rather should try to gain more intelligence, to arrive at more knowledge of truth, and to develop finer character.

I have been careless of what many care for—wealth, and military office, and family interests, and speaking in the as-sembly, and plots and parties. Reflecting that I was really too honest a man to be a politician and live, I did not go where I could do no good to you or to myself, but where I could do the greatest good privately to every one of you. And I sought to persuade every man among you that he must seek virtue and wisdom before he looks to his private interests.

While I have life and strength I shall never cease from the practice and teaching of philosophy, appealing to anyone whom I meet, to interrogate and examine and cross-examine him, and if I think that he has no virtue in him, but only says that he has, I will reproach him.

Care most about improving your souls. I say that money does not bring virtue, but rather that from being virtuous one can attain money and many other good things.

Socrates worked every day of his life to "strengthen his soul" in four ways:

- Self-control

- Authenticity

- Self-discovery

- Self-development

We see him striving to achieve one or more of these in virtually every dialogue. And each of them was expressed in a vivid incident or metaphor.

Socrates' *self-control* was regularly acknowledged by his friends. While he enjoyed the pleasures of the flesh, he never succumbed to them. His friends mention often that while he joined them in drinking at their frequent symposia, Socrates never ended the evening in a stupor but was always ready to continue the dialogue after others had fallen asleep. And Alcibiades tells the raunchy story in the "Symposium" of how he attempted to seduce Socrates when they were together on military maneuvers by getting under his blanket at night. Socrates was impervious.

Socrates' commitment to *self-discovery* was expressed in the amusing story of the Silenus (see sidebar, page 162). His friends used to compare him to the little statues sold in the agora that portrayed a grotesque figure, a homely troll-like creature much like Socrates himself. But the secret of the Silenus was that within one out of every fifty the sculptors would imbed a tiny golden figurine of a lovely creature. To get to that prize, you had to be willing to break your Silenus with the hope that you would be rewarded by discovering the treasure within.

Socrates' friends said that he was like the Silenus: off-putting because of his grotesque appearance but worth getting to know because, when you broke through that forbidding surface, you found a golden soul inside. Socrates himself was constantly challenging himself and others to break through to the authentic self within.

Socrates revealed his commitment to *self-development* when he compared his life-work to that of his father, the stonecutter Sophroniscus. Socrates would have liked Michelangelo's remark that he created his statues by seeing the finished figure within the stone and then removing everything that was not part of that vision.

Socrates uses an appropriate phrase to associate this soul-work with the work of the craftsman like his father. *Techne tou biou* translates as "craft of life." For Socrates, the spiritual life was not a reverential submission to a divine authority; it consisted of using the tools at our disposal, with the highest craftsmanship possible, to shape ourselves and our circumstances. His tools for that "craft of life"—the chisel and mallet for shaping oneself—were the strategies we have explored in this book:

- Know thyself.

- Ask great questions.

- Judge for yourself.

- Free your mind.

- Grow with friends.

- Speak your truth.

- Strengthen your soul.

SOCRATES' SPIRIT IN OUR TIME

One of the best contemporary exemplars of a person who cultivated his soul in the ways that Socrates did was the psychologist Carl Jung.

Just as Socrates spoke often of his daimon, that inner voice that he could not disobey, so Jung declared at the end of his life, "There was a daimon in me. It overpowered me, and if I was at times ruthless it was because I was in the grip of the daimon. Since my contemporaries, understandably, could not perceive my vision, they saw only a fool rushing ahead." Socrates might have said the same thing.

Jung devoted much of his life to strengthening his soul in the ways we will explore in this chapter. He created the time and a place to invite his soul: a stone tower in a remote location. Building it with his own hands over many years, he discovered that every four years he would make a major addition, not according to some preconceived plan but as his daimon dictated. (For Jung the number four signified wholeness.)

When he retreated to this special place, Jung devoted himself to the soul-work of "going within" to seek authenticity, self-knowledge, and self-creation. He painted on the walls. He engaged in reverie and recollection. He recorded his dreams and visions. His soul-work is expressed in the title of his memoirs, *Memories, Dreams, Reflections*.

Jung wrote about his hours and days and weeks in the tower: "I have done without electricity, and tend the fireplace and stove myself. Evenings, I light the old lamps. There is no running water, and I pump water from the well. I chop the wood and cook the food. These simple acts make man simple; and how difficult it is to be simple" (a great lesson of our own Henry David Thoreau, who did much the same thing in his cabin at Walden).

Throughout history, thoughtful men and women have, like Jung, created special places to strengthen their souls. Spiritual leaders like the Christian saints and Eastern mystics went on retreats in the desert or elsewhere. The great humanist Montaigne and the Irish poet W. B. Yeats built themselves towers in which to write and think.

We can, however, follow these examples without retreating to a remote location. We can dedicate a part of our living quarters to soul-work. One friend of mine has in a corner of his bedroom a little writing desk left to him by his father, a miniature water fountain that bubbles up relaxingly when turned on, and several spiritual artifacts, including a tiny Ganesh from India. This place is for him a refuge from the pressures of life and a place to enjoy inner peace. "This is the bedrock of my spiritual life," he says. He generally spends fifteen minutes there with a cup of tea first thing in the morning to capture and reflect on the night's dreams, and anticipate the day ahead.

Other people I know get the same benefits from a tai chi class or stopping into a favorite small museum or taking a walk at a nearby creek. "Modest forms of retreat can serve the spiritual needs of the soul," advises Thomas Moore in *Care of the Soul*. "Spirituality need not be grandiose in its ceremonials. Indeed, the soul might benefit most when its spiritual life is performed in the context it favors—ordinary daily life. But spirituality does demand attention, mindfulness, regularity, and devotion. It asks for some small measure of withdrawal from a world set up to ignore the soul."

CHALLENGES, EXPLORATIONS, AND APPLICATIONS

 1. Enhance your "spiritual literacy."

Socrates had few possessions, yet he lived a rich and fulfilling life. He enjoyed himself and his friends with immense gusto. "All in all he was fortunate," declares historian Will Durant. "He lived without working, read without writing, taught without routine, drank without dizziness, and died before senility, almost without pain."

What Socrates enjoyed and thrived on were *experiences*—of friendship, insight, creativity, self-mastery, and fulfillment of his destiny. Today, many people are embracing this ideal of living a rich life by savoring the significance of their experiences rather than by accumulating possessions and power. Two carriers of the flame who have provided wonderful practical help in cultivating this lifestyle are Frederic and Mary Ann Brussat. They have developed a repertoire of techniques that they call "spiritual literacy." Their book, so titled, is the best single source of ways to care for your soul.

This everyday spirituality does not require that we become masters of certain religious texts or that we climb to a high rung on the ladder of enlightenment. Indeed, it is the very opposite of such elitism. It is the

Strengthening Your Socratic Spirit

- Do you have a repertoire of simple spiritual practices that enables you to enjoy and enrich your life, regardless of your circumstances? (Exercise #1)

- Do you know how to reach inside yourself to tap your intuitive wisdom? (Exercise #2)

- Do you practice an art or craft that is good for your soul? (Exercise #3)

- Do you maintain control over your emotions so that they motivate you in productive directions rather than cause you problems? (Exercise #4)

- Do you cultivate a "sound mind in a sound body," by taking care of your physical well-being? (Exercise #5)

- Would you like to master a simple technique for activating "the Socrates in you" and in others with whom you are thinking things through? (Exercise #6)

- Do you regularly draw inspiration and guidance from great souls with whom you feel a special kinship? (Exercise #7)

- Do you recognize the "stages of the soul" that foster your growth and self-fulfillment? (Exercise #8)

- Do you benefit from the "soul of your work"—the values that give meaning and direction to your job or profession? (Exercise #9)

- Do you have clear and strong values that impel you to "do the right thing" even in the face of the greatest temptations? (Exercise #10)

knack of lingering with our experiences and seeing our daily world with ever-fresh eyes.

The key to finding meaning in everyday activities, say the Brussats, is to look for certain markers of the spiritual life. They have identified thirty-seven spiritual practices common to all the world's religions that

SOCRATES AND THE GODS

Socrates' way of thinking about the gods exemplified his way of approaching every issue. He

- questioned conventional thinking

- demanded clarity

- learned from everyday experience

- came to his own conclusions

Conventional religious thinking among Socrates' fellow Athenians was a mishmash of contradictory notions. Legends about the Olympian pantheon of gods—Zeus, Aphrodite, and Apollo—had proliferated and taken grotesque turns, as examplified by the tale of Zeus taking the form of a swan or a bull in order to rape mortal women. Most sophisticated Athenians considered these fictions at best as metaphors for human emotions. However, there was widespread conviction that "the gods" were likely to punish human beings for such things as hubrus (excessive pride or confidence) or even just great good fortune.

Socrates required clarity. He found it in a place where few of his fellow Athenians looked: within himself. Ever since he was a child, Socrates had experienced a "divine sigh"—a voice within which we might call his intuition. This voice regularly told him that certain things were not right for him to do, and he had learned that it was never wrong. From this everyday experience, Socrates derived his spiritual convictions.

This inner sense of what was right for him led Socrates to three conclusions: First, the gods cared for all people; otherwise they would not have instilled this divine spark in a mere stonecutter's son. Second, the gods were good: They wished well for human beings, rather than behaving as the capricious and vengeful creatures portrayed in the ancient tales. Third, the gods required goodness from human beings. The best way to show respect for the gods was to be the best human being you could be.

enable you to read the world this way. Below is their "Alphabet of Spiritual Literacy."

Pick one or two that resonate for you, and work on practicing one of them for a week, reading it every morning, carrying it on a card with you, and seeing how many times each day you can find occasion to put it into practice. For still more ideas, go to their website, www.SpiritualityHealth.com.

A

Attention: Pay attention. Stay awake and totally alert. See with receptive eyes and discover a world of ceaseless wonders.

B

Beauty: Walk the path of beauty. Relish and encourage its inward and outward expressions. Acknowledge the radiance of the creation.

Being Present: Live in the present moment. Don't obsess about the past or worry about the future. All you need is right here now.

C

Compassion: Open your heart, mind, and soul to the pain and suffering in the world. Reach out to others and discover the rewards and obligations of deep feeling.

Connections: Cultivate the art of making connections. See how your life is intimately related to all life on the planet.

D

Devotion: Express your praise and adoration through devotional practices. Pray with words and pray through your actions.

E

Enthusiasm: Celebrate life with this intoxicating passion. It adds zest to everything and helps build community. Hold nothing back.

F

Faith: Recognize and accept that there is a dimension to life other than that which is obvious to us. Live with obstacles, doubt, and paradox, knowing that God is always present in the world.

Forgiveness: In both your private and public lives, discover the sweet release that comes from forgiving others. Feel the healing balm of being forgiven and of forgiving yourself.

G

Grace: Accept grace, and your world will be larger, deeper, richer, and fuller. Look for its intimations everywhere. Let this seed of the Giver of Life bloom in your words and deeds.

H

Hope: Let this positive and potent emotion fuel your dreams and support your service of others. Through your attitudes and actions, encourage others never to lose hope.

Hospitality: Practice hospitality in a world where too often strangers are feared, enemies are hated, and the "other" is shunned. Welcome guests and alien ideas with graciousness.

I

Imagination: Give imagination free rein in your life. Explore its images and ponder its meaning-making moments, and it will always present you with something new to be seen, felt, or made known.

J

Joy: Rejoice and be exceedingly glad. Find this divine energy in your daily life and share it with others.

Justice: Seek liberty and justice for all. Work for a free and fair world where oppression and inequality no longer exist.

K

Kindness: Let spirit flow through you in little acts of kindness, brief words of encouragement, and manifold expressions of courtesy. These deeds will add to the planet's fund of goodwill.

L

Listening: Cultivate the art of deep listening, in whose practice you lean toward the world in love. All things in the universe want to be heard, as do the many voices inside us.

Love: Fall in love over and over again every day. Love your family, your neighbors, your enemies, and yourself. And don't stop with humans. Love animals, plants, stones, even the galaxies.

M

Meaning: Constantly try to discover the significance of your experiences. Seek further understanding from sacred texts and spiritual teachers.

N

Nurturing: Take good care of the best that is within you. Self-exploration and personal growth continue throughout our lifetimes and equip us to tend to the needs of others.

O

Openness: Hold an open house in your heart for all people and all things. Be empathetic with others and receptive toward the universe.

P

Peace: Protect the earth's future by promoting peace every day. Your small steps will link you with others who are combating violence in the world.

Play: Be playful. Express your creative spirit in spontaneity. Rejoice in the pleasures of being, and let loose your laughter.

Q

Questing: Savor questions and thrill to the quest. See your life as a journey that quickens your faith and deepens your soul.

R

Reverence: Practice reverence for life. The sacred is in, with, and under all the things of the world. Respond with appropriate respect and awe.

S

Shadow: Give up trying to hide, deny, or escape from your imperfections. Listen to what your demons have to say to you.

Silence: Slow down. Be calm. Find a place where you can regularly practice silence. There you will find the resources to revitalize your body, mind, and soul.

T

Teachers: : Be willing to learn from the spiritual teachers all around you, however unlikely or unlike you they may be. Always be a sensitive student.

Transformation: Welcome the positive changes that are taking place in your life. Open up the windows and let in some fresh air. Wholeness and healing are waiting in the wings.

U

Unity: In this age of global spirituality, respect differences but affirm commonalities. Work together with those who are trying to make the world a better place.

V

Vision: Practice the art of seeing the invisible. Use the wisdom of your personal visions to renew yourself and your community.

W

Wonder: Cultivate a vibrant curiosity and welcome the reports of your senses. The world is alive and moving toward you with rare epiphanies and wonderful surprises. Remember you are standing on holy ground.

X

The Mystery: Accept the unknown as part of life. Don't try to unravel the profound mysteries of God, human nature, and the natural world. Love the ineffable.

Y

Yearning: Follow your heart's boundless desire. It takes you out of yourself and fosters an appreciation for the multidimensional pleasures of life.

You: Accept that you are a child of God. Sing your own song with gusto. Fulfill your mission as a copartner with the Holy One in the unfolding drama of the universe.

Z

Zeal: Be passionately aroused by life. Cherish every moment, honor your commitments, and treasure your kinship with all.

SEARCH THE WEB WITH THE ALPHABET

Use the Alphabet of Spiritual Literacy to search a database of more than 800 reviews of new books, movies, videos, and spoken-word audios at www.spiritualrx.com. New reviews are posted every Friday on the site.

 2. Get in touch with your daimon.

Socrates referred often to his daimon, a spirit that motivated and guided his life. In modern times, highly developed carriers of the flame like the poet W. B. Yeats and the psychologist Carl Jung have testified to their version of the same drive. Jung writes:

> We know that something unknown, alien, does come our way, just as we know that we do not ourselves *make* a dream or an inspiration, but that it somehow arises of its own accord. What does happen to us in this manner can be said to emanate from mana, from a daimon, a god, or the unconscious.

(Jung himself actually preferred the term *unconscious,* but readily acknowledged its origins in Socrates' daimon.)

Socrates' regimen for getting in touch with your daimon is strikingly similar to some of the most powerful strategies used today by people who seek to live their lives to the fullest. It is basically the same as the process you would undergo in good psychotherapy to learn how to live more wisely and enjoyably. Here is how Jonathan Lear compares the two approaches in his brilliant *Open Minded: Working Out the Logic of the Soul,* a book in which he carries the flame of Socratic inquiry into our contemporary world of psychiatry. It is a profound prescription for getting in touch with your daimon:

- *Make the unconscious conscious.* Socrates' method of cross-examination is designed to elicit contradictory beliefs that have remained hidden inside you. In that sense, Socrates is engaged in an effort to make the unconscious conscious.

SOCRATES' PRAYER

Having sought for authenticity by "going within," Socrates then sought to express that authenticity with his friends. His aspiration is expressed in the one prayer of his that comes down to us. Made one summer afternoon in the cool of a many-shaded grove, it was a plea to be and seem the same.

> *Beloved Pan, and all you other gods*
> *Abiding hereabouts,*
> *Grant that I may become handsome within!*
> *May I appear to be that which I am.*
> *May I regard wisdom as the only wealth,*
> *and may my own wealth*
> *be no more than I can bear.*

- *Ask: "How shall I live?"* Socrates had a fundamental question, "How shall I live?" which is also the fundamental question of therapy. We make ourselves distinctively human by our efforts to ask and answer this question. That is why, for him, the unexamined life is not worth living. (See Exercise #8 in Chapter 1.)

- *Be honest with yourself and others:* Socrates' fundamental rule—state only what you believe—bears a family resemblance to the fundamental rule of psychoanalysis. The point of the Socratic rule is that (you) must be committed to what (you) say. It is precisely because you are committed that if you become aware that your position is contradictory, you will be changed by your awareness.

- *Improve your psyche:* For both Socratic and psychoanalytic practice, the fundamental task is the improvement of one's psyche. For Socrates, it was the only truly important task.

A wide variety of strategies can help you get in touch with your daimon. The Brussats (see the previous section) point to a dozen people they know well, who have used diverse means to do this. (I'm pleased to have turned up as the fifth one on the list.)

- Several women get together once a month to take turns answering one question. They share their deepest concerns and the stories of their lives.

- A retired couple come to the beach every day with their dogs. They carry garbage bags and pick up litter as they walk. They love the beach and make a habit of caring for it.

- A jogger runs in the park every morning, come rain or shine. At a certain point, her movement seems almost effortless.

- A woman teaches in the Sunday school and serves as an officer of the women's group at her church. Through her daily demonstrations of enthusiasm for church work, she inspires others to become involved.

- A wise and creative entrepreneur, who occasionally expresses an aversion to religious matters, has pioneered the field of informal lifelong learning with innovative seminars, speeches, and articles. Learning is his spiritual practice, and it enables him to give full expression to his gifts and skills.

- A young couple have just had their first child and decide to return to the synagogue. They want their boy to relish his ethnic roots and to experience the practice of Judaism.

- A group of therapists gathers on a weekday afternoon to talk about their night dreams and to do mental imagery exercises as a way of getting in touch with their inner lives.

- A woman in a stressful job attends yoga class every other day. This combination of body work and meditation relaxes and revitalizes her.

- A woman has two close encounters with death in as many years. She accepts them as wake-up calls and reorders her life, giving herself more time for self-nurturing. She sees a spiritual

director and makes room in her busy schedule for daily
devotional reading and prayer.

- A small circle of people meets each month to talk about the
story of a movie in relation to the stories of their own lives;
they call the process they are going through together "soul
making."

 ### 3. *Practice a personal craft or art.*

Socrates' favorite hangout in the agora was the stall and workshop of
Simon the Sandal Maker. (If you ever visit the ruins of the agora in
Athens, you can actually stand in the place where this shop stood, thanks
to the dedicated work of the archaeologist at the American School of
Classical Studies.) As we have noted, Socrates' talk was full of the jargon
and wisdom of potters, horse handlers, jewelers, and other craftspeople.
He clearly saw that the discipline of making useful and lovely things was
the best pursuit for the "craft of life." Even in his jail cell, while awaiting
the day of the hemlock, Socrates spent some of his time writing poetry
(an activity I recommend to you).

Pursuing a craft or art is one of the most enjoyable and powerful
ways you can care for your soul. Among my friends, colleagues, and acquaintances, the following arts and crafts are the most popular:

- Watercolor painting

- Sculpture

- Choral singing

- String quintet

- Sketching historical homes

- Flower arranging

- Bird-watching

- Just being in Nature

SOCRATES CONSULTS HIS DAIMON

In the "Apology," Socrates describes his lifelong practice of heeding his inner voice:

> You have heard me speak at sundry times and in diverse places of an oracle or sign which comes to me, and is the divinity which Meletus ridicules in the indictment. This sign, which is a kind of voice, first began to come to me when I was a child; it always forbids but never commands me to do anything which I am going to do.

And toward the end of his defense, Socrates explains that he has come to his trial without fear because he knows it is the right thing to do:

> When I was leaving my house this morning, or when I was on my way to the court, or while I was speaking just now, my internal oracle made no sign of opposition. In nothing I have said or did has the oracle opposed me. What do I take to be the explanation of this silence? I will tell you. It is an intimation that what has happened to me is a good, and that those of us who think that death is an evil are in error. For the customary sign would surely have opposed me had I been going to evil and not to good.

- Hang gliding

- Sandal making

- Quilting

- Gourmet cooking

- Gardening

- Carpentry

To find the right art or craft for yourself, think about one for which you once had great enthusiasm but have let languish. How would it feel to return to it now and make a place for it in your life? We almost all have such "ghost hobbies," as Michael Gelb calls them—great enthusiasms, even passions that we once pursued but then gave up and that we might greatly enjoy reviving.

The pursuit of such an art or craft can be immensely enjoyable and can also benefit your whole life. One of the most memorable demonstrations of this positive effect occurred when I spoke at the annual convention of the Directors of the American Association of Blood Banks, immensely important organizations on which all our lives depend. My presentation helped some of these dedicated professionals to see that the demands of their work—for rigor, discipline, precision, analysis, and control—did not give them any opportunity to express some other aspects of their personality: spontaneity, appreciation of beauty, insight, sensory delight.

So, in the aftermath of that meeting, a number of those in attendance took one of my suggestions and started writing haiku—those tiny Japanese poems which invite just such kinds of expression. One of them sent me a little pamphlet of his haiku about a year later, saying: "This practice has changed my life. It may even have SAVED my life!"

How to Write Haiku

The purpose of writing haiku is to seize and share a momentary perception that means something to us, even if we don't know at the moment what that meaning is!

> *on a barren branch*
> *a raven has perched—*
> *autumn dusk.*
> —BASHO

Many of us were taught in school that the haiku should have seventeen syllables, arranged in three lines of five, seven, and five syllables, respectively. Don't worry about that, unless counting the syllables is appealing to you. The important point is that "looking for haiku" is a way of nudging yourself to be more perceptive, open, and aware—just as the Brussats advised in those "ABCs" of Spiritual Literacy!

Find Your Muse

A wonderful classical guide to finding your own inspiration is *The Nine Muses: A Mythological Path to Creativity* by Angeles Arrien (Tarcher/ Putnam). Arrien uses the nine daughters of Zeus, so well known to Socrates, to illustrate how we can awaken our own gifts and talents. The book is an artistic work itself, replete with illustrations from Greek art, mythical tales, and exercises.

> The Muses invite us to adorn our lives with creativity and beauty. . . . They appear in our lives in both direct and subtle ways. . . . They are often found in our relationships, especially in those where each partner or important friend encourages each other's creative achievements and where each fosters mutual support for the emotional well-being of the other.

 4. Nurture your emotional intelligence.

As we have seen, Socrates was renowned among the Athenians for his understanding and control of his emotions. The allegory of the charioteer vividly portrayed the struggle this entailed. We, too, must become adept at the task of the charioteer in his great metaphor. We must learn to understand and control our most powerful emotions. Unrestrained, our emotions can bring us to grief despite our rational intelligence. But understood and controlled (not merely ignored or stifled), they can become our wellspring of motivation and passion for life.

This realm of emotional intelligence has been mapped by Daniel Goleman in his bestselling book *Emotional Intelligence*. Here are Goleman's five dimensions of emotional intelligence:

Self-awareness

- Tune in to your emotional states.

- Express your feelings to others in an appropriate manner.

SOCRATES' ALLEGORY "THE CHARIOTEER"

The challenge of controlling our emotions was dramatized by Socrates in his allegory of the charioteer with two powerful steeds.

Of the nature of the soul, let me speak briefly, and in a metaphor: a pair of winged horses and a charioteer. One of the horses is noble, and the other is ignoble, and driving them is immensely difficult.

The right-hand horse is upright and cleanly made—he is a lover of honor and modesty and temperance; he needs no touch of the whip, but is guided by word only.

The other is a crooked lumbering animal; he is insolent and proud, shag-eared and deaf, hardly yielding to whip and spur.

This vicious steed goes heavily, weighing down the charioteer to the earth because he has not been thoroughly trained: this is the hour of agony and extremest conflict for the soul.

The charioteer must drag the bit out of the teeth of the wild steed, force his legs to the ground, and punish him sorely. When this has happened several times, and the horse has ceased from his wanton way, he is tamed and humbled, and follows the will of the charioteer.

Self-regulation

- Accept responsibility for your emotional responses.

- Learn to manage emotional "triggers."

Self-motivation

- Strive to be "in the moment" with work tasks.

- When setbacks occur, resist self-defeating thoughts.

Empathy

- See the world through the eyes of others.

- Recognize and respond to everyone's emotions.

Effective Relationships

- Use EI to influence and persuade others.

- Build consensus and support for team goals.

Try this exercise in empathy, to see how rewarding it can be to cultivate your emotional intelligence.

WALK A WHILE IN MY SHOES

Sit down with someone with whom you have a significant relationship at work or in your personal life. Agree to spend an uninterrupted fifteen minutes to look together at one activity in which you both participate and over which you sometimes feel there is less than complete understanding or empathy.

To start, you talk about how you understand and feel about what the other person does on those occasions. For example: "Mary, when we work together at the end of each month on the payroll figures, my understanding is that what you do is . . . That makes me feel . . ."

Then, have the other person correct, augment, or revise your understanding. "Ron, that's not all there is to it. You see, at the same time that I'm doing that, I am also called upon to . . . That makes me feel . . . So when you ask me if I'm going to have the figures on time, I feel . . ."

Now, reverse roles. Mary now tells how she sees my role on these occasions, and I get to explain to her that "That's not all there is to it . . ."

When both of you feel that you have expressed the facts as well as the feelings involved in the situation, explore together whether there are ways to make it a more successful experience for both of you. Keep in mind that the purpose of this exercise is not to complain; it is to understand each other's roles better and to find ways to improve the relationship.

For more on this serviceable strategy, visit the Walk-the-Talk website, at www. Walkthetalk.com

 ## 5. Body and Soul

The classical Greeks were the first to propose the ideal of "a sound mind in a sound body." Socrates would have concurred. While he enjoyed food and drink, his friends all admired his self-control and moderation.

Research has established that a regimen of physical fitness, including regular exercise, healthy eating, and avoidance of damaging practices or toxic environments, contributes significantly to one's mental and indeed spiritual well-being.

- A workout is a the key to unlocking a door to your inner self. Inside each of us is an incredible force. Physical and mental fitness are processes that help release this force.

- A workout makes you better today than you were yesterday. It not only strengthens your body, but relaxes your mind and toughens your spirit.

- A workout is the mark of an organized, goal-oriented person who has taken the steering wheel and who chooses which road to travel for success.

- A workout is a personal triumph over laziness and procrastination. When you finish a workout, you don't just feel better—you feel better about yourself.

 ## 6. Activate "the Socrates in you."

By now, you have learned a great deal about Socrates. You have undoubtedly created an image of him in your mind. You've probably pictured him in the agora, at an evening symposium, or at his trial addressing the jury. In your imagination, you may even have given Socrates a voice, "hear-

SOCRATES' HEALTHY LIFESTYLE

Socrates led a simple but healthful lifestyle. When a wealthy friend once presumed to commiserate with his modest lifestyle, Socrates retorted:

> Have you ever known me to stay home because of the cold? Or to push and shove into a shady spot because of the heat? Or to refuse to walk to save my feet? Aren't you aware that exertion makes weak people strong, whereas sloth makes strong people weak. Don't you realize that a little self-discipline will help prepare you for sickness, battle, and old age?

As a result of this hardy regimen, Socrates fared well in terms of health, longevity, and vitality. He seems to have avoided major illness, even during the plague years that killed one out of every four Athenians. He was renowned for his stamina both on military marches and encounters. And best of all, he reached the age of seventy at the peak of his powers.

ing" him speak some of the words that you have read. Perhaps you have felt what it would be like to be talking with him. In short, Socrates' personality and character have worked their way into your mind and heart.

In this exercise, I invite you to experiment with a way to use everything you have learned and felt, to activate "the Socrates in you." This technique will enable you to "become" Socrates—your own version of Socrates, based on those aspects of him that you find most compelling. It's based on a principle proclaimed by Gene Hackman, portraying a con man in David Mamet's movie *Heist*. Hackman is asked by one of his partners-in-crime, "How come you always know what the really smart move is?" Hackman answers, "I just think about some guy who's much smarter than I am, and then I do what that guy would do."

I have used this technique myself for over ten years, and I employ it in my presentations, workshops, and meetings of my Socrates Café. Participants find it enjoyable, exhilarating, and productive.

The technique is simple: You don a headband, which signifies your commitment to thinking like Socrates. Of course, you'll be self-conscious at first. But please give it a whirl. After all, using a piece of headgear to indicate a role we are adopting is a common device. We've all heard the expression "put on your thinking cap." And we're all familiar with a wide variety of headgear that signifies that the person wearing it is performing a certain role: a chef's hat, a fireman's helmet, a young person with a baseball cap on backward, a construction worker's hard hat, an artist's beret, a dunce cap!

To signify that you are entering your Socratic role, you will use an elastic headband of the type used for workouts or jogging. If you have one at hand, use it for now. If this exercise works well for you, I would want you to obtain three new ones, just for this purpose, in colors that you find most suggestive of Socratic thinking. Eventually, you might even want to design and decorate your own with motifs that have special meaning for you, as I have.

Anytime you want to use your mind to the utmost, put on this headband. It will do five things for you:

- It is a simple but vivid way of declaring to yourself and others that you want to carve out some time to use your mind productively or enjoyably.

- Once you've donned the headband, feeling it in place is a gentle incentive to "stay on task"—to focus on the thinking task you have set yourself.

- The headband will call to mind your favorite among the Socratic strategies you have learned and the ones that might be most useful to you in your particular situation.

- Each successive use of the headband will draw strength from your previous successes. Each time you put it on, you will be reminded that you have demonstrated your capacity to lift your thinking to a higher level. This should increase your confidence and success.

- If you are talking and thinking with others, the headband signals that you are committed to doing your best thinking and that you expect the same from them.

Most people find very quickly that headbands like this really do trigger better thinking. In my workshops, almost all of the participants want to take their headbands home with them for further use. (For that reason, I've learned to provide attractive heavy paper bands rather than expensive elastic ones!)

 7. Enrich your soul by touching other great spirits.

Socrates constantly alluded to other great souls as mentors for living. The most dramatic instance of this is at the end of the "Apology," when he welcomes death because it may offer the opportunity to encounter other great souls from the past.

> When the pilgrim arrives in the world below, he is delivered from those who profess justice in this world, and finds the true judges who are said to give judgment there, sons of God who were righteous in their own life. What would not a man give if he might converse with Orpheus and Musaeus and Hesiod and Homer?

> I will be able to continue my search into true and false knowledge. I shall find out who is wise, and who pretends to be wise and is not.

> What would not a man give, O judges, to be able to examine the leader of the great Trojan expedition; or Odysseus or Sisyphus, or numberless others, men and women too. What infinite delight there would be in conversing with them and asking them questions.

Throughout this book we are lifting our spirits by embracing Socrates' high standards of intellect, integrity, and friendship. Your success in doing this will make it much easier to continue the process by further enriching your soul through contact with other master spirits.

One outstanding resource is *How to Think Like Leonardo da Vinci* by Michael Gelb, a superb companion volume to this book. Exploring a second great spirit, after your experience with Socrates, can launch you on a lifelong series of such apprenticeships to greatness.

There's no more exciting way to grow than to study and emulate those great spirits whom you most admire. As Wordsworth proclaimed:

> *There is One Great Society alone on Earth,*
> *The Noble Living, and the Noble Dead.*

Da Vinci is, of course, considered the supreme "universal human"—artist, inventor, musician, astronomer, botanist, humorist, philosopher. But in your work and your life you call on the same skills that Leonardo used at the genius level, as Gelb demonstrates. He exemplifies the Socratic virtues of:

- Managing ambiguity and change

- Learning from experience

- Seeing the connections among all the elements

- Constant learning and improvement

- Awareness of the connection between top mental functioning and the physical body and its environment

- Whole-brain thinking

These are some of the traits that Gelb has teased out of Leonardo's extraordinary performance. We can all cultivate them to a much greater degree.

Start by cultivating the following three traits shared by Leonardo and Socrates:

Learning from experience: Your most important learning comes from your own experience. Continual education is essential, but nothing beats reflecting on your work every day. Learn from every project, every meeting, every encounter, and you will continually improve. (Leonardo called this ability *dimostrazione*.)

Seeing the connections among all things: The bane of our lives is disconnectedness. We pile challenge upon challenge, responding to this demand and that. But often we fail to ensure that all these pieces, each excellent in itself, reinforce each other. At the worst, the plethora of involvements fractures our experience. Seek to select and shape your activities and commitments with more unity and coherence. What are the largest goals you want to achieve? Sharpen your answer to that question, then look ruthlessly at your plethora of current commitments to *focus* and *simplify*. (*Connessione* was Leonardo's term for this skill.)

Whole-brain thinking: In your work relationships and your personal ones, seek a balance of people who are logical and those who are imaginative. Thrive on a mix of people who are devils for the details and those who make your soul soar. Admire both kinds of "genius" and cultivate them both in yourself. (Gelb calls this trait *arts/scienza*.)

If you want to go even further in this direction, I highly recommend Gelb's *Discover Your Genius: How to Think Like History's Ten Most Revolutionary Minds.* The geniuses with whom Gelb acquaints you in this wonderful book are Plato, Brunelleschi, Columbus, Copernicus, Elizabeth I, Shakespeare, Jefferson, Darwin, Gandhi, and Einstein.

 8. Live "the stages of the soul."

We have explored the journey of the soul in the allegory of "The Cave" in Chapter 4. The prisoner who escapes from the cave goes through the five-stage process we will revisit in this exercise.

Socrates' life, from the time he heard "the call" from the Oracle at Delphi, through his struggles with his fellow Athenians, to his final choice to take the hemlock, is a dramatic illustration of this process. You also experience it each time you open the *Dialogues* and start reading about one of Socrates' encounters. In every case you will find a call to explore some new area of the world of ideas, a search for the right perspective on it, a struggle with misleading ideas, a breakthrough when the initial position is transcended by fresh understanding, and a return to daily life.

We've all become familiar with the idea that, as adults, we go through these phases and stages in our growth and development. Carl Jung first proposed this provocative thesis, and Eric Erikson refined it. Gail Sheehy popularized the notion in her book *Passages,* drawing on the

SOCRATES' WAY OF "LOOKING WITHIN"

Socrates sought *authenticity* by regularly "going within"—removing himself from his fellows and closing his eyes in a trance-like state. We have seen how he came late to the symposium because he took time to stop in a portico up the street to meditate.

Even more dramatic was an incident that occurred on a campaign north of Athens, the seige of Potidaea. It was a summer morning, and there was no action in prospect. There wasn't much to do except sentry duty, sleeping, and talking about home.

Around noon, Socrates was observed standing on a small hill, where he had been since dawn, barefooted and silent. He seemed completely oblivious to his surroundings. His fellow soldiers tried to attract his attention, but Socrates was completely absorbed in his own thoughts. After awhile most of them wandered away.

Through the entire night, Socrates stood there, with a few soldiers sleeping nearby as the stars gleamed above. The next morning he was still there and joined them for breakfast, refreshed and robust as ever. Socrates never spoke about what he had been thinking, but he often explained his mission in life as one given to him by the gods, as a soldier gets his commands from his general. So it may well be that during that day and night of contemplation, Socrates found his soul-work.

work of Daniel Levinson. But this useful literature leaves out the spiritual element of our development as adults. Harry Moody, a carrier of the flame who is a philosopher and activist, has filled that gap with a dazzling book, *The Five Stages of the Soul,* written with David Carroll.

Recall a time in your life when you went through this process.

- *The Call*—You received some signal that you needed to change your life in some way, or that a change was going to be imposed on you.

- *The Search*—You undertook a search for what you needed to do to cope with that change.

- *The Struggle*—You took an action that sometimes involved struggle to achieve the goal you could see.

- *The Breakthrough*—You experienced some kind of change or insight.

- *The Return*—You brought the results into everyday life.

Now, use this heightened awareness of how you have gone through this process to discern where currently or in the foreseeable future you are going to experience it again.

 9. Find your soul in your work.

Socrates found his soul in his work and implored others to do the same. His call was for excellence in whatever craft, trade, or profession people found themselves in. Whether you're a potter or a doctor, a helmsman or a diplomat, what matters is understanding what constitutes excellence in that field and dedicating yourself to it. Socrates would have agreed with John Gardner that if a philosopher despises his plumber, neither his theories nor his pipes will hold water.

Many of us are searching today for more meaning in our workplace or profession. How does one dare yearn for something more when so many workplaces seem totally committed to financial survival and profit making? How do we get work done amidst the demands and tugs on our soul?

David Rottman addresses these serious questions in his book *The Career as a Path to the Soul*. As vice president for Career Services at J. P. Morgan Chase in New York, he has personally and with the help of his staff assisted thousands of employees at all levels to find career fulfillment. Rottman's basic belief is that "there is a sacred premise"—an "antique soul" as some like to call it—behind every profession. You can use this principle to experience your work as part of something larger—the meaningful enterprise of humankind's journey.

To see your work in this way, consider it without reference to its current context. What is its "Platonic ideal"? For example, it is true that these days lawyers have a poor reputation among many people. But ask yourself: "In its essence, what is the legal profession supposed to do? What is the timeless ideal function of the Law?" This is its sacred premise.

This is exactly the approach Socrates used. He sparked dialogues on what constituted the essential ideal or virtue of each craft or profession, from asking the potter what makes one pot better than another to inquiring into the soul of the good stateman.

Rottman suggests where to look for the soul of certain professions:

- The Librarian is the keeper of the sacred flame, responsible for the continuity of knowledge and the treasured legacy of our accumulated wisdom.

- The Journalist ascertains the facts as they really are, so that people know what is going on and can make the right decisions.

- The Actor enables an audience to have significant vicarious experiences that sharpen their feelings and thoughts.

a. What is the sacred premise of your profession, occupation, craft, or art?

b. How well are you succeeding in serving this sacred premise?

c. How could you rededicate yourself to the higher purpose of your work?

 ## 10. Do *the right thing.*

"Crime does not pay," we all learned as children. But Plato's allegory "The Ring of Gyges" raises the challenging issue "What would happen if people discovered as adults that crime *does* pay?"

David Denby, the *New Yorker* journalist and film and culture critic, read "The Ring of Gyges" when he returned to Columbia University at the age of forty-eight, to spend two years reading the Great Books with undergraduates. Here is how the myth sparked him to fantasize on what he would do if he could put on the Ring of Gyges:

Let's see, *lunch,* lunch at at Le Cirque! Yes, head straight for the kitchen, one of New York's proudest, and there remove

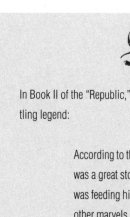

THE ALLEGORY OF THE RING OF GYGES

In Book II of the "Republic," Socrates' friend Glaucon challenges him with a basic moral issue by telling this unsettling legend:

According to the tradition, Gyges was a shepherd in the service of the king of Lydia. There was a great storm, and an earthquake made an opening in the earth at the place where he was feeding his flock. Amazed at the sight, he descended into the opening, where, among other marvels, he beheld a dead body of stature, as it appeared to him, more than human, and having nothing on but a gold ring; this he took from the finger of the dead and re-ascended.

Now the shepherds met together, according to custom, that they might send their monthly report about the flocks to the king. Into their assembly he came, having the ring on his finger, and as he was sitting among them he chanced to turn the collet of the ring inside his hand, when instantly he became invisible to the rest of the company and they began to speak of him as if he were no longer present.

He was astonished at this, and again touching the ring he turned it outward and reappeared. He made several trials of the ring, and always with the same result—when he turned it inward he became invisible, when outward he reappeared.

Whereupon he contrived to be chosen one of the messengers who were sent to the

Henry Kissinger's *brochette de quenelles* as it was waiting to be served, and eat it in the corner. . . . No, this was pathetic, it lacked virtuosity. Snatching the morsels from his fork would be more like it, and then impeding his arm as he lifted his glass to drink, my own lips meeting the glass for a swallow. That was better, more like Harpo, who always wore the Ring of Gyges.

Fantasizing more ambitiously, Denby realizes that the cloak of invisibility could be put to more socially responsible use:

court. As soon as he arrived he seduced the queen, and with her help conspired against the king and slew him, and took the kingdom.

Suppose now that there were two such magic rings, and the just man put on one of them and the unjust the other. No man can be imagined to be of such an iron nature that he would stand fast in justice. No man would keep his hands off what was not his own when he could safely take what he liked out of the market, or go into houses and lie with any one at his pleasure, or kill or release from prison whom he would, and in all respects be like a God among men.

Then the actions of the just would be as the actions of the unjust; they would both come at last to the same point.

And this we may truly affirm to be a great proof that a man is just, not willingly or because he thinks that justice is any good to him individually, but of necessity, for wherever any one thinks that he can safely be unjust, there he is unjust.

For all men believe in their hearts that injustice is far more profitable to the individual than justice, and he who argues as I have been supposing, will say that they are right. If you could imagine any one obtaining this power of becoming invisible, and never doing any wrong or touching what was another's, he would be thought by the lookers-on to be a most wretched idiot, although they would praise him to one another's faces, and keep up appearances with one another from a fear that they too might suffer injustice. Enough of this.

Off to work. Head to Baghdad, where I find a knife in a street bazaar, make my way to Saddam's headquarters, bypassing the guards, and plunge the knife into the dictator's . . .

But quickly he realizes that despite having the power to do these things, he still would be constrained by the person he is:

Snapping out of it, I realized with a pang of disappointment that I wouldn't do any of this. Well, maybe the bit with the *quenelles.*

But even if I were invisible, I could not kill Saddam Hussein, though I wouldn't mind if someone else killed him. Glaucon, I thought, was wrong—at least in my case. I would remain "just." Long maintained habits of obedience to the law would probably keep me honest, nonviolent, and even faithful. I wouldn't want to sleep with any woman who would sleep with an invisible man. (Perhaps I was closer to Groucho than to Harpo.) All right, *once,* for a kick.

Eventually, Denby concludes that we may *already* have too much leave to do whatever we want:

The truth is, I thought that too many people in America acted as if they were already wearing the Ring of Gyges. The dream of total invisibility—the hope of getting away with murder—was one of the things hurting us. The first time I read the *Republic,* when I was eighteen, I might have taken the ring. But now I wanted peace and civil order and accountability.

Challenge

Think about these questions yourself, and raise them with friends:

a. Would you be ethical if you knew there were *no* possibility that your unethical behavior would ever be discovered?

b. Would others?

c. Why? On what principles? For what reasons?

d. Recollect an occasion when you had the opportunity to wear the Ring of Gyges, i.e., when you could do whatever you chose, even if it was something that others would regard as unethical, with complete assurance that no one could ever find out what you did. What did you do? Why?

SOCRATES' FAREWELL TO HIS FRIENDS

Gathered in his jail cell waiting for the hemlock to be prepared, Socrates' oldest friend Crito asks the him a simple question:

CRITO: What can we do to please you best?

SOCRATES: Nothing new, Crito. Just what I am always telling you. If you look after yourselves, whatever you do will please me and mine and you too. . . . On the other hand, if you neglect yourselves and fail to follow the line of life as I have laid it down both now and in the past, however fervently you agree with me now, it will do no good at all.

CRITO: We shall try our best to do as you say.

SOCRATES' WAY FOR WOMEN

> To judge a person's capability by gender
> is like judging a man's intelligence by the
> amount of hair on his head.
>
> SOCRATES, IN XENOPHON'S "CONVERSATIONS"

ON HIS WAY to a great public funeral, as Xenophon tells us in "Memoirs," Socrates met an acquaintance who asked him pointedly: "Do you think you could speak yourself if they asked you to?"

"Not a problem," replied Socrates, "considering the very capable coach I have in that art."

"Who is he?" asked his companion.

"'He's a *she*," Socrates answered. "Aspasia. Only yesterday I heard her composing an oration about these very dead. She repeated to me the sort of speech which she felt should be delivered. Parts of it were from one that she'd obviously composed for Pericles; other parts she improvised on the spot."

"Can you recite any of it, Socrates?"

"I ought to be able to, for she taught it to me and she was ready to beat on me because I kept forgetting."

Though Socrates himself admired women, there aren't any among the participants in the Socratic *Dialogues*. Despite all the "glories that were Greece," it wasn't so glorious if you were a woman (or a slave or a "barbarian") in fifth-century Athens. The majority of women were excluded from politics, business, the arts, sports, and the military.

The unnatural male predominance in Socrates' world diminished its quality for both men and women. Just imagine what would have happened if Socrates had been born female—if that masterful intellect and imagination had been embodied in a woman. History would have been altered. There would have been no Socrates as we know him, but rather Socrata (as I've dubbed this imagined woman), who would have been unschooled, confined to the house, and deprived of the companionship of other budding minds. She would have been precluded from participation in political, military, social, and economic life. Yet in our time women often exemplify the best of the Socratic approach: asking great questions, thinking things through deeply, encouraging dialogue, and cultivating their souls.

In this appendix we will explore the enduring value of the female spirit in Socratic terms:

- How Socrates himself saw through his patriarchal society and proudly counted women among his most treasured comrades. (And how his fellow Athenians admitted the value of women in their arts, myths, and religion.)

- The evidence that Socrates' approach comes naturally to women and that their propensity for it will improve their prospects in the twenty-first century.

- How you can use the Socratic approach to enhance your life, and to secure your rightful place in our society.

SOCRATES AND WOMEN

Throughout his life, Socrates respected and learned from women. He honored them for their intellect, vision, understanding, and wisdom—the qualities he most respected in any person.

- Phaenarete, Socrates' mother, provided him with the model for his life work. He often evoked her profession of midwifery as the model for his role as a "midwife" of the mind.

- Diotima was Socrates' teacher in the only subject on which he claimed to have expert knowledge. In the "Symposium" he says: "Now I will give the account of Love which I once heard from a woman of Mantinea, called Diotima. She had other accomplishments as well . . . but what concerns us at present is that she was my instructress in the art of Love."

- Aspasia, the life-partner of Pericles, was admired not only by Socrates but also by the entire elite of fifth-century Athens as a visionary, policy maker, and writer. She was reputed to have "ghost-written" some of Pericles' most important official speeches.

According to one scholarly study on the status of women in Greek antiquity, *Pandora's Daughters* by Eva Cantarella:

> Socrates was particularly well disposed toward women and did not limit himself to abstract recognition of their capacities; he listened to their advice and even admitted that some of them were wiser than himself.

THE ATHENIANS AND WOMEN

Like Socrates, many of the most thoughtful and creative Athenians recognized the value of women and expressed it in their works. All the major playwrights of fifth-century Athens portrayed magnificent women. Just recall Aeschylus' Clytemnestra, Sophocles' Antigone, and Euripides' Medea. The audiences for those plays were clearly receptive to works that featured strong, powerful, effective women.

Euripides, the playwright closest to Socrates in his thinking, was a passionate champion of women. He dramatized the injustices they suffered in the macho world of ancient Greece. He and Socrates were denounced as "fellow conspirators" by contemporaries like Aristophanes. Their roles in challenging Athenian orthodoxies were captured in the popular opinion that "Socrates lit the kindling for Euripides' bonfire."

In addition to *Medea*, Euripides based plays such as *Phaedra* and *The Trojan Women* on female protagonists who eloquently defined their tragic situation.

> *Men say we women lead a sheltered life*
> *At home, while they face death amid the spears.*

The fools! I had rather stand in the battle line
Thrice, than once bear a child,

says Medea. Nothing like that is expressed in Western literature until Ibsen's *A Doll's House.*

The comic playwright Aristophanes also got into the act with such plays as *Lysistrata,* in which the women organize themselves to put a stop to the men's mindless pursuit of militarism. He portrays an Athenian wife and mother who expresses the group's view on the doings of their husbands:

Too many times, as we sat in the house,
we'd hear that you'd done it again—
man-handled another affair of state
with your usual staggering incompetence.
Then, masking our worry with a nervous laugh,
we'd ask you, brightly,
"How was the Assembly today, dear?
Anything in the minutes
about Peace?"

In religion, too, the Athenians implicitly acknowledged the importance of women. They literally worshiped female divinities. For example, their city was, they believed, founded by Athena, whose statue reigned majestically inside the Parthenon. Furthermore, it was the female Muses who inspired virtually all the arts and sciences the Greeks revered, from epic poetry and theater, to history and astronomy.

Most telling of all, women were powerfully present among their highest divinities. "The Olympian pantheon is anything but chauvinistic," notes Murry Hope in *Practical Greek Magic.* "There is an equal number of gods and goddesses. Hera is the mother of the gods. Aphrodite, Athena, Artemis, and Demeter symbolized the most important qualities a human being could cultivate." So meaningful are these goddesses that there's a wonderful book about how women today can use them as "archetypes" of spiritual growth: *Goddesses in Everywoman* by Jean Shinoda Bolen (see Exercise #6).

The Socratic Spirit in Our Time

The entry of women into the mainstream of American life has benefited our culture and society with a fresh influx of the Socratic spirit. Such gadflies as Betty Friedan, Gloria Steinem, Jean Houston, Clarissa Pinkola Estés, Maxine Hong Kingston, Bella Abzug, and Marian Wright Edelman have been among the foremost Socratic figures of our era. And carriers of the flame in other fields have exemplified Socrates' independence of thought (see Exercise #4, below). These well-known women have their counterparts in virtually every area and region of the nation, working in every kind of profession and business.

"To make my contribution I must Ask Questions, Speak the Truth, Think for Myself, and Care for My Soul," says Linda Meyer, founder of the famed Meyer Learning Center in Denver. Meyer's life-work is to help children and families to overcome learning and educational challenges. She works with "gifted," learning-disabled, and typical students as well as their parents and teachers. Her unique methods are the basis of her widely used book *Helping Your Child Learn.*

Meyer conceives her function as a tutor in Socratic perspective. The vision statement for her center reads in part:

For most of Western history, parents who could afford the best, engaged private tutors to help educate their children. Classical Greeks sent their sons to the gymnasium with their personal teachers, and some of the brightest of them sought out Socrates, the model for excellence in teaching, who did his work not in a classroom but one-on-one with this students.

Meyer herself exemplifies the Socratic spirit and uses it in her work and life in these ways:

- *Know thyself.* "First, I help my students to become aware of their own learning styles. The schools rarely do this. Yet such self-knowledge is the foundation of enjoyable and effective learning."

- *Ask questions.* Meyer diagnoses each student to discover his or her unique strengths and problems. But her approach is much more Socratic than the "instruments" used by most psychologists. While those are part of her repertoire, her diagnostic process is more like a Socratic conversation. "My chief tool is to ask the right questions, and really listen to the answers," she explains.

- *Think for yourself.* Meyer calls it "deep processing"—using her years of training plus all of her own "learning styles" to process information. "Like Socrates, I know I need to take the time to think things through, review critically what people think they already know, and tap my informed intuition. I resist the temptation to come to fast and firm conclusions, preferring to give rein to my thoughts and intuitions. Sometimes this looks a little like one of Socrates 'trances'!"

- *Speak the truth.* "To tell a mother some hard truths about her child, which she has been denying for years—and yet to give her hope—is the hardest part of my job," says Meyer. (But parents I have interviewed about Linda's work regularly say: "My conferral with Linda about my child was the most important conversation of my life as a parent—because it not only explained what was wrong, but offered a solution.")

- *Free your mind.* Just as Socrates had to question the dominant beliefs of his time, Meyer had to free herself from an upbringing in conventional small-town American Protestantism, which was reinforced throughout her college years and as a young wife and mother:

    "When I began to discover my own spirituality, I was rejected by my fellow Christians. It was a painful paradox: on the one hand, I found myself spiritually exhilarated by Nature, by striving to be a better person, even by fitness training. But my conventional neighbors made me feel that I was losing my soul, rather than finding it.

    "It helped me greatly to learn how Socrates suffered this same way. His whole life was driven by his personal piety—yet his fellow citizens sentenced him to death for irreverence and 'introducing new gods.'"

- *Strengthen your soul.* Like other successful counselors, coaches, and therapists, Meyer has learned that she must care for her soul if she is to give her clients her best and avoid "burnout." "I've learned that to give my best to clients, I need to be sure to meet my own needs—for Nature, for physical fitness, and for growth."

CHALLENGES, EXPLORATIONS, AND APPLICATIONS

 1. Identify the "Socrata" figures in your life.

Identify at least six women who have played significant roles in your life. They may include your mother, sister(s), best friends, colleagues, or mentors.

Strengthening Your Socratic Spirit

- Are there women who have been important figures in your own life, whose Socratic virtues have left their mark on you? (Exercise #1)

- Are there ways in which you have already or are now exemplifying Socratic qualities in your life? (Exercise #2)

- Have you identified, explored, and nurtured those Socratic traits that you likely share with other women? (Exercise #3)

- Have you acquainted yourself with the lives of outstanding women who have successfully achieved some of the goals you seek? (Exercise #4)

- Do you have regular opportunities to talk with other women about the issues that mean the most to you in your life, particularly in the areas where you aspire to make your mark? (Exercise #5)

- Have you explored "the goddesses in you"—the strengths symbolized by the female Olympian divinities like Athena and Aphrodite? (Exercise #6)

Now, consider how each of them influenced you in one or more of these Socratic ways:

- Helped you know yourself better

- Asked questions that stimulated your thinking

- Freed your mind from false or pernicious ideas

- Encouraged your growth through friendship

- Told you the truth when it might hurt, but could also help greatly

- Strengthened your soul by enabling you to see new depths and dimensions in yourself

a. Choose one of these women, and let her know again how she affected your life in this way.

b. Is there someone in your life now whom you can help in one of the ways that you were helped?

 2. Discover that you are already on the path.

If you have not already done it, do the exercise on pages 34–36, "Defending Your Life," based on the movie with that title in which a woman leads the way, reevaluating and upgrading one's lifestyle.

 3. Explore your Socratic ways of thinking as a woman.

"Women's Ways of Knowing" has emerged as a fruitful field of study over the past fifteen years. This body of research and thinking has firmly established that women have some distinctive "Socratic" strengths in developing their minds to their full potential. These "natural talents" of women are especially serviceable in the emerging world of the twenty-first century, argues Helen Fisher in *The First Sex*:

> As women continue to pour into the paid workforce in cultures around the world, they will apply their natural aptitudes in many sectors of society and dramatically influence twenty-first-century business, sex, and family life. In some important parts of the economy, they will even predominate, becoming the first sex. Why? Because current trends in business, communications, education, law, medicine, government, and the nonprofit sector all suggest that tomorrow's world will need the female mind.

Fisher identifies seven Socratic traits among the talents that will put women at the forefront. In the space below each one, please note:

1. One example of how you have used or are currently using this trait in your life or work.

2. A way you can further strengthen this trait in yourself through training or self-development.

3. An opportunity that you can foresee to capitalize on it even more over the next year.

- Women think about things in the larger context.

- Women have superior verbal abilities.

- Women have greater people savvy.

- Women have patience.

- Women have the ability to do and think several things simultaneously.

- Women have a penchant for long-range planning.

- Women have a preference for cooperating, reaching consensus, and leading via egalitarian teams.

 ### 4. *Inspire yourself with the lives of women you admire or find interesting.*

Using great lives to inspire our own is a classical strategy for self-development that has recently been revived by such writers as Wayne Dyer in his wonderful book *Wisdom of the Ages* and by Michael Gelb in his book *Discover Your Genius*.

This strategy is even more important for women, since they have fewer models to emulate. To find one or more for yourself, the most useful resource is the National Women's Hall of Fame, at *www.infoplease. com/people.html*. Here, you will find a roster with brief bios of women honored for their contribution to society in every field. For most of them, you can easily find a biography or an autobiography at your public library. (Few people will recognize all the women in these diverse categories, which is why reviewing this roster can be so exhilarating.)

- Businesswomen like Carly Fiorina and Donna Karan

- Scientists like Barbara McClintock and Margaret Mead

- Writers like Judy Blume and Maya Angelou

- Media personalities like Christiane Amanpour and Oprah Winfrey

- Artists like Judy Chicago and Helen Frankenthaler

- Athletes like Kristi Yamaguchi and Sarah Hughes

- Political figures like Carol Moseley-Braun and Hillary Clinton

Many of these women are, of course, notable carriers of the flame, and some of my personal favorites are among those least known to the general public. Scientist Barbara McClintock, for example, is a Socratic figure who attributes her achievement to the fact that she stayed outside the mainstream of academic science. (She won the Nobel Prize in medicine in 1983.) "The importance of her story lies in her independence," declares her biographer Evelyn Fox Keller in *A Feeling for the Organism: The Life and Work of Barbara McClintock*.

 5. Engage in dialogue regularly with other women.

Find or create your own opportunities to "dialogue" with other women on important topics of common interest and concern. You will find that the strategies and techniques provided in Chapter 5, "Grow with Friends," can be used to locate or launch groups especially for women. Among them are:

- a car pool with women who share your interests and concerns

- a brown-bag lunch group at your workplace

- a salon or Socrates Café

 6. Discover the goddesses in you.

We have seen that the fifth-century Athenians revered goddesses as a major part of their pantheon of divinities. Athena, for example, was extolled in the Parthenon and watched over the entire city as its protector. The classical Olympian array of higher powers was composed of both male and female figures.

Those female divinities were much more than decorative figures. They each represented a basic force in human life and human affairs, including such powerful drives as love, nurturing, autonomy, and wisdom. These are forces and drives that still shape the lives of women today.

In her book *Goddesses in Everywoman: A New Psychology of Women,* Jean Shinoda Bolen, an M.D. and clinical professor of psychiatry at the University of California, San Francisco, demonstrates how understanding these "archetypes" can facilitate self-knowledge. She introduces seven archetypal goddesses, or personality types, with whom most women can identify. She shows you how to identify your ruling goddesses (from the autonomous Artemis and the cool Athena to the nurturing Demeter and the creative Aphrodite), how to decide which to cultivate and which to overcome, and how to tap the power of these enduring archetypes to become a better "heroine" in your own life stories.

Here are the Olympian goddesses and the psychological strengths and difficulties they represent. Which of them do you recognize in yourself?

a. Complete this sentence about each of the goddesses who you feel are expressed in you.

"Like _____,

I _____."

For example:

"Like Artemis, I enjoy and thrive on being immersed in Nature, and feel a freedom and kinship with animals and birds."

"Like Artemis, I take pride in my capacity to set my own goals, stay on track, and achieve them."

"Like Artemis, I sometimes find myself angry when my purposes are thwarted."

Aim for three or four versions of the sentence for each goddess, with at least one of them including one of that goddess's "difficulties."

Goddess	Jungian Psychological Type	Psychological Difficulties	Strengths
Artemis	Usually extroverted Usually intuitive Usually feeling	Emotional distance, ruthlessness, rage	Ability to set own goals and reach them, independence, autonomy; friendships with women
Athena	Usually extroverted Definitely thinking Usually sensation	Emotional distance, craftiness, lack of empathy	Ability to think well, to solve practical problems and strategize; form strong alliances with men
Hestia	Definitely introverted Usually feeling Usually intuitive	Emotional distance, lack of social persona	Ability to enjoy solitude, to have a sense of spiritual meaning
Hera	Usually extroverted Usually feeling Usually sensation	Jealousy, vindictiveness, rage; inability to leave destructive relationship	Ability to make a lifetime commitment; fidelity
Demeter	Usually extroverted Usually feeling	Depression, burnout, fostering dependency, unplanned pregnancy	Ability to be maternal and nurturing of others; generosity
Persephone	Usually introverted Usually sensation	Depression, manipulation, withdrawal into unreality	Ability to be receptive, to appreciate imagination and dreams; potential psychic abilities
Aphrodite	Definitely extroverted Definitely sensation	Serial relationships, promiscuity; difficulty considering consequences	Ability to enjoy pleasure and beauty, to be sensual and creative

b. Now consider which of the other goddesses you might want to express more fully, to resolve the "difficulties" you encounter with your chosen goddesses.

Dr. Bolen suggests that once you get to know your goddesses well, you can summon their help when you need it, with such invocations as:

- Athena, help me to think clearly here.

- Persophone, help me to stay open and receptive.

- Hera, help me to make a commitment.

- Demeter, help me to be patient and generous.

- Artemis, keep me focused on my goal.

- Aphrodite, help me to love and enjoy my body.

- Hestia, honor me with your presence; bring me peace and serenity.

c. Once you have become familiar with these goddesses, introduce the idea to a good friend who you think would also enjoy it, and compare notes on your answers to these questions.

d. When you find yourself in situations where one of your chosen goddesses should come to the fore, consider how you can go even further by using other of her qualities you have learned about.

e. Finally, after considerable experience with your goddesses, you may want to have a conversation with one of them! Dr. Bolen describes how you can do this:

> Once a woman becomes aware of the goddess archetypes (in herself), she has two very useful insight tools. She can listen with a sensitive ear to the voices within herself, recognize "who" is speaking, and become aware of the goddesses that influence her. When they represent conflicting aspects of herself that she must resolve, she can tune into the needs and concerns of each goddess, and then decide for herself what is most important.
>
> Since all the goddesses are innate patterns in every woman, an individual woman may realize the need to become better acquainted with a par-

ticular goddess. . . . Actively imagining goddesses can help a woman know the archetypes active in her psyche. She might visualize a goddess, and then, once she has a vivid image in her mind, see if she can have a conversation with the visualized figure. . . . She may find that she can ask questions and get answers. If she is receptively attuned to hear an answer that she does not consciously invent, a woman using active imagination often finds herself as if in a real conversation, which increases her knowledge about an archetypal figure that is a part of herself.

Socrates would approve of this process. As we have seen, he regularly consulted his inner daimon to discover what was right for him.

APPENDIX A

READING THE SOCRATIC DIALOGUES

Nothing will keep your mind keener than spending a little of your life among Socrates and his friends, as my father taught me to. Here's some help on getting started.

You've already sampled Plato's and Xenophon's *Dialogues* in the epigraphs that opened each chapter on the seven keys. We started with Socrates' conversation with Euthydemus about self-knowledge and ended with words from the "Apology" about tending to your soul. Here, I want to recommend a short selection of Plato's *Dialogues*—the ones that give us the most accurate and vivid portrayal of Socrates in action. (Plato continued to write Socratic dialogues for decades after the death of his master. But increasingly these writings expressed Plato's own developing views rather than reflecting those of the Gadfly.)

I recommend the Penguin Classics paperback editions, which are widely available, freshly translated, have lively introductions and serviceable notes, and are attractively printed.

- "Symposium." The best introduction to Socrates and his circle. A Greek symposium wasn't an academic colloquium, but a drinking and thinking party. At this one, the subject is love, and the guests, among them the comic poet Aristophanes, who lampooned Socrates in *The Clouds,* compete to define it. Midway, in bursts the drunken Alcibiades, who tells the tale of how he tried unsuccessfully to seduce Socrates by crawling into his bed when they were on military maneuvers. Are *your* dinner parties this lively?!

- "Apology." At the high point of his trial, Socrates addresses his accusers, his jury, his contemporaries, and posterity in this brilliant justification of his life and thought. With wit and profundity he proclaims the personal and social need to know thyself, ask questions, free your mind, speak the truth, and strengthen your soul.

- "Crito." The night before his death, Socrates' oldest friend pays an unexpected call to his jail cell, to try to convince the doomed man to accept a foolproof plan for his escape into exile. As the night wanes, Socrates poignantly explains why he chooses to accept the verdict of the court. The dialogue is at once a poignant portrayal of friendship and a classic formulation of the doctrine of "civil disobedience."

- "Phaedo." Socrates' friends gather with him in his jail cell as he prepares to take the hemlock. Some cannot bear what is about to happen, and the prisoner himself must try to ease their pain. Right to the end, Socrates displays the deep conviction that comes from knowing that he is doing the right thing.

- "Gorgias." Does might make right? So demands Callicles in this important dialogue whose bitter tone strongly suggests that it was written shortly after the death of Socrates.

- "Protagoras." Socrates goes toe-to-toe with the most renowned "sophist" of the day, while an appreciative crowd savors the fracas.

- "Euthyphro." On the way to the courthouse pursuant to his trial, Socrates runs into a young friend who is on his way there to prosecute his own father. More intrigued by this provocative case than by his own, Socrates cannot resist interrogating the other man about the values and logic that have impelled this provocative action. By the time Socrates is finished, Euthyphro—and we—have come to see why it is so necessary to critically examine the bases of our actions.

- "Meno." Here, too, Socrates engages in conversation with a fellow who is supremely confident about his own ideas—in this case, that wealth indicates virtue and that poverty is a sign of personal failing. Along the way, we see how Socrates demonstrated that a slave boy with no knowledge of geometry could be guided to solve a Euclidean conundrum, demonstrating how much we can learn if our innate capacity is activated by the right questions.

- "Phaedrus." Socrates rarely left his beloved Athens to savor the joys of the countryside. ("Trees are lovely," he said, "but you can't dialogue with them.") So this conversation on the banks of a vividly evoked waterway is uniquely charming. In the course of demonstrating that the arts of rhetoric are only acceptable when firmly based on the truth, Socrates uses one of his powerful metaphors: the chariot of the soul.

APPENDIX B

BEST BOOKS ON SOCRATES AND OUR CLASSICAL HERITAGE

Socrates by Anthony Gottlieb (Routledge, 1999).

This little paperback is my choice for the first fifty pages you should read on Socrates' life and ideas and how they have shaped our thinking. As might be expected from the executive editor of *The Economist,* the book is well written, nonacademic, personal, and critical. His theme is that Socrates was "philosophy's martyr." But he says of the "Apology" that "from a legal point of view, Socrates' speech is a miserable performance."

The Trial of Socrates by I. F. Stone (Little, Brown, 1988).

Another journalist-scholar weighs in with this maverick view of Socrates' trial. Stone undertook this study as his retirement project at the age of seventy, and learned classical Greek so he could read and judge the sources with the same independent judgment he had applied to "The Pentagon Papers." He comes to unconventional conclusions and even has the dazzling audacity to rewrite the "Apology" to make the points he thinks Socrates should have made. Along the way he illuminates the man and his times in vivid and provocative prose.

Socrates, Ironist and Moral Philosopher by Gregory Vlastos (Cornell University Press, 1991).

Vlastos was the most distinguished Socrates scholar of the last generation, and this was his final masterwork. It is a model of true scholarship and profound reflection. Moreover, the author exemplified Socratic virtues in his life and career. As a young scholar, he scrapped the manuscript of a book that would have earned him tenure because his own daimon told him it was inauthentic and untrue to Socrates' spirit. And he wrote in the front of his last work, published when he was in his seventies and awarded every honor his profession could bestow: "I have made mistakes in the past and will doubtless make more of them in the future. Anyone who points them out to me is my friend." Socrates must have given Vlastos a glorious welcoming "symposium" when he reached Elysium.

Socrates Café: A Fresh Taste of Philosophy by Christopher Phillips (W. W. Norton, 2001).

You met Chris Phillips, whose life was changed by the Socratic spirit, in Chapter 5. This book recounts his conversion experience, portrays the Socrates Cafés he's started, and plumbs the Socratic spirit throughout Western thought and in our time. Phillips is both inspiring and thought-provoking. "The one and only firm and lasting truth that has emerged from all the Socrates Café discussions I've taken part in," he concludes, "is that it is not possible to examine, scrutinize, plumb, and mine a question too thoroughly and exhaustively. There is always more to discover. That is the essence, and magic, of what I have come to call 'Socratizing.'"

Socrates in the Agora (American School of Classical Studies at Athens, 1978).

This precious little pamphlet distills the findings of a decades-long project to excavate the Athenian agora. I used it to tramp around the site, following in Socrates' footsteps. "Since Socrates was most truly at home in Athens' agora," writes author Mabel Lang (who, with scholarly diffidence, eschews a byline on the title page), "it should be possible to follow his career in the remains there and rebuild in ideal form the surroundings in which he practiced what he preached." Wonderful photos show everything from the floor plan of the kind of house in which the "Symposium" took place to the thimble-size terra-cotta vessels from which Socrates drank the hemlock.

City of Sokrates: An Introduction to Classical Athens by J. W. Roberts (Routledge & Kegan Paul, 1984).

"In any assessment of the city the key witness must be Sokrates, who was both a devoted son of Athens and her most radical critic." That's the premise of this reconstruction of Athenian society by Eton scholar Roberts, who vividly evokes the public ceremonies, including the dramatic festivals, as well as art in general. He shows how Athenian self-esteem expressed itself in imperialism and does not skirt the fact that the freedom of the citizens was predicated on the unfreedom of their slaves and their subject allies.

Courtesans and Fishcakes by James N. Davidson (St. Martin's, 2000).

And now for something completely different . . . ! Here's a lively example of the new school of "bottom-up" history, which focuses on everyday life and common folk instead of on the rich and famous. The author chronicles Athenian customs in eating, drinking, and prostitution. The book opens and closes with portrayals of Socrates as exemplifying the Greek approach to pleasure as vigorously rationalistic and humane. Davidson concludes: "While Buddha is commemorated as a skeletal figure meditating under a Bo tree and Jesus is monumentalized in triumph over the flesh on a cross, Socrates is best remembered in conversation at a lavish symposium . . . arguing gently in favor of the small cups" (the use of which signified enjoyment of wine, but in moderation).

The Art of Living: Socratic Reflections from Plato to Foucault by Alexander Nehamas (University of California Press, 1998).

"Socrates' major accomplishment is that he established a new way of life, a new art of living," contends Professor Nehamas of Princeton. This book explores how several major thinkers—Plato, Montaigne, Nietzsche, and Foucault—have endeavored to do the same thing, inspired by Socrates but not imitating him. These robust and courageous thinkers show us how following Socrates' Way entails finding our own.

Who Killed Homer? The Demise of Classical Education and the Recovery of Greek Wisdom by Victor Davis Hanson and John Heath (The Free Press, 1998).

An impassioned call to arms from two acclaimed classicists, this book argues that if we lose our knowledge of the Greeks, we lose our understanding of who we are. The Hellenic heritage, they contend, explains why Western culture is so uniquely dynamic and why its tenets of democracy, personal freedom, market economy, civil liberty, and constitutional government are now sweeping the globe.

The authors are ruthless about the failings of their academic colleagues: "Most of these senior professors do not look like those who held the pass at Thermopylai. They do not talk like the condemned Socrates or see the world at all as Sophocles saw it. America's stewards of the Greeks are not even flippant like Archilochus; they lack both the humor of Aristophanes and the solemnity of Thucydides. How do we grow so utterly distant from those to whom we have devoted our lives?"

Barefoot in Athens by Maxwell Anderson (Sloan, 1951).

A wonderfully readable play about Socrates that inspired my lifelong interest in him.

Of course, I also hope you will sample Socrates' own favorite books:

Homer's *Odyssey* and *Iliad*

The plays of Aeschylus, Sophocles, Aristophanes, and especially those of intellectual comrade Euripides

The works of the historians Herodotus and Thucydides

If you think they may prove to be dull, think again! Here's how one teacher, Victor Davis Hanson, describes their impact on his working-class students in California:

The Hellenic spirit thrives among my students working at Burger King and among night-school returnees, who, once hooked on Thucydides' blood and guts, then begin to appreciate the power of his thought. They welcome a tough guy like Thucydides who shows how their brutal experiences are universal, even banal, and thus explicable . . . Thucydides' honesty comes as a welcome touch of realism. With him there is no "feeling your pain," no pretense of cheap compassion, and there are no easy apologies for what we are and what we have done.

SOCRATES
AND HIS WORLD
ON THE WEB

by Chrysoula Economopoulos

Media Relations Director,

American Hellenic Institute

ON SOCRATES

The Death of Socrates (painting)
www.ccla.org.uk/aecd/unit1/ped8.htm

Here is Jacques Louis David's monumental painting portraying the death
of the Greek thinker (which appears on the front jacket of this book).
Provides also a brief description of the painting and the artist as well as an
overview of the scene being portrayed and the significance of Socrates
and the manner in which he led his life and influenced others.

    This is one page on the Adult Education for Citizenship and Democ-
racy's website, "a new learning programme exclusively concerned with
the promotion of democracy and active citizenship." It is part of the Pop-

ular Education for Democracy and European Citizenship project, which is supported by the Socrates Programme of the European Union.

Socrates Quotes
www.lyfe.freeserve.co.uk/quotesocrates.htm

To browse a selection of some of Socrates' better-known quotes, click on this page and watch his words of wisdom scroll across your screen.

Socrates on Encarta
encarta.msn.com and search on "Socrates"

A good basic starting point for obtaining general information on Socrates, his education, his teachings, and his times. Contains links to a number of articles on the philosopher himself, on his beliefs, on the Socratic method, and on biographers and scholars. Articles are concise and written in layman's terms, yet serve as a solid foundation from which to delve deeper into a study of Socrates, how he was influenced, and who he in turn influenced with his thinking.

The Last Days of Socrates
socrates.clarke.edu

For a nice tutorial on reading the "Euthryphro," "Apology," "Crito," and the death scene from "Phaedo," here's analysis and insight into the characters and the situation in each of these classical pieces of literature. However, anyone interested in reading these particular works should visit this site, which contains annotated hypertext versions of Plato's most important dialogues and audio clips of some of the texts. Included are definitions and background information on particular concepts, characters, and words, as well as photographs and maps to transport you to the particular time and place in focus. Notes are available on a sidebar to clarify and highlight the deeper nuances in the texts. Finally, test your knowledge of the works presented with a quiz that is available on the site.

Exploring Plato's *Dialogues*
plato.evansville.edu/

By searching on the term *Socrates,* this site's search engine turns up more
than 350 articles and texts related to the great philosopher. Complete in its
nature, it includes references and links to definitions of words appearing
in the texts and more. Archived are full hypertext versions of Plato's *Dialogues:* "Crito," "Phaedo," "Phaedrus," "Symposium," and "Republic,"
as well as an overview of Plato's life (including important influences such
as Socrates) and a substantial bibliographical listing. With this abundant
information, the site meets its goal of producing an interactive learning
environment that uses technology to enhance the study of Plato in ways
previously unavailable.

Dear Socrates
www.philosophynow.demon.co.uk/socrates31.htm

According to the column's introduction, "Having returned from the turn
of the fourth century B.C. to the turn of the twenty-first A.D., Socrates has
eagerly signed on as a *Philosophy Now* columnist so that he may continue to carry out his divinely-inspired dialogic mission." Following
along the lines of the "Dear Abby" column, this webpage has Socrates,
rather than Abby, answer readers' questions in only the way Socrates would.
The "Dear Socrates" column appears on the *Philosophy Now* website
(the newsstand magazine for everyone interested in philosophy) and allows readers to submit their own questions to the famous philosopher-
turned-columnist.

The Socrates Argument Clinic
www.mindspring.com/~mfpatton/sclinic.htm

A comical approach to understanding Socrates and his methods of end-
less query. Fact tempered with comedy helps the user to connect with a
virtual Socrates. Log onto this page on Patton's Argument Clinic, a website designed to introduce "the good, the bad and the idiotic debates in

modern philosophy" in a humorous manner. You will embark on a series of questions and answers with the great philosopher, choosing from four themes of debate: What is truth; What is justice; What is courage; and What is beauty. Debate on one of these themes continues. But beware: a "sycophantic response may bring on the ridicule of others. Your challenge is to complete the argument without making Socrates drink the hemlock."

RELATED SITES ON THE CLASSICAL HELLENIC WORLD

Top Sites

PBS—The Greeks: Crucible of Civilization
www.pbs.org/empires/thegreeks/

One of the best interactive sites available on the Internet regarding ancient Greece. Spun off of the PBS documentary *The Greeks: Crucible of Civilization,* this website contains an organized, visually appealing, and hi-tech presentation of information. Included is a time line, spanning from 1400 B.C. at the founding of the Oracle of Delphi; through the eras of Cleisthenes, Themistocles, Pericles, Aspasia, and Socrates; and ending at 337 B.C., when Athenian democracy came to a close. Most notable is the 3-D animated footage of the Parthenon and Acropolis and audio capability that allows the user to hear how the ancient Greeks spoke. Don't forget the five-part questionnaire, which helps users gauge their would-be rank and profession in Athenian society based on family background, gender, work experience, and other key determinants of status. An excellent links page found under "Educational Resources" completes this hi-tech site and includes a selected bibliography, student-friendly websites, lesson plans, and other links that help to define and illustrate the culture, society, politics, economy, and all other realms of ancient Greek life. For the full effect, download Quick Time Player and an audio player of your choice to your PC.

Perseus Digital Library
www.perseus.tufts.edu

Excellent and comprehensive, Perseus is *the* on-line encyclopedia and dictionary reference source for classical studies. It modestly describes itself as "an evolving digital library, engineering interactions through time, space, and language" and is part of the Department of the Classics at Tufts University. Perseus achieves its primary goal of bringing a wide range of source materials to as large an audience as possible and seeks to inspire inquiry into and further discoveries related to the classical world.

The Perseus site contains a search capability as well as an index of classical authors, including Plato and other contemporaries of Socrates. Within each search generated are links to definitions, photos, bibliographical references, and more. It also contains hypertext versions of classical works. In addition to the website's exhaustive search capabilities are links to a Greek history overview, arts and architecture catalogues, and more.

Internet Classics Archive
classics.mit.edu/index.html

"Bringing the wisdom of the classics to the Internet since 1994," this archive boasts a selection of 441 works of classical literature from fifty-nine different authors, primarily from the Greco-Roman world. It also includes links to other classical and electronic text resources and reader-recommended websites for each work that is available.

Odysseus (Web server of the Hellenic Ministry of Culture)
www.culture.gr

The Hellenic Ministry of Culture's Odysseus server does an excellent job of providing a listing of all the cultural wonders, past and present, that Greece has to offer. The mission of the site is to display "the millennia of artistry, the centuries of outstanding art, the achievements of the human spirit, the routes on which the western civilization strode in order to reach its current form." The site achieves a dual purpose by listing descriptions, photos, and hundreds of links to important museums, artwork, maps, monuments, and archaeological sites while also providing contact information and hours of operation for many of these historic landmarks. While all periods are touched on, the classical Hellenic period is complete and worth exploring.

Ancient World Mapping Center
www.unc.edu/depts/awmc/content/xhtml/index.html

To see how the world looked back in the times of Socrates and his contemporaries, this website is the tool to use. The AWMC is an on-line atlas of the ancient Mediterranean world designed for a broad cross section of groups interested in the study of the classics: from high school students and teachers through the university level and beyond. Notably, the site allows you to download and print high-resolution maps from the ancient world. But the site doesn't stop there. Also included are links to news and events, published work, and other ancient world map sites on the Internet.

Electronic Resources for Classicists
www.tlg.uci.edu/~tlg/index/about.html

Among the most complete and organized index of significant links to the classics on the Internet. Headings under which links are categorized include: information gateways, databases and information servers, electronic publications, bibliographical indexes, images, course materials, fonts and software, professional organizations, on-line seminars, K–12 resources, e-text archives, classics departments, discussion groups, and others.

Classics and Mediterranean Archaeology
classics.lsa.umich.edu

Hosted on the University of Michigan's website, this on-line index boasts hundreds of links related to the classics and Mediterranean archaeology. It is a links-only website, providing information under the categories of: texts/projects/journals/bibliographies, indexes of links, exhibits and image sources, field reports and archaeological site pages, associations and organizations, departmental descriptions, course material and teaching resources, museums, atlases and geographic information, news groups and mailing lists, and more.

The Costumer's Manifesto: Ancient Greece and Environs Costume Links
www.costumes.org/pages/greeklinks.htm

Look here to access the on-line catalogue of fashion in ancient Greece and the surrounding world. This website compiles the hottest links on the Internet that display clothing for men, women, and children for many different occasions. Links are conveniently listed on the homepage and are filed under the categories of: general information (including history), women's dress, men's dress, textiles, theater costume, armor and weapons, jewelry and accessories, hair and headdress, cosmetics, and related information. This site also incorporates an on-line bookstore focusing on costume-related books from all eras.

The British Museum: Greece
www.thebritishmuseum.ac.uk/world/greece/greece.html

The Department of Greek and Roman Antiquities of the British Museum boasts one of the most comprehensive collections of antiquities from the ancient civilizations of Greece and Rome, with over 100,000 objects. These mostly range in date from the beginning of the Greek Bronze Age (about 3200 B.C.) to the reign of the Roman emperor Constantine in the fourth century A.D. While the website for the collection does not display all of its treasures, some of the key exhibits highlighted include the Parthenon sculptures, with links to papers focusing on this topic. This is a must-visit for those interested in the debate on the Parthenon Marbles currently being waged between those who view Greece as their rightful home and those who believe the frieze should remain at the British Museum.

Also available is the COMPASS on-line database of nearly 5,000 objects on display at the British Museum, including artwork and artifacts from ancient Greece.

Other Sites Related to Socrates' Times

The National Archaeological Museum of Athens
www.culture.gr/2/21/214/21405m/e21405m1.html

Available via the Greek Ministry of Culture's website—*www.culture.gr*—this link lists and describes the various exhibits housed in this renowned museum and presents photographs of selected artwork and artifacts. The museum is described as "the most important archaeological museum in Greece and one of the richest in the world concerning ancient Greek art. Its collections are representative of all the cultures that flourished in Greece." With this in mind, the website is an important one to visit for a preview of what the museum has in store for its virtual and real visitors. See also *dboals.virtualave.net/archath1.html* for on-line photographs of exhibit items.

Louvre Museum: Greek, Etruscan, and Roman Antiquities
www.louvre.fr/anglais/collec/ager/ager_hp.htm

Includes photos from a selection of ancient Greek works on exhibit at the renowned Louvre Museum in Paris. Art is categorized chronologically, with eleven pieces of art from Socrates' era displayed on-line. Also offered is a description of how the artwork in this particular collection was acquired, a basic map of the Mediterranean world, and other pertinent information about the collection.

The Ancient City of Athens
www.indiana.edu/~kglowack/athens/

For an oft-cited photographic archive of the archaeological and architectural remains of ancient Athens, explore The Ancient City of Athens, sponsored by Indiana University. The primary purpose of the website is to supplement class lectures and reading assignments for students of classical art and archaeology, civilization, languages, and history at Indiana University. However, the site will be of use to anyone more generally interested in archaeological exploration and "the recovery, interpretation, and preservation of the past." Images presented are from the personal slide collection of Kevin T. Glowacki and Nancy L. Klein of the Department of Classical Studies at Indiana University, Bloomington.

American School of Classical Studies in Athens
www.ascsa.org

Now the largest of fourteen foreign advanced research institutes in Athens, the American School of Classical Studies in Athens' website contains general information, publications, a school directory, a listing of school-related excavations and surveys, and fellowship and grant information. It is targeted primarily at scholars and those interested in researching the classics. Its stature as the first and largest American overseas research center in terms of assets, programs, and constituency makes it a worthwhile place to visit on the web.

Classics Resources
artsci.wustl.edu/~cwconrad/classics.html

Classics Resources is essentially a no-nonsense links page that can take you to most places you would want to go on the Internet involving the classics. Links fall under the following headings: general classics listings; texts, general; specialized sites; Greek language; Greek authors; maps/sites, ancient world; Classics e-journal; Perseus resources; classics departments; e-list archives; Latin-related sites; classics publishers; classics associations; and other pages of note.

Archives for Greek/Latin Discussion Lists
omega.cohums.ohio-state.edu/hyper-lists/

To join in an on-line chat or discussion related to Greek and Latin civilizations, log onto one of the moderated sessions hosted on this site. Also included are related job listings, grants, scholarships, events, and conferences. The webpage is simple and straightforward.

Exploring Ancient World Cultures (EAWC)
at the University of Evansville, Indiana
eawc.evansville.edu

EAWC is available through the University of Evansville, Indiana's web-site. The EAWC strives to demonstrate the modern-day importance of studying ancient cultures, and achieves that goal with links to a number of ancient civilizations, among them that of Ancient Greece with a spe-cific reference to Socrates and the social organization of Athens during his time. This website hits all the major philosophers of the ancient Greek world. The value of this website is in its drawing together a diverse array of ancient civilizations. With this picturebook glimpse across history and cultures, the reader can compare and contrast each of the civilizations from one virtual vantage point.

Cultures that can be explored on this website include: Ancient Near East, Ancient India, Ancient Egypt, Ancient China, Ancient Greece, An-cient Rome, Early Islamic World, and Medieval Europe.

Ancient Greece (from Universal Artists)
www.ancientgreece.com

The Ancient Greece site provides an excellent overview of the environ-ment in which Socrates lived. It doesn't stop there, however. This site in-cludes information, photographs, and web links on the broad topics of: art and architecture, geography, mythology, people, history, Olympics, wars, and other resources to help the user form a complete image of the various facets of daily life in ancient Greece. Also useful is the site's on-line bookstore, presented in association with Amazon.com. Books, which can be browsed by general topic area or by plugging your key words into the Amazon.com search engine.

The Ancient Greek World
www.museum.upenn.edu/Greek_World/Index.html

The Ancient Greek World challenges the viewer to "discover the story of life in ancient Greece." This on-line resource from the University of Pennsylvania Museum of Archaeology and Anthropology will transport you back in time by detailing daily life in this ancient world culture through the use of images and essays. The artifacts on display vividly depict daily ancient Greek life by examining four subcategories: land and time, daily life, economy, and religion and death.

Land and Time: An overview of the physical landscape and climate of ancient Greece and a time line of important events.

Daily Life: Covers all aspects of daily life in ancient Greece, including home life, facets of both women's and men's lives, and roles at home and in society.

Economy: Includes photos and explanations of various coins, a description of the means of exchange in society, including an overview of trade and manufacturing, goods traded, and the significance of pottery in the whole process of exchange.

Religion and Death: Provides an overview of ancient Greek religious beliefs and customs. Interestingly, this portion of the site details the conception of the afterlife during those times.

Women, Children, and Men
mkatz.web.wesleyan.edu/cciv243/cciv243.CIHAGChapter.html

This chapter from Marilyn Katz's book *The Cambridge Illustrated History of Ancient Greece,* provides a detailed representation of life in ancient Greece. Among other things, Katz tackles the difficult question of gender roles in society during those times. While art and literature may portray the social ideal as consigning men to the public realm and women to the private realm, she points out that "when we examine more closely some of the details of ancient Greek social and cultural practices, the reality looks quite different." Also discussed are the polis, the legal system, social classes, the agora and trade, drama, demographics, and home life and the role of men, women, and children in these realms. This site complements The Ancient Greek World site well in its focus on daily life.

Greek Civilization for Middle Schoolers
www.historyforkids.org

A frequently referenced site on the Internet, this teaching and learning tool is targeted at middle-school students (ages 11–14) and urges investigation of Greek civilization of the Classical period.

Launch your research by logging onto the History for Kids homepage and clicking on "Greek Civilization," or run a more targeted search on "Socrates" to produce a concise, easy-to-understand overview of his life and times and the challenges that confronted him and his contemporaries in society. General categories on the Greek Civilization link include: history (with time line), environment (with maps), religion, philosophy, clothing, people, language and literature, food, sports (the Olympics), science, art, architecture, suggested books on Greece, crafts and projects, teachers' guides, and gifts about Greece.

Ancient Greek Music at the Austrian Academy of Sciences
by Stefan Hagel
www.oeaw.ac.at/kal/agm/index.htm

To hear fragments of music enjoyed during the times of the ancient Greeks, explore this site and tune into one of more than twenty musical melodies.

According to the website: "This site contains all published fragments of Ancient Greek music which contain more than a few scattered notes. All of them are recorded under the use of tunings whose exact ratios have been transmitted to us by ancient theoreticians (of the Pythagorean school, most of them cited by Ptolemaios). Instruments and speed are chosen by the author. The exact sound depends on your hard- and software."

This site also contains a link to Homeric Singing and Classical Greek Pronunciation, which will help you to better envision what Socrates and his contemporaries heard and spoke. A fascinating compilation that transports the "surfer" back thousands of years.

People of Ideas in Ancient Greece (1500–325 B.C.)
www.newgenevacenter.org/reference/greece2.htm

Navigate your way to this site for a consolidated listing of ancient
Greece's most important thinkers, from Homer to Aristotle, including a
brief overview of their lives and significance as well as links for further
exploration.

Didaskalia
www.didaskalia.net/listings/listings.html

For the arts and culture aficionado, or for those simply interested in enjoying the classics on a modern stage, visit the Didaskalia website.
Didaskalia, an English-language electronic publication about Greek and
Roman drama, dance, and music in today's world, publishes listings and
reviews of performances, conferences, and other events. The site keeps
readers informed of forthcoming events, but is also a valuable historical
archive. The site provides capability for on-line submission of upcoming
events and reviews as well.

The website, whose name is taken from the inscriptions used to
record the outcomes of drama and music festivals in Athens, was created
in association with the Drama Committee of the American Philological
Association. The recipient of numerous web awards for content and
theme, Didaskalia has a very well-organized, easy-to-follow format.

The Stoa Consortium
www.stoa.org

From the word for "colonnade," stoa.org is "a consortium for electronic
publication in the humanities." Similar to a colonnade, stoa.org lends its
support to and exists as a source of coordination for electronic scholarship in the humanities, with a special focus on on-line publication of texts
related to the ancient world and the classical tradition. For those who
seek to have their work published, to contribute to an electronic publication underway, or to view currently available texts, stoa.org is an excellent resource and channel for achieving any or all of these objectives.

Diotima
www.stoa.org/diotima

Diotima, part of the Stoa Consortium, is a resource dedicated to the study of women and gender in the ancient Mediterranean world. It includes course materials, a searchable bibliography, and links to many online resources, including articles, book reviews, databases, and images.

The name of the site is borrowed from a reference made in Plato's "Symposium" by Socrates, who claims to be passing on to his friends what he has previously learned about Eros from a woman named Diotima from Mantinea.

Greek Alphabet Table
faculty.washington.edu/smcohen/alphabet.html

Hosted on the University of Washington's website, this provides a quick review of the Greek alphabet, including the letters (capital and lowercase) in Greek, their sound, and the name of each letter.

Foundation of the Hellenic World
www.fhw.gr/fhw/en

This site's missions are to illustrate and communicate Hellenism and its contribution to the development of civilization, to create an awareness of history through the dissemination of Hellenic cultural traditions, and to promote Hellenic spirit and history as a reference point and source of inspiration for the present and future. The Foundation of the Hellenic World's mission closely parallels that of the Socrates Project, and links provided on the foundation's website help to fulfill all three project missions. Of note is a 3-D and virtual reality link that reconstructs Hellenic architectural monuments and sites that today are either nonexistent or in ruins.

Argos
argos.evansville.edu

Looking for a very specific item related to Socrates or his times? Direct your browser to the Argos limited area search of the ancient and medieval Internet. This search engine for the ancient world, developed and maintained by Anthony F. Beavers and Hiten Sonpal at the University of Evansville, has an impressive array of associated sites including, among others, Cambridge Classics, Exploring Ancient World Cultures, the Perseus Project, and Diotima.

Museum of Reconstruction
www.reconstructions.org

A special page hosted on the *Scientific American* magazine's website, Restoring Virtual Ruins displays the work of the Museum of Reconstructions, a nonprofit organization formed in 1995 to use cutting-edge 3-D computer modeling methods to re-create lost or damaged works of art and architecture. Of note are the fruits of the organization's recent collaborative efforts with archaeologists at Princeton University and at the Greek Ministry of Culture to virtually restore the gateway leading into the Athenian Acropolis. The Museum of Reconstructions hopes that visitors to their site will soon be able to stroll on-line through their virtual reconstructions. It will be worth keeping an eye on.

Sites Not Directly Related to Socrates or to the Fifth Century B.C.

The Examined Life On-line Philosophy Journal
examinedlifejournal.com/index.shtml

Though not directly related to Socrates or Hellenism, this website offers a glimpse into what philosophy is all about, including links to philosophical discussions, chat sessions, access to the on-line journal *The Examined Life,* philosophy and interdisciplinary search engines, a listing of philosophy events, and a downloadable database of quotations from famous and not-so-famous philosophers.

The Examined Life's mission is "to offer a communication forum for the professional, student, and amateur philosopher. We hope that through the love of philosophy, our readers will develop a stronger appreciation of the philosophical positions of others and their own. We believe by offering a forum for the dialectic of philosophy to continue, that we will enhance and develop such an experience for the professional, student and amateur philosopher."

American Philological Association (APA)
www.apaclassics.org

Visit the website of the "the principal learned society in North America for the study of ancient Greek and Roman languages, literatures, and civilizations." Among the APA site's notable offerings is The Agora, an online listing of interesting links useful "to anyone interested in what the Classical Greek and Roman world has to say to modern America." Also included is a page with links to North American and international associations and research institutes devoted to the classics, journals, selected sites, and a listing of lectures and conferences among many other offerings.

ACKNOWLEDGMENTS

Socrates was nothing without his friends. This book would not exist without *my* friends, who are listed below. They provided inspiration, guidance, advice, criticism, encouragement, and, in the instances noted, financial support.

For early encouragement of the project I am grateful to Ms. Helen Philon and Ms. Connie Mourtoupala of the Greek Embassy, Ambassador Loucas Tsilas of the Alexander S. Onassis Public Benefit Foundation (USA), and John Psarouthakis.

For wise advice on the project I appreciate Sondra Myers, Ken Fischer, and Jean Houston.

For reviewing and critiquing the entire manuscript I (and the reader!) must thank Roben Torosyan, David Gow, and Peter Gross.

For reviewing and critiquing selected chapters I am grateful to William Caspary, James Allen, Jay Carney, Burt Bauman, Henry Lipman, Emiliano de Laurentiis, Kathy Akins, Ruth Weinstock, Kimeiko Hotta Dover, Edward Pores, Dorothy and Leon Puryear, Allan Brooks, Buzz Gummere, Jane Beckhard, David Rottman, Charlotte Fleisher, Mab Gray, Marilyn Gilbert, and Peter Rojcewicz.

Dan Green has been the *éminence grise* of this project as of so many other publishing ventures.

For invaluable assistance in providing photos, drawings, and other illustrative materials for this book, I am grateful to Constantine Hliavoras and Vicki Antonaraki of the Greek National Tourism Organization in New York City. They went far beyond any reasonable expectations in being resourceful and creative in finding images that fit the needs of this work. (And they also, along the way, contributed significantly, from their own reading and experience, to my understanding of Socrates.) Their successor at the GNTO, Demetra Mitropoulou, has also been extremely helpful.

In a few instances, permission could not be obtained, despite diligent efforts, because of publishers going out of business. Any omissions will be gladly corrected in future printings upon notification.

For the illustrations specifically commissioned for this book, I thank the gifted artist Kana Philip.

My editor at Tarcher, Mitch Horowitz, contributed crucially to shaping the book and informing it with his own wisdom, skill, and integrity. Jeremy Tarcher's breathtaking imagination confirmed my initial dream of bringing Socrates back to life.

I also appreciate the regular input and inspiration provided by the Rocky Mountain Learning Coalition, coordinated by the Meyer Learning Center in Denver, and the Center's founder-director, Linda Meyer. Their keen interest and critical review of the project at every phase contributed greatly.

For the deepest and widest support, I thank my life-partner, Bea Gross, and my daughter, Elizabeth Cohn.

I am grateful to the University Seminars at Columbia University for assistance in the preparation of the manuscript for publication. The ideas presented have benefited from discussions in the University Seminar on Innovation in Education. Professor Robert Belknap, Director of the University Seminars Program, has been a valued supporter of the work. (Please see page 166 for the Socratic significance of this program.) The connection between the seminars and the Socratic tradition is covered on page 166.

For additional financial support for the project, I am delighted to thank the Foundation for Hellenic Studies (a program under the auspices of the American Hellenic Institute) and the chairman of its Foundation's Advisory Board, Professor Van Coufoudakis.

For additional financial support I am pleased to express my gratitude to the Educational Foundation of the American Hellenic Educational Progressive Association (AHEPA) and its chairman, Dr. Pandeli Durbetaki.

THE SOCRATES PROJECT

This book is a product of The Socrates Project of the University Seminar on Innovation in Education, one of the University Seminars at Columbia University in New York City. The project's goal is to enhance the knowledge, appreciation, and application of the Hellenic heritage by Americans today. The project is directed by Ronald Gross, co-chair of the seminar.

Initial support for The Socrates Project has been generously provided by:

- the Foundation for Hellenic Studies (a program under the auspices of the American Hellenic Institute)

- the Educational Foundation of the American Hellenic Educational Progressive Association

In accordance with its goal, the project also organizes appropriate seminars, provides presentations, publishes other materials, and generates Web-based information. To be kept informed, please contact:

THE SOCRATES PROJECT
Administrative Offices: 17 Myrtle Drive, Great Neck, NY 11021
E-mail: GrossAssoc@aol.com   Tel.: 516-487-0235   Fax: 516-829-8462

GRADUATE PROGRAMS

IN THE CLASSICS

IN THE UNITED STATES

AND CANADA

Here is a roster of schools with graduate programs in the classics, compiled by the leading learned society in the field in North America, the American Philological Association. The association's *Guide to Graduate Programs in the Classics* provides up-to-date information on each program's admission and degree requirements, curricula, facilities, costs, and financial aid. It is designed to assist prospective students and their advisors in choosing an appropriate graduate program. The guide is available for $15.00 from the association at:

> The American Philological Association
> 293 Logan Hall
> University of Pennsylvania
> 249 South 36th Street
> Philadelphia, PA 19104–6304

Two related publications are *Careers for Classicists* and *Teaching the Classical Tradition*. The association's website is an important source of information about classical culture: www.apaclassics.org.

*University of Alberta
University of Arizona
University of Arkansas
Boston College
Boston University
*University of British Columbia
Brown University
Bryn Mawr College (Classical/Near Eastern Archaeology)
Bryn Mawr College (Greek, Latin, Ancient History)
*University of Calgary
University of California–Berkeley (Classics/Classical Archaeology)
University of California–Berkeley (Ancient History)
University of California–Irvine
University of California–Los Angeles
University of California–Santa Barbara
Catholic University of America
University of Chicago
University of Cincinnati
City University of New York
University of Colorado
Columbia University
Cornell University
Duke University
Florida State University
University of Florida
Fordham University
University of Georgia
Harvard University
Hunter College, CUNY

---

*Throughout, indicates an institution located in Canada.

University of Illinois, Urbana–Champaign

Indiana University

University of Iowa

Johns Hopkins University

University of Kansas

Kent State University

University of Kentucky

Loyola University, Chicago

University of Maryland–College Park

University of Massachusetts–Amherst

*McMaster University

University of Michigan (Classical Art/Archaeology)

University of Michigan (Classical Studies)

University of Minnesota

University of Missouri–Columbia

University of Nebraska–Lincoln

*University of New Brunswick

New York University.

University of North Carolina–Chapel Hill

Northwestern University

Ohio State University

University of Oregon

University of Pennsylvania

University of Pittsburgh

Princeton University

*Queen's University at Kingston

Rutgers University

San Francisco State University

University of Southern California

Stanford University

State University of New York–Albany

State University of New York–Buffalo

University of Texas

Texas Tech University

*University of Toronto

Tulane University

Vanderbilt University
University of Vermont
*University of Victoria
University of Virginia
University of Washington
Washington University–St. Louis
Wayne State University
*University of Western Ontario
University of Wisconsin
Yale University

A COURSE ON SOCRATES

Here is the syllabus for a course on Socrates as taught by a first-rate classics scholar, Professor Dirk T. D. Held of Connecticut College. It has been excerpted and abridged from *Teaching the Classical Tradition* by Emily Abu and Michele Valerie Ronnick, published by the American Philological Association (see previous section for information on the association).

In this seminar for freshmen and sophomores, the philosophical ideas of Socrates as they appear in the ancient evidence, primarily that given by Plato, are examined. In the latter weeks of the course, attention is turned to more recent views on Socrates of two major thinkers of the nineteenth century who hold quite divergent views on the ancient philosopher (Kierkegaard and Nietzsche) as well as a political theorist from the twentieth century (Hannah Arendt).

WEEK 1   Introduction

WEEK 2   Plato, "Apology" (in *Four Texts on Socrates*, ed. West); Xenophon, *Socrates' Defense Before the Jury*.

WEEK 3   Plato, "Crito"; Xenophon, *Recollections of Socrates*, Book I, ch. 1–2, pp. 3–19.

W. K. C. Guthrie, *The History of Greek Philosophy*, vol. III, pp. 325–59; 378–90; 398–408. (The identical material can be found in W. K. C. Guthrie, *Socrates*, pp. 5–39; 58–70; 78–88.)

WEEK 4   Plato, "Euthyphro"; Xenophon, *Recollections,*
Book II; A.R. Lacey, "Our Knowledge of Socrates" in
The Philosophy of Socrates, ed. G. Vlastos, pp. 22–49.

WEEK 5   Plato, "Laches"; John Ferguson, *Socrates: A Source
Book,* pp. 90–97, items #2.5.2.1; pp. 101–102, #2.5.4.1;
pp. 106–107, #2.7.2; in addition, skim pp. 21–29 and p. 189
and following. L. Versenyi, *Socratic Humanism,* pp. 73–110.

WEEK 6   Plato, "Charmides"; Xenophon, *Recollections,*
Book III.

Reserve reading: R. Robinson, "Elenchus: Direct and Indirect;
Socratic Definition" in *The Philosophy of Socrates,*
ed. G. Vlastos, pp. 78–124. (The identical material can be found
in R. Robinson, *Plato's Earlier Dialectic,* pp. 7–32; 45–60.)

WEEK 7   Xenophon, *Recollections,* Book IV; G. Vlastos, "The
Paradox of Socrates" in *The Philosophy of Socrates,* ed.
G. Vlastos, pp. 1–21.

WEEK 8   Plato, "Meno"; C. J. De Vogel, "Who Was Socrates?"
in C. J. De Vogel, *Philosophia I.*

WEEK 9   Aristophanes, *The Clouds;* Freeman, "Ancilla to the
Presocratics," pp. 87–89 (Diogenes of Apollonia, an example
of the Greek scientists) and pp. 131–33 ("The Sophist Gorgias,"
proving the innocence of Helen of Troy); G. Kerferd, *The
Sophistic Movement,* pp. 24–41; Guthrie, *History of Greek
Philosophy,* vol. III, pp. 164–175, 250–60, 359–75. (The same
material is in Guthrie, *The Sophists,* pp. 164–75 and 250–60,
and Guthrie, *Socrates,* pp. 39–55.)

WEEK 10   Plato, "Phaedo"; J. E. Raven, *Plato's Thought in
the Making,* pp. 79–104; W. K. C. Guthrie, *History of Greek
Philosophy,* vol. III, pp. 467–88.

WEEK 11   Nietzsche, *The Birth of Tragedy,* pp. 19–42, 46–59,
76–112, 121–46.

W. Dannhauser, *Nietzsche's View of Socrates*, pp. 80–87, 92–103, 119–129. (Of possible interest, but not required, is Dannhauser's critical exposition of *The Birth of Tragedy*, found on pp. 46–75.)

WEEK 12   Kierkegaard. Assignments and selections will be passed out prior to the class.

WEEK 13   Hannah Arendt, "Thinking and Moral Considerations," in *Social Research*, vol. 38 (1971), pp. 417–46.

INDEX

ABOUT THE AUTHOR

More than 100,000 professionals, businesspeople, students, and educators have met Socrates, as portrayed by Ronald Gross, at major national conventions and conferences. He is the author of such books as *Peak Learning, The New Professionals, Radical School Reform, Individualism,* and *The Lifelong Learner.*

Formerly associate director of the Education Program of The Ford Foundation, Gross currently co-chairs the University Seminar on Innovation at Columbia University in New York City and is an on-line columnist for About.com.

More information about his speaking and consulting, including numerous publications for reading and downloading, are available at the websites *www.ronaldgross.com.* and *www. SocratesWay.com.*